A Remarkable True Story

The *Circle of Many,*

The *Path of One*

... On the journey to the Light within.

"Each Light is a voice that places words upon the pages
of life to teach, inspire and bring hope." **Parkah**

by

Glenda Faye Thornton, PhD

Published by …

 **Awe Inspired**

Publishing House
Victoria, British Columbia,
Canada, V9Z 0S6

Library and Archive Canada: Legal Deposit - September 2018

ISBN 978-0-9731844-2-6 (Paperback)

ISBN 978-0-9731844-3-3 (eBook)

Blessings Judy

Dedicated to my sisters,

Rosie and Heather,

my son, Ryan

and granddaughter, Dayna.

J J Thornton

Nov 2019

Please Note:

There is power in the energy of all things,
including words and thoughts.

The energy of the words you will come to know
while reading this, or any other book, are no exception.

The energy of this book and
the energy provoked by your thoughts in contemplation of it
will affect your Energy Signature.

These words will alter your Energy Signature;
warmly if you are engaged with the Light,
in more reactive ways, if you are not.
You may be unaware of any of these effects
- at first, but

Watch for the signs -
as important clues rise to show you
where you are in the Cosmos
right now.

G. F. Thornton

Table of Contents

G. F. Thornton

PREFACE

I remember the very first day. Transfixed, I stood amongst the many shelves and wondered where to start. How would I know? What was I about to learn? Would these authors poison or taint my journey, or would they add to and brighten what I already knew?

The Library was a quiet landscape of multi-colored spaces containing rich, new and amazing wisdom, and subtle, sensitive and intimate secrets. This place held the history of the vast expanses and landscapes of the Universe. Each book written was the grace and wisdom from the Circle of Many on the journey toward the truth and each had marched along on their personal Path of One. Standing there on that day in that place of captured wisdom, I was called to consider as many as I dare.

This book was birthed and the pregnancy was long. It was foretold of 54 years ago when I received my first message that 'I would write a book one day that would make a difference.' And today I can see how my life has coursed to bring it into the world and send it skipping out to others. Not a page would arrive however until I found the inspiration and connection to the Light from which it would emerge. It is the time as we are being called to learn and share Sacred Wisdom. The journey to this end is the stuff of miracles, the wonder of the Universe and the fairy dust that falls upon it all.

I share with you the gratitude I have for my Mother; bless her beautiful First Nation Spirit and for swearing I would never know prejudice as she had. I honor her kindness, her crazy sense of humor and her fairness and love for everyone. Mom knew all too well the burn of prejudice as a child in the 1930s. Yet she had overcome in a gentle way and managed to live above her inner sadness. She had been a welcoming Spirit and an undeniable friend to whoever passed through her door. Mom had been a devoted mother and wife and deeply loved us all. While there was always something buried inside us that made us feel so different from the world, it would take decades to understand what. Yet my mother filled my childhood with precious memories and plenty of laughter.

G. F. Thornton

As I got older life taught me valuable lessons on what not to do, how not to react and who not to trust. Without the pain and sorrow from these lessons I never would have been able to appreciate the Light quite as much as I do. There had been many angels in my life too: spiritual women, strong and bold women, with whom I worked and befriended and who believed in me and encouraged this path to the end as they whispered "never leave the dream unfinished." Thank you to Jennifer for the day she came into my office and whispered, "You're wasting your time here!" It was a call to move beyond the ordinary and catch a glimpse of what else was possible. Adele, Dawn, Anu, Val, Wilma, Kathleen, Alison, Karen, Miranda, Iris, Sandra, Vicky, Sara, Tracy, Sharon, Cathy, Emily, Ruth, Brenda, Geetha, April, Leslie, and so many others; you have been my sentinels reminding me regularly of what is possible. Even if you didn't realize what your energy meant at the time, I thank each one of you for your support.

To the lovely Spirits who edited and commented on this book, I cannot possibly thank you enough. Dear Dawn, Bonnie, Heather and Rose, you offered the greatest gifts of your time and attention as you helped to validate and assist with Spirit's book. I honor you immensely.

I have to boast about my sister, Heather, as someone who always brightens my day and who makes me feel the Light whenever she is around. Younger, yet taller in height, I had looked up to her. And I still admire the sunny smile, her shiny blue eyes and her infectious energy. It could be said she is an unusual-looking First Nation woman, but it is her heart that has always been connected to the truth of our heritage, especially today as we travel this Spiritual path together. You have been my constant, my blood, my hope and more than just my sister. I am so grateful we are on this journey together.

And last but certainly not least, I wish to thank my mentor and best friend for opening her heart up to our friendship nineteen years ago. I wish to thank her for being so loyal and steadfast and for always being there when I needed her. Rose was a star of Canadian Women's Softball in her day, recipient of a World Silver Medal in 1979 for a smorgasbord of pitches. Earning a Master's Degree in Education Psychology also, even with dyslexia, she has become the Registered Clinical Counselor extraordinaire. Through her kind heart, generous debriefings and immense counsel she continues to help me as I file and sort through my closet full of lessons. My sister and Rose now travel this Spiritual path beside me as we dance in the Light together. Blessings are sent to you, my friend, for offering me a safe place to test these waters and encouragement to do this work. I could not have done any of it without you.

A Note: I learned in the eleventh hour that all of our lives are filled with messages from the Universe. If we're awake, we'll hear them, and if we're not, we won't. Rose said to me just yesterday that some of the Elder's wisdom resonated with things we considered nearly twenty years ago. And my response came from the insight gained during the writing of this book. I said, "The stuff in this book isn't new. This information has simply been rewrapped in a different colored paper to make it seem new and shiny. It was guided by wisdom from the Universe and is meant to become a gift for anyone who is looking for another way to understand."

I have been so fortunate to have traversed this life as I have, to have been awakened to the value of the Light even in my fiftieth year. To my readers, I wish you all the Light and inspiration promised to each and every one of you through Spirit. I invite all of you who wish to find and know the Light to come forward and join this wondrous new Tribe which will lead the world into peace and a brighter future. The magic is already in the air. The new Tribe will be instrumental in ending poverty, inequality, disease, greed and war... for all time. No pressure!

To those of you who will come to embrace Spirit's book, blessed is your journey. Thank you for welcoming the Universe into your inner sanctum. And the Elders and I are honored to take this journey beside you too.

Blessings

Glenda Faye

> While the stories in this book are true,
> the names have been altered
> to protect the identity of those involved.

G. F. Thornton

PART ONE
Mystery & Magic

The Elders would speak and I would listen.
They would teach and I vowed to learn.

And they would stay close to remind me often
that within each of us is the Light of the Universe.

G. F. Thornton

Chapter 1

Evolution of Light

YOU WERE LIGHT BEFORE YOU WERE BORN. Light is the Force of life; the animating energy of every living thing. On the day you were conceived, Light touched down within the first cells of your body and continued to fill every cell and every DNA strand thereafter. Written within this Light is the sum of the Universe and your very own purpose and truth." **Wahwaskenah**

There have been at least six **Peak Experiences** in my life. The following was the one that catapulted me toward the Light in 1999. I called it my Bubble of Peace (BoP). It was such a profound event I was drawn to seek that same peace, very consciously every day since because I really wanted to live there forever. This placed me on a path that would take me into a mysterious corner of my inner self where I would discover there was a much softer way to travel this thing called life.

Peak Experience: an event of a profound Spiritual Energy; an event of a miraculous nature.

Peak Experience: Bubble of Peace

It had happened in our first year together. I had left him then too. Once he found me, he worked very hard to convince me that he'd never attack me again. So I went back. After six peaceful years however and out of the blue on March 26th 1999, I would become his victim again.

My husband had to pack up and leave the house after I reported the attack to the authorities and had placed a restraining order on him - as advised. While I was away for four days trying to make sense of what had just happened, my husband was doing a fine job convincing everyone we knew that he had been my victim. He spread word to everyone, including my family, that I had attacked him and was trying to destroy his business. No one knew I had financed everything. This made me more wary of his agenda and more determined to not ever be his victim again.

Affiliates, a married couple, had booked an appointment with me the following month to convince me to stay put. I expected my husband had sent them. I wasn't looking forward to a confrontation or having to defend myself but I was determined to avoid another attack and was preparing to face financial ruin to do so.

The couple arrived on schedule and we made our way to the living room where we sat on opposing sofas. Peter began by stating a few of his reasons why I should stay, including one of his previous comments to me about the attack, "Aren't you taking this a bit too seriously?"

Shortly after we started the meeting, something began to shift. Their voices started to fall away as if distance was stretching them thin. I noticed there was a blur around my peripheral vision. I blinked my eyes and leaned in to find my adversaries had slipped even further away. His body was animated while his voice had become a mere whisper. I took note that he seemed to be on a roll – throwing what were obvious verbal cannon balls in my direction, his flailing hands used for emphasis. I sat back into my Bubble simply wanting to enjoy the peace.

I took stock of me. There seemed to be a smile on my face, which was a surprise, and thought I must have looked like a bobble head sitting on that sofa, nodding mindlessly up and down. Every now and then I would hear myself say, "Interesting," as if I actually was. Then the best observation of all was that there wasn't an angry, fearful or judgmental thought or feeling anywhere to be found within me. I was enveloped in total peace inside and out. I had been so prepared to fight that day, I marveled at how this could possibly be happening under the circumstances.

When they ran out of steam, we all stood up as if on cue and walked to the door where we hugged, smiled and said goodbye as if we'd just had a tea party. They even turned and waved as they headed down the walkway to their car, quite certain they had managed to change my mind. I shut the door and fell back upon it – in shock!

"WHAT THE 'BLEEP' WAS THAT?!"

The next question was obvious. Could I go back to that place of peace again whenever I wanted to? It was the day I committed to myself to find the answer. I would do plenty of work on me over the next ten years and I would come to trip over many more questions and answers I could never have imagined at the time.

What exactly had happened that day? Where had I gone? What did this mean? I began a conscious turn to an inner corner of my own self where I started to look into my own eyes to find out what really made me tick. Exactly how had I taken part in my own chaos and pain in the past? As new questions cropped up, one thing would become very clear; the Bubble of Peace happened inside of me, exclusively, and it had nothing to do with the outer world. In fact, it had rescued me from the chaos of those days and made me sit in my own presence for once. Suddenly I wanted to take notes! It would seem as though I had slipped into a great hall of secrets and wonder in the depth of cosmic space …and I was there to learn the truth.

Occam's Razor: if several hypotheses are offered to explain something, the simplest hypothesis that accounts for most of the observations is the most likely and should be considered first.

The Bubble of Peace stepped up my lifelong search for 'something better' and it piqued my curiosity. I would labor diligently for the next ten years at something I had never done before - learn about myself and my own role in the life I was living. While I continued to work at my j-o-b, days off would be filled by diving into that past. I was drawn to challenge all the things I knew had poisoned me and that I had to do something about - besides suffer them. This time I would find a better way – and a special energy would rise inside me to validate the path at every turn. I also knew, without a doubt, how important it was to take this journey on my own as if only I could find the key that would unlock the door. I expected I would have to be vigilant, awake at all times and cautious of life's distractions to stay on track.

Years later, after gaining a better understanding of myself by focusing intently on the real me, I began to recognize something else; the messages. There were messages that seemed to be coming to me from somewhere. Whispers started catching my ear as remarkable thoughts began arriving as if on the wind. I knew something unusual was happening even though much time would pass before I would become convinced about their origin. Through these messages I would be informed that I was to be guided and that I was to follow along and be patient. What had I stumbled into?

My Theory of Light

In 2013, a project I was working on kept offering up bits and pieces of information on light that I could no longer ignore. My brain was such that it loved to connect one dot with another and suddenly there was a host of dots being linked up. Light was not just fundamental to life. Science was discovering light was an animator and communicator. And this light was not just ordinary light. It would turn out to be the fundamental energy from a Field that permeated and connected the entire Universe.

Information, or dots, from totally unrelated materials and books started to coalesce into what I would come to call my **Theory of Light**. I even remember the moment it happened. The revelation was that life is quite simply the **Evolution of Light**! I skipped in and out of a state of skepticism too - as you did just now. What a crazy idea, right? The more I tested the theory in my own life however, the more valid it became. I would be encouraged by further messages to at least consider the possibilities.

I had to entertain that the messages must have been coming from another realm and maybe not just from *the other side*. In 2016, I began to see shadows, then a circle of shadows then I sensed Beings in the darkness of night when my eyes were closed. These lights heralded the arrival of more messages and information about their origin. I was connecting with Light Beings, visitors from another place. They were Elders and old souls from many generations and places and they were from another realm of time and space. One day they whispered that my theory could not be mine, nor could it be a theory at all. "The Divine," they said, "doesn't need to do theory." Eventually they would explain that the messages, including what I thought was my Theory, had actually been directed by Intelligent Energy. The Elders were using this Energy and directing it, not to me - but through me, and I was meant to capture it. I would eventually realize all of the messages were meant for the book I had been told so many years ago that I would write one day.

I could no longer barrel blindly forward without justification nor should I be swayed by my own opinions or beliefs. The Elders had touched the Spirit energy within me and they had my attention. I was tethered to this strange new energy like a ribbon at the end of a kite. My fascination kept me listening and watching with curiosity and awe. The messages would increase in depth and complexity and eventually would reveal an even bigger purpose. I began to wonder if this was going to change everything.

Indeed, the Elders would become my teachers and I would become an eager student. My role was changing. Instead of the author, I would become a story teller and a channel as the Elders began filling pages of paper with messages. Over time, I would find there were many other people from all over the world who were receiving similar messages. Again and again there would be evidence that the world was waking up. I wasn't alone.

"These events are the precursors of great change and this time will mark the darker moments just before a brighter dawn." **Wahwaskenah**

Shifting

Whether you believe the poles are shifting or Nibiru will be upon us soon, this shift is bringing a renewed Energy that is Spiritual and feminine in nature. What happens to one, happens to all …what happens here, will happen there. The Universe was coalescing Spiritual Energy toward our little planet.

My Spiritual experiences would take me out of the limiting left brain and into the expansive and creative right Mind many times over the following years. One day, the difference between the brain and the Mind would be validated by Jean Bolte-Taylor in her famous TED Talk where she tells of what happened to her during a left-hemisphere stroke [a bleed in her brain]. A Neuroanatomist, someone who studies the brain, she recounted the details during her stroke.

When her left brain was out of commission, on and off over a period of a few hours, she noted that her concept of the world totally changed. At one point she could no longer discern where her arm stopped and the wall started. When the left brain was shut off, Jean felt expansive and unlimited, powerful, loving and brilliant as she melted into the ether of the Universe untethered by the limits of her tiny physical-ness. Jean wondered how she could ever fit all of her expansive amazing self into her tiny physical body ever again. She was astounded to realize how much the left brain determined the boundary of her limited physical body.

The question had to happen. Could it be a mere collection of gray matter, mere biology that stops us from connecting with the Energy of the Universe? I had been on a constant search for clear, real-world information to validate what and who I was and how everything worked in the physical world and for me Jean's revelations were profound. What was the real scope of the left brain? Does it give rise to conflict, fear and divisiveness too when we are unaware of what stretching it means to finding peace and love and wonder as big as the Universe?

How much of what we understand of our own life is determined by this governor? To what degree do these limitations deter our ability to move outside the box, to go beyond old paradigms and beliefs or usurp repeated patterns of error and mistakes - generation after generation? And, more importantly, is it possible to reach past it – simply because we want to?

From this new century, I saw my own limiting beliefs in the 80s. I had been unwilling to acknowledge an ability to channel messages no matter how they arrived, what they offered or if the ability had been validated or not. I would take the easy road and be of the mind that psychic talent was a fantasy, a sideshow or an illusion at best. Evidence Spirit had always had hold of my mind, my pen and indeed my life would show up regardless, and piece by piece I would be drawn to reconsider.

As you read the stories from my life, you will begin to see threads that wove throughout my past. Yet it would take several Peak Experiences to accept that messages had always been sent and received and that I had been blind and deaf and in denial ...until I was ready to open that door. This entire learning process would one day validate that when we focus attention on something long and hard enough we wake up to unlimited possibility. We can open up our minds and look inside anything to find surprising meaning and value – but we must be ready. Shutting off, ignoring or missing the messages was far more common than listening to them.

My very first message was that I would "write a book one day that would make a difference." It had arrived in 1963 even though I hadn't realized it was a message at the time. It had perched just over my left shoulder every day for more than five decades. There was no indication of what the subject of the book would be however. Finding the subject must have been the gentle nudge that kept me searching and kept me moving forward until I found it. What could I possibly write about? What subject or story could I relay that would help others - when I was so lost myself?

They say authors should write about what they know. And so, I had sat down many times to write about surviving all kinds of nightmares from rape to physical and emotional abuse to being kidnapped. Writing about a period I called my 30 Years of Darkness turned out to be a terrible immersion into doom and gloom for long enough to write this story. Each time I would start, the negative energy would quickly sour the paper. I couldn't quite understand that if I was meant to write a book and should write about what I know, what else could I draw from than my sordid past? As I set the book aside time and again to wait for a more plausible subject, I wrote other books; a fantasy about addiction called Angels Over Bubble Gum, and a novel of unrequited love called Sunset Point. And for years I wrote reams of what I considered to be scribble ...until I learned something else.

Auto-writing; receiving messages through a stream of consciousness; a form of channeling messages to paper without conscious effort.

In my 20's and 30's when tossing and turning at night attempting to get to sleep, I would often have to off-load the day. As if it was a simple dump of excess stuff in my brain, I would turn on the light, grab a pen and paper from nearby and started recording whatever came up. There was never any conscious engagement in the writing and I would just let the pen go where it needed to. I felt it was kind of cool and it had been more effective than a sleeping pill. It would be a ritual for many years without acknowledging what was really happening. There was no indication that the writings were from the ether, from the other side or that they were from messengers, and I simply ignored the possibility. Occasionally reading some of the scribbles weeks later, they seemed to be insightful and deeper in meaning than just nonsensical offloading. Unfortunately their importance and true source had been denied for years.

Another strange thing would happen every time I'd sit down to write. A word would pop into my head while composing a sentence. The word would be uncommon or unfamiliar and on occasion I wouldn't even be able to spell it. I'd finish the sentence, read it again and again and stare at that odd word wondering if it fit. I would shake my head every time then go to a thesaurus to find that 99% of the time the word fit - perfectly. This still happens. Where were these words coming from? I had never been a reader. In fact, I wondered many times how someone could be a writer without being a reader. Once I realized I was channeling and once I accepted that Spirit had always touched me, this phenomenon became less of a mystery. Most of those words, those books and all that auto-writing had not come from me but through me. They had been beacons and clues that could have bloomed into lessons and insight had I been awake. These had been the first messages. Looking back at sixty years of history, there would be many of them to acknowledge and much to reconsider.

It wasn't until 2013 that the subject of the book would arrive and I actually sat down to write. This long-awaited subject would be about the spiritual journey I found myself on after the Bubble of Peace in 1999. As the book started to form, I would ease my grip on what I thought was reality and I would give Spirit more and more leeway. Words and paragraphs would randomly be switched. There would be cause to delete whole chapters or move them around from back to front – and all without a care. I, on the other hand, being a die-hard sequential would cringe at the mere thought of such antics. Again, not me! Editing was next. Over and over again as I read through the book, I found information I had no earthly recollection of writing or better yet, of knowing. And this still happens too. Over time, this project would change from my book to Spirit's book, from my theory to Spirit's design, ipso facto, from my little story to one about all life and the Universe.

After years of sorting through the past, I found lots of stories that had rolled out like so many I had heard from others. Some of my stories would come to be counted as miracles. The details would be different from others but the pain and joy were the same. You will, in fact, be able to relate to these stories as they touch your own. They will validate how much we are alike and how easy it is to wander off in the wrong direction or get stuck in the mud along the way. They would serve as a stage or a common landscape to connect with everyone's story. "They will make the book more human," they said, "and the information more accessible."

I set out with plenty of information to write the book; evidence of Light, research information, new scientific evidence, ancient & religious text and true stories in a tidy little plan. I was excited to finally be writing the book I had dreamed of for so long. Spirit had a different plan. As messages arrived over several years, this book would morph into Spirit's book. This process however was about to change the outer chaos and the innermost heart of my own life too.

As the consummate seeker of the very information to which I now seemed privy, I kept my head down and leaned further into this wind. I had to trust it. There was a hunger to understand the Bubble of Peace experience, what its source had been and better yet, how to return to that peace again. I had to trust the search would become the fuel which would stoke the fire that burned inside. I would become caught up in the cosmic sparks as Spirit slowly earned my undivided attention over the five years it took to write the book.

There was that question again; had I become psychic? So unusual and all-encompassing were the messages, I had to sit back and literally observe as one chapter reached out and touched the next. Words would skip about in my mind then find space on just the right page - all without a plan. In the middle of the night, a spark would cause me to sit up and start writing. The way the book was shaping up had to validate the power of Spirit's truth. Few would ever write a book in such a fashion without at least a magic wand! "The Universe is the source of all and everything," they would repeat many times, and that would include me, my theory... and this book!

I would become a student on a journey deep into my inner self. Reworking my understanding of the past, I would find golden insight and ruby-colored gems in the strangest places. When I stopped trying to keep up and started to just go with the flow, the easier the messages arrived. Again and again Spirit would add more depth to this thought, more clarity to that chapter and more insight to this concept. Coming to terms it was a circle of Elders who were channeling through me, taught me that regardless of our lot and regardless of what happens on this Earthly plane, there is a path laden with stars and lit by liquid glitter. I could count on the process.

Dread

I usually have good dreams, but for decades I would wake up from each one and a feeling of dread would slowly leak into my peaceful mind - and the world would grow dark again. It had been so common that it was just how things were, I thought. Even though I had grown so tired of the dread, there didn't seem a way out. For at least one weekend in six or eight, I would hide in my bedroom, close the blinds tight and sleep. It had been necessary to refuel and it was the only way I managed a life that was so much work and filled with such fear and chaos. Each night, I wondered if I would ever escape or if the tears would ever stop. And each morning reality would remind me again as the dread seeped slowly back into my awareness - as if right on cue.

I would change. The more time I spent focused on my inner world, the less I focused on stupid things or the injustices of the world and the less frustrated I felt. My anger began to evaporate into the air to be whisked away. One day I would notice a smile on my face for no reason and even the ice would start to melt in the coldest corner of my heart.

Chemistry Class

In the very first chemistry class in high school the teacher had us observe and write a description of a common everyday object. He handed each of

us a candle and a lighter. The assignment was to view a burning candle as if we had no previous knowledge of one, and then we were to record our observations. The exercise was designed to teach the scientific method - to observe; to study and evaluate without preconceived opinions, beliefs or limitations. We were to view this common item from a totally new perspective from the one we had before class. The candle flickered and the scent of burning wax filled the room. How could I possibly explain what this was as though I knew nothing of it? I stared for some time as the flame moved back and forth tickled by the subtle breezes of the room. Can we not know what we know?

My mind was trying to bend as I pushed back what I knew. Observing the candle as if for the very first time wasn't as easy as it sounded. This exceptional experience had been a simple event yet one I would relate to many times over the years. Opening up the mind to cosmic possibilities, to the ethereal mysteries of reality and to the Light would take the same kind of mind-bending.

There was a whole new world to be discovered inside of me and throughout the past. New meanings would pop up and clues would surface to what made me tick, how I became so angry and why I seemed so stuck. The past would be filled with pearls and every one of them spoke a new meaning of what had happened. It would become strangely personal. I was starting to feel insightful when I had the courage to look honestly into my own eyes. This spoke to why it is folly to interfere in another's story too. While you can perhaps see what I am blind to, I will never be able to understand it - if I use only your eyes. Within your story resides the insight too. It is bold and real enough to paint a new landscape - when the old one no longer fits. And all it really takes is honesty.

Somewhere over the rainbow on this cosmic journey, it was very rewarding to come to things of such value. We are here to create and be and not to simply endure. Finding my purpose would show me I was clearly stuck in the mud of the middle where I had lived between two opposing cultures. This exposed it all; the pain and joy and everything in between on the way into a deep ocean of experiences. And in the end, Light would heal me as it set the trauma and losses of that muddy past into a little box marked: Done.

My destiny would unfold and I vowed to let it happen. I would find many clues along the way that this was the music I was meant to hear from the beginning. If I dare take this journey I was hoping to be led back to the Bubble of Peace. As every destination starts with the first step, I started counting from one.

While the stories in this book are true, this book is not about me. My stories create a picture, a landscape of hills and valleys, of wonder and mystery, miracles and magic, sadness, loss and pain. Mine is merely one human story. The details are different from yours but it is the emotion that unites us all. Our sunshine and hope are the same. We all seek safety where we can be without pain or worry. We all want a place to belong where we know our life matters in some way. We all need to find those who will hear us and witness us as we live our story. We all want simple happiness and peace and safety so we can thrive. This human-ness unites us all.

This book is not for everyone either for one must be ready to hear another ending to their story before they can open up to it. I hadn't been ready for far too many decades – and I had even been looking! The 'Note' at the beginning of this book reminds all of us that words and thoughts have their own energy and those which have been placed in this book are here to change you whether you are aware or not, ready or not. Rest assured that if you are not open to the energy of this book, you will notice an uncomfortable, restless and unsure feeling until you can sort through what it is that you need to understand first. For those who are ready to take this path, you will find evidence that this book shifted you forward in a welcome way – also regardless of whether or not you were aware or not at the time. They said this was by Divine Design.

Wait for it!

Chapter 2

First Nation

I AM FIRST NATION, even though there was no reason to acknowledge the fact, nor did I know how important this would be in the grand scheme of things. Not until just the other day would I fully understand what this ancestry meant and how profoundly it had affected who I was and who I would become. Over time I would find a surprising new faith and trust in this ancient culture as I found out how deeply it was rooted within me.

They were Elders but not just First Nation Elders. They were Elders of the Universe and they would visit regularly. They were an impressive group from another realm and they would share their energy through whispers, pictures and messages. They would teach of the Spiritual, Conscious, Intelligent and Light energies that streaked through all time. They would teach that by design, knowledge is retained in each respective Light that would weave through many incarnations. "Every inch gained in this life," they said, "would be one less tear to shed in the next."

> "The bravest thing you can do in this life is to look honestly
> at your own truth." **Parkah**

Parkah would come first. His words would be bold and solid. He would bring others forward too when they had wisdom and insight to share. They were a circle, a cluster of great energy sent to shine Light into this world through willing channels, of which I was apparently one. Over five years of writing this book, they would task me to discover the truth while they urged me to test everything in my own reality first. I was a skeptic and hard to convince. Yet this book would become a living, breathing being, one that was born and would grow and progress over time. It would become a home filled with messages, intimate and profound, with conversations and thoughts hashed out, contemplated, learned, tested and applied. This counsel could only have come from **Sacred Energy**, the wisdom of which is born from the Universe. It was my destiny to make this book concrete and real and now in your hands. And I take very little credit.

*   *   *

When she was a child, my First Nation mother suffered incredible prejudice. Yet she had been organic; clear and real, pure and plain. While the taunting she had suffered created deep scars, she became a kind and generous person. She would never sit in the sun for fear of darkening her skin that would make her feel dirtier than she already felt. She disliked her hands and had called them 'claws' saying they were big and awkward. She felt heavy and clumsy, yet her 5 foot 6 inch frame maintained a normal weight throughout her adult life. She was a paradox; a contradiction in terms. She could quickly spot anyone who was the least bit pretentious or who lived in an illusion of grandeur. She knew no one was better than any other yet she had felt lesser than most. As painful and as simple as her life had seemed in part, her journey was to spread equality, fairness and laughter wherever she went, and as designed, she would.

She swore above all else that her children would not suffer the same prejudice she had known. She chose a blonde, blue-eyed man from an ordinary white family and my sister Heather and I would be raised as little white girls. I had been dressed in fancy clothes, frilly socks and patent shoes with ribbons and ringlets in my hair. We lived in a Mainstream neighborhood and attended their schools. And we rarely spoke of our First Nation heritage as if it didn't really exist. Perhaps our ancestors had denied their heritage too to avoid the battle of assimilation.

I had that very blood in my veins and it would paint me with the color of that heritage, even if I hadn't actually lived in it. Unknowingly, the discord of these opposing worlds, the First Nation and Mainstream, caused my life to unfold unevenly. I had always sensed the awkwardness. I knew there was something different about me that sat at the base of who I was but I didn't have a clue what it could have been.

I didn't see the world the same as other kids. I remember not understanding why they behaved as they did. I couldn't find them in me or me in them. By the time I was in high school, I had settled in my mind that I was simply more mature having spent my first five years of life without a sibling and surrounded only by adults. Those years with doting aunts and uncles, cousins and grandparents must have had an effect, I thought. The most influential people had been the Native side. They had been a link that had never quite severed a secret past from the present. I wouldn't understand until my late forties that the First Nation blood had made a huge difference in everything. I would discover that blood eventually; one Elder, one event, one story at a time.

The children in our family had always been included. By the time I was seven I could play difficult card games like Canasta and Cribbage. I would join in whatever game was the flavor of the day and I felt grown up and valued when invited to play with the adults. Heather and I tended bar and prepared snacks at their parties and gatherings, looking after the adults as they played just as they looked after us when we played. These were the times that had built a confidence and sense of belonging within a large, happy family as diverse and colorful as any. No one taught us to include everyone or that this was a page from our First Nation past. This was simply just what we did and how it was. Everyone was welcome – always.

It was my mother's father, Bill Buss, or Boo as I had nicknamed him, who I spent many dusty summer days with and who unknowingly had breathed upon me his secret culture. His silent knowledge to this day remains unmatched. He wasn't a perfect person, by any means, yet he held everyone captive as the story teller, the prankster, the entertainer and the family cornerstone. I had felt privileged to spend time with him, especially to go fishing and to learn whatever he was teaching. There had been many times I had sat in his great shadow with the yellow sun melting our bond on a warm summer day. He taught me things young white girls would not normally learn: how to prepare bait precisely, how to name, catch and clean fish *properly*, how to read the ocean and horizon, how to skin a dear, kill a chicken, tan a hide...and ready the Rock Soup.

Rock Soup

I found him on his knees working in the side garden one summer day when I was about eight years old. I slipped silently up to watch and learn as I loved to do. Boo was weeding and removing the relentless array of rocks that were common to the soil of our Island. I noticed a perfectly round one about the size of a five-pin bowling ball still nestled in its place as if it belonged there. He moved to another section. I had to ask as I pointed to that rock, "Aren't you going to take that one too?" He stopped for but a second to look over at the rock. "Nope, that's a special one and it's not finished growing yet." I had to ask, "Growing?" He never missed a beat as he responded, "Yup... before I can use it in the Rock Soup."

He had said it so nonchalantly that I felt I should know all about Rock Soup, and so I never questioned him further. And, I never had another bowl of soup from the kitchen that hadn't been thoroughly searched for bits of rocks first. This was how he affected my world. I never quite knew what he meant or when he was only kidding. It was all part of his mystery and the kind of magic that held me spellbound for decades.

He had left that rock there for his own reasons, and one day I will ask him why.

Mom grew up in a log cabin in Dashwood that Boo had built in the 1920s. He had logged the wood from the lot to build it while he lived in a tent by the Little Qualicum River along with his cow. He would marry my grandmother, Daisy in 1920 and she would join him on the river. How they met has been lost to time... but I'll bet a fishing pole and a boat were involved.

This is a picture of me, my young cousins and the log cabin I loved.

Boo never wasted anything. He fashioned strange and wonderful things from whatever he found just lying around, like a left-handed jug made from a silver plate and garden planters made from old tires that were wedge-cut, turned inside out and painted white. Some bits and pieces from those tires ended up as knee pads for gardening. He used empty tobacco cans for many things. Two such cans, their bottoms screwed to the log house held the garden hose as it wound between them, back and forth in a lazy figure eight. The nozzles were safely stowed inside the cans and the lids would hide them away. He taught me how to cut kindling in the wood shed and warned me to not go into his work shop in the washhouse - unless he was with me. It was just one more mystery.

There, amid the scent of oil, soap and old cedar, the blackened walls thick with decades of soot from the little wood stove lived a history unto itself. He would show me the ancient tools, arrow-heads and walrus teeth while an assortment of tools hung on the walls and treasures were tucked into the wooden drawers that had been worn smooth from use. His fishing gear hung from the ceiling and tool boxes held more secrets as if they were shrines of magic. All the items were like props on a stage, always conjuring up his great stories from days gone by.

He had been a logger by trade, but he was more famous for trapping, hunting and fishing. He was the one man in the area who could catch fish when no one else was having any luck. Boo and Daisy had quite the reputation when they operated the Boat House on Qualicum Beach in the 50's. I was so proud to tell the tourists about him as I played on the sandy beach. "Go see Boo at the Boat House," I'd point, "and he'll show you where the fish are!" He was a local hero in many ways, and he never wasted time, energy or anything for that matter. There was something about him; a knowing, a special brand of simple knowledge. When I think back to these times, my First Nation ancestors must have hid the treasures of their heritage long past that I could glimpse it in the here and now. Passed silently down through generations, this heritage was the stuff of legend, of ritual, magic and tradition. And Boo and Mom had been my link to it all.

Their log cabin became a home for me and many others every summer. No one could ever drive by on the highway without stopping for some laughter, a cup of tea and some goodies from the chilly kitchen pantry. The cabin barely had a square corner to count, yet it housed a family of five, six and seven as everyone had been welcomed. Two lost teenagers had taken them up on the invitation to stay and made this place their home too. They would blend into the family easily and never leave.

The cabin remains where it was built on the hill above the main highway that buzzes through Dashwood today. Sadly, since 1996 after Daisy's death this special place is being reclaimed by nature. The house that held a mountain of love and laughter is slipping into memory and history under brush and roots and moss. When I visit, as I often do, I can still hear the laughter. It is one of those things that will forever be burned into my heart. Many years ago I had a wooden sign made that had hung on the back porch that said it all.

It wouldn't be until I was in my fifties that I would learn my unique way of seeing the world was mainly because I travelled the middle road, lost somewhere between the First Nation and White culture. The future would show me how this had been what had given root to my confusion. Growing up in the white world meant I was stuck in the mud of the middle –

suspended somewhere between two very opposite cultures. I had one foot in each - yet I existed wholly in neither.

Robert

Throughout this book you will read the story of a unique character in my life. We were star-crossed lovers and soulmates. Robert was First Nation and grew up in the Mainstream too. When we met in 1986, a spark ignited between us that spanned centuries and connected vast secrets. Decades after meeting, I would realize ours had been a very different experience from what I first thought. This single relationship, beyond all others, would serve as one of the most amazing revelations of my life for reasons no one could have dreamed. Our story may have seemed short but it was as vast and deep and mysterious as the Universe.

When I was 56, I would land a job as assistant to the First Nation Advisor for the provincial government. While in training, I would meet a gaggle of elders and one pretty important chief; mine. It wasn't until this job when I found myself ensconced in this culture and surrounded by First Nation people I would begin to appreciate what had created the confusion within me. This job would offer up a fresh river of information to this unique and important energy from the past. My heart began to sense a familiar rhythm of an ancient and sacred energy more fitting than my own skin. My eyes would fill up with gratitude and respect and my throat would choke every time I drew near.

Meeting My Kind

After the job interview with two Elders and a Chief, I woke up wandering around the city as if on a vacation. My heart felt soft and full. Colors and sounds were striking and the sunshine held new warmth. I was moving along the street feeling light and airy and wonderful. Reality started filtering back into my awareness and I tried to recall the interview. It wasn't part of my memory. Days later the phone call came that I had the job. The office where I would work was connected to the First Nation Friendship Center and I would suddenly be surrounded by reminders of a culture I thought I didn't know.

I would come to meet a host of First Nation people; members, Elders and Chiefs from many tribes around the province. Each time I came into a room where an Elder was sitting, my throat would choke with emotion and tears would roll down my cheeks. It felt as though I was in the presence of Spiritual Royalty. As unlikely as it was for me to have nothing to say, I would often have no voice with which to say it. There was so much to learn, and yet I didn't know what I didn't know. A sense of honor and sadness when amongst them always filled me and this exists to this day. I had no clue to what was happening but I spent many hours apologizing to my boss, Diana, for not being able to speak or for needing another tissue. Diana took it all in stride as if it was quite natural. Years would pass before I would understand and appreciate what the tears had meant.

Our family found that connecting with our heritage on paper would be impossible as Mainstream records dried up in the late 19th century. To gain some kind of link to the past, there would be no records to assist. Uncle Jack tried several times to gain a link - to no avail. I wrote to our tribe, trying not to intrude, but wanting so badly to hear of others with the same last name. Questions burned inside about who they were and why it felt so important to connect with them. There are few remaining members of the family who are still connected to our history as the old cabin slips silently into the past.

Even though the memories fade more with each generation, this same energy is found in my son and granddaughter and they validate the strength of this blood further. Uncle Jack has kept closer ties to our past, to our heritage, to the stories and the way in which we had made such special memories together ...that I miss so dearly. I could not know the depth and effect of my First Nation heritage. Yet regardless of how I had been raised, of whatever my mother's intention had been, I was a product of that history and philosophy, at least in part, be it through family, blood or DNA, or our connection through a common energy - it really didn't matter.

There are many things First Nation people have been forced to forget and so there is much to gain in recapturing their truth from the past. I am proof we are forever connected and bound to our past even if we have a difficult time believing it. We are all meant to make use of the wisdom gathered and honored over many generations. The First Nation people were custodians of what makes a community, of cooperation and honor and how to protect

Mother Earth. When anyone, of any Nation, is forced to bend in the wrong direction or is forced to forget what's in their blood, it threatens their very survival. FNs were forced to deny what had been written in their Light and it has devastated their path ever since.

All words and thoughts have a unique energy – one that can affect and move and change us. When a word resonates within, it brings an energy with it, a confirmation or denial that speaks directly to us. This resonance is unique to each word and phrase and even to each story. Looking for and finding those bits of information, your personal confirmations that resonate within you, takes being conscious and living in the moment. When something resonates, it becomes yours. It becomes a valuable clue to your truth and you are meant to take note. Many times over the past few years there had been a treasure of wisdom or meaning that I needed to sit with and take in. Each bit that resonated would herald the clues of what to pay attention to and what really mattered …for me.

The following are some other clues that tell us there's something we need to pay attention to…

- Unexpected tiredness or exhaustion.
- Subtle muscle aches and pains.
- Colds and flu-like symptoms.
- All or nothing thinking: the brain goes with too big or too small, or is just plain stuck.
- A muddled mind, lack of focus, inability to concentrate.
- Inability to sleep soundly for very long.
- A new or unfamiliar excitement.
- Increased sensitivity; often reacted to when misunderstood.
- Increased emotions that can be good ones or not so good ones.
- Recurring situations of deep loss, sadness and anger.

Emotions

Parkah spoke many times about emotion. "Emotions are the bridge to your Spirit. Your heart is how Spirit lets you know when you are on track and when you are not."

Understanding that our emotions are connected to the wisdom of our own unique Spirit offers us a path to learn of our strength, to be guided by it and to be able to discover our own wisdom which can take us to new heights. While white culture teaches that being emotionally sensitive is a sign of weakness - it is nothing of the sort. In truth, to be sensitive means you have a clear emotional bridge to your hidden inner wisdom. Emotion is the language and the path to that wisdom and learning how to access and understand it is a gift of the Light - and in the Light - everything is perfect.

Spirit; pure, Sacred Essence within; likened to a seed, Spirit will burst forth with whatever is contained within it. When you give Spirit a chance to speak and bend your ear, Spirit is your cosmic guide.

We begin as Spirit, as the Light from the Source. When we're born we enter a strange and unfamiliar physical life where we spend years being distracted by the world outside of us. Slowly we begin to accept that happiness is out there or found through material things, relationships, money, career or achievements. The yearning for the Light within grows stronger and the feeling that something is missing expands. After suffering for decades, we finally realize nothing out there has brought lasting peace or happiness. It is the time when we realize we have been yearning and missing the peace of our inner Light all along. Imagine how life would be if we knew this from the beginning.

Chapter 3

Spirit & Light

THE BUBBLE OF PEACE and my desire to return to it caused a path of self-reflection that would produce a few surprises. My lifelong search for something better would change the more I was guided to dig deep inside for that place of peace instead of finding it out there in the world. My attention had to become conscious. I started to identify a different dialogue in my thoughts that seemed unusual and special at the same time. Listening with a purpose, I learned how to recognize a message. Eventually I captured one that had to have come from somewhere else because it had not been in my memory bank. I was to let go of my grip on the outer world and what I thought I knew and open up to let the truth out. I somehow knew I had to test each message and integrate the ones that proved to be true. It would soon become impossible to separate this Spirit from the running commentary of my life, past, future and present.

Coherent Light: a concentration of photons; a singular beam of concentrated light.

The Elders are going to jump right into the deep end and give you the most important part up front. And just so you know, I couldn't take some of this at face value either when I first heard it. I had been skeptical too. Don't let this stand in your way however. If you follow through to the end of this book, it could well change your life as it changed mine. It is important to not avoid new information or be afraid to let go of what you think you know because the wonder of the Universe might just hang in the balance.

> "Biological bodies of all types offer Light a vehicle
> and a means of expression in the physical." **Orella**

Light Energy

Today scientists tell us that throughout the entire Universe there is only Energy and matter, and that the matter is the insignificant part. The essence of everything is energy. Within the spaces between galaxies and between the nucleus and electrons of an atom, thought of as a vacuum of empty space, is a vast field of energy - Light Energy. We were taught that mass was the significant weight in the center of each atom. Yet if you could stop the electrons from whizzing around the nucleus of every atom in your body …you would disappear. The matter from 6.5 billion people currently on Earth would leave something about the size of a sugar cube. This is how much the matter …doesn't matter!

Spirit: pure, sacred essence; a stream of The Source; The Light; God; Goddess; Higher Self; Consciousness; God Mind; Life Force; Universal Wisdom; Inner Light

Spirit and your aura, the photonic you – is made of Light. Light is the vital animating energy in all life. Now hold on to your hats for this next one.

The biology offers Light a way to be expressed, to progress and respond, move, change and create on a physical plane. There is a fully intelligent energy in the Universe, as most of us will agree. It is the ultimate Love and Wisdom. This is the Light that lives within you. Through this Light you are the Conscious Intelligence of the Universe *from* a distant and brilliant *future* space and time: more on that mindbender later.

Science tells us that Light is stored in every cell and every DNA strand in our body. Light is made of photons which are vibrations and frequencies. This Light is a collection of energy, a coherent beam that embeds into all living things. The body facilitates the expression of this Light. Light becomes therefore an abundant energy which responds to other energy. Light is creative and makes up our emotional energy in order to signal possibility, wonder, happiness, knowledge and wisdom. Through a range of frequencies, Light communicates from within each biological vessel. Light is aided by water and together they are potential, balance and the Sacred Essence. You know plants use Light to make energy. Can you stretch your mind to see that Light makes up the intelligent energy within you too?

> "Light is progressive. The Light in you comes from
> the Perfect Light that exists only in the future." **Parkah**

Whether you believe in creation or evolution, Light was present in the very first living cells. Light energy hopped a ride inside a vessel and life was animated. Together they created a symbiotic relationship where one would facilitate the other. The vessel would offer things like movement, response, possibility, procreation, creation and potential. The Light provided animation, information, energy, recordkeeping and instant communication. Over time, greater and more complex life on the physical plane progressed giving Light a way to progress as well. We are Light.

One molecule responds to another creating a transfer or an exchange of energy. This reaction causes blood to flow, movement and digestion and this same exchange works similarly across the full spectrum of life. The Light is an ever-present energizing force of capacity and accumulated knowledge. As a result Light has progressed in a single direction with divine purpose and meaning. Just as our bodies provide a symbiotic environment for trillions of bacterial life so too does it offer a vessel for the expression of Light.

> "The Light is the Conscious Intelligence of the Universe
> and you are its expression in physical form." **Wahwaskenah**

Each one of us is a singular Point of Light in the cosmic fiber optic lamp of this physical reality. And by divine design, when we connect Spirit to

G. F. Thornton

Spirit, the amazing energy of that bond moves the Earth - a tiny bit. We can't take this lightly; pun intended.

What is the difference between a life form that is alive and one that isn't? What is missing? When the biology has worn out or ceases to function, what happens to the Light energy inside of it? **Wahwaskenah** would answer, "The Light leaves the body when the vessel can no longer provide its purpose. The bond is broken. The function of the vessel is no more. One cycle has completed and the Light will prepare for the next. Light inhabits each biological vessel to facilitate its own progress, eventually toward Ascension. And you are made of this Light. Your Light is your sentient consciousness which connects you to the Conscious Energy of the Universe. Its source is Divine Perfect Light *from the future.*"

> "You inhabit the biology and it plays a role but
> you are not just biology." **Buck**

We are losing the battle. Our moral compass is in distress. We tether tighter and tighter to the physical illusion and so much so that most of us are not able to separate from our body. And fewer are abiding by the sacred essence of the Light which is love, compassion and ethical energy. Balance, faith and trust are dissipating into a soup of anger and greed. Many have never connected with the Light, and so they are wandering a barren landscape to be scattered in unidentifiable directions. Religions and doctrines of faith disappoint as God seems to have left the building. Some use religion as a reason for crime and war. When blind to the Light, we can easily be dragged into the storm.

More and more of us however are beginning to feel the shift in the energy of the planet. We intuitively sense that something fundamental is changing. In our short lifespan it can be difficult to notice what this is because it happens so slowly over many years. Yet everything in the Universe changes and moves forward toward its purpose. All energy is in constant flux. All life shifts from birth to death and back again, even the biology. How many of us have been taught or are aware of this symbiotic relationship? Do we know how it affects the meaning of everything else?

The good news is that the truth of who we are and why we're here is written in this Light. It is the Inner Light, the Universal spark and quantum magic. There is a unique identity and purpose in each Light beam. Plants, flowers and trees are alive with Light too. They communicate with each other, take care of their young and can adjust to their own community. Animals are aware of themselves. They are intelligent, emotional and protective and feel pain and loss. Their Light shines out from them for the world to see, even when we don't notice. It is a calling for life to follow its purpose and to revel in the reward of its fulfillment. We are to consciously make choices to focus on and exercise the gifts of this amazing Light.

"When the Universe guides you, control isn't necessary." **Simi**

Imagine having a way to tap into a resource that would shed a light on the very best choices, much like the way God is meant to be a guide. What if you discovered just such a resource to use at your beck and call? What if I told you that the Light is such a resource? What if this is the promise made to all of us?

Energy = Consciousness = Spirit = Light = Energy

[These words are used interchangeably throughout this book.]

You may not be famous, a princess or songster, as seems to be the desire these days. The fulfillment of your expression on Earth may not be big or famous or even out there. No one Light is more than any other as the essence is quality versus quantity which means every Light is a perfect value. The color of your skin or your address makes no difference to this energy. All life is valuable - gems in the cosmic crown - no less or greater than any other. We all have gifts. The Light inside of you is the perfect place to keep your purpose, destiny and self-wisdom safe from the world. There it will remain untouched and unchanged until you are ready to find it. Where better to secure the divine truth and beauty of your life than to hide it in the Light that lives within you? This is wisdom!

It is by divine design that when we connect to our Light we begin to fully understand and experience this physical life as we are meant to. And thankfully, when connected is also when the Light softens the edges and calms the waters of all other experiences in every way. The need for material wealth, greed, acts of war and hate naturally wane in the presence of Spiritual Light, so profound is its purpose.

Willo, an Elder with a gentle voice, remarked, "Every Light comes from the perfection of the Source. This pure and perfect Light is made of the full color spectrum which is Love Energy. Within you is the door."

Was I able to fathom this? Would I be able to realize I had all I needed in order to uncover the gifts? Once reconnected, I began to understand the value of all life and what love, joy and presence was possible. To step away from the chaos of the world out there was a welcome relief too. It is a promise in fact for all who seek solace and respite from the chaos.

Reconnect: not to travel to something new, as in 'connect to the Light', but to return to where you began as in 'reconnect with the Light'.

Willo continued, "Life is the result of a fundamental course that has happened since the beginning. Progress was even the precursor to the beginning. Nothing in the Universe has ever been static or has not progressed forward - ever. All vibrations and forms progress all the time from one state to the next as knowledge is accumulated and stored. Why would such a course not include Consciousness?"

Yet the Light is a constant animating Energy of the Universe. Light is unique as it denies and supersedes other laws. Quantum physics offers that there is only Energy. It was Light Energy that animated the Universe 13.8 billion years ago at the Big Bang. Light energy burst forth and lit up the ultimate burst. Over millions of years it cycled from the Bang to darkness and back to stars to ethereal energy then on to imperfection to progress to physical perfection. Light sparked acids and proteins toward an animated reproducible form called life. Once instilled within these forms, Light could capture information, transmit and retain it. Light would then expand, express and progress to its own destiny when it will take the simple physical expression to ascension and the ultimate perfection.

Earth is not the only planet which bears such magnificent stuff. Why would Earth bear the only life in the Universe? If life is here, why would it not be there? As time passes, it is becoming less and less likely we are as alone as we once thought. One day life will cross the fine line from unknowingness in the deep sleep to knowingness in the Light. It will be a day when life will progress past the pain. Even though all life has access, not everyone is prepared, able or ready. At no other time in human history have we been so close or as prepared as we are at this moment. Herein lies the future.

Veil: life distractions that form a block between the physical and the spiritual; that which blocks the inner Light from one's access, focus or view.

Not all of us recognize inspired moments as being connected to Spiritual energy. To live from the Light and to know how to sustain the connection is the challenge as life itself is the greatest distraction. Centered in our bodies keeps us distracted from our natural connection with the Light and consequently the Universe. We all receive messages but they can easily be hidden beneath the white noise and chaos of life.

While the Earth's shifting Energy is stirring our Inner Light, many others; authors and teachers, guides, psychics and metaphysicians are becoming instruments. There are many Elders busy communicating with those who can align with them. As a result, there is a new army of Spiritual Lights who will help to awaken those who are still asleep. Old paradigms and ancient ideologies will give way to a brighter, clearer and more relevant energy. Spiritual Beings will be sparked by ancient thunder and the unscathed little people with good intention will renew the Earth and our human-ness. Sacred Energy will bloom from within - just as it is meant to.

There was evidence of the Light in other books and historic wisdom, some from the sciences, religion, philosophy and others. Books would fall at my feet to offer validation and hope as I moved along on this path. The Elders would reveal more and more. Our human population, and indeed all life, is poised for this next step. And you're it – ready or not.

Parkah would explain that centuries of masculine physical and intellectual energy came to a close near the end of the Mayan calendar in 2012. Humanity entered into an era that would bring the feminine energy forward. Like a vibrant bloom on a summer day, the shift in the Energy of the Earth is the new Emotional-Spiritual Era. The feminine Energy will rise gently. Today women are running governments, institutions and corporations. They are executives, monks, sages, metaphysicians and medicine women. **Parkah** says that the Love Energy tucked inside of all of us, men and women alike will flow more freely and bring about a greater peace. Today may seem like a tumultuous time but it is only the final resistance before the old hierarchical fire burns itself out.

G. F. Thornton

To answer the age-old questions about who we are and why we're here, we no longer need to come from hope or faith alone. Today as you look for and sense the shift in the Earth's Energy and as this new Era awakens us we will find more confirmation of the Light. And this vital Energy will ripple out into the world: no matter the place, age, gender, race, religion or belief... and it will change everything.

Energy Signature: the frequency and vibration of your unique Light; the average of the total energy from within you.

What did this new information mean? Once I started to grasp it, I knew it was okay to trust again. There was a desire to take it in and to bask in this simple sunshine. Spirit would resonate and these new vibrations would become links to greater meaning. The Light will always resonate to good and meaningful tomes. It would be a new guide as I tested everything at every stage.

The meaning of things changed. I became more resilient to and less tolerant of toxic energy. I adopted a new awareness and a need to distance from lesser energies. I would begin to feel lighter, less stressed and more in control of my inner energy. I needed to be able to recognize when I slipped back into old habits or when I was returned to my human-ness. Old words and thoughts and old habits began to feel grating and awkward. Little bursts of happiness would suddenly bloom from nothing. I found a renewed faith as the Light softened the meaning of the world. And as I progressed, I felt a new trust in the process of life again as I would find my Bubble of Peace inside little moments of each day.

Matrix: the total energy field throughout the Universe in which everything swims and through which everything is connected.

Spirit led me to my own Coherent Light, a beam that began centuries ago. All of my incarnations and all I learned had been recorded in this Light. We bring all of our accumulated knowledge and any Karmic Debt with us into each incarnation. It was important to trust what was happening and to not cut myself off from greater energy. I knew the messages were from another realm as they added something of immense value, opened up my eyes and changed how I viewed the world. Spirit was seriously closing old doors and opening new ones. Letting go and trusting that this new Spiritual wind would hold me up was next.

44

Spirit is sharing this and more - with all of us. The Earth's Energy shift is upon us. Many of us are silently and unknowingly listening, others are talking and many are responding even if they're not aware of what they're responding to. The renewed energy is exciting us and waking many of us up to be witnesses, to take part, to be supportive and peaceful soldiers of hope. The next leap is near. We are on the cusp, waiting with breath held as we sense the subtle changes in the music. It makes perfect sense that the Light would shine the brightest just as we are about to place a foot upon a new path toward the next exciting leg of our journey.

Spiritual Design

"Spiritual Design is life, abundance, peace and fulfillment, not just for the lucky or the fortunate but for all life; humans, plants and animals." **Sarah**

All species and all things are interdependent, connected by a web of energy, regardless of whether we acknowledge it or not. We are social beings and we experience innate connections with each other all the time. We don't, nor do we want to, do this life alone. So, why can't we get along, and why isn't there peace and happiness when to connect with each other is so inherent? Why must anyone do without when we have the ways and means for abundance for all? Why has humanity been condemned to suffer when there clearly is a better way? Why isn't life fair …when it can be? Why do we not move beyond hate and greed when we can?

> "Karma will keep score every time you forsake your inner code
> to linger in or choose lesser vibrations." **Willy Bear Paw**

Simi spoke of Karma. "Karma is the Law of Cause and Effect which ensures that what you intend for others you do foremost to yourself - by default. If it is your intention to hurt someone in some way, your intention will point the finger of pain and ignorance at you – as the cause. Make no mistake that Karma is always keeping score."

We cannot escape the truth. The victim may be impacted but the victim becomes the effect of 'the cause'. The cause will bear the only burden and they will suffer the Karmic debt. I will have to pay with my happiness quotient to balance the debt I create – certainly in this life and maybe even the next. Each journey will be influenced until the debt is rebalanced –

which will take considerable effort and understanding. An imbalance brings conflict, confusion, pain, sadness, loss, anger and frustration. While they may suffer, a victim does not bear Karmic debt like the perpetrator. Jesus gained no Karmic Debt when he was killed. He begged God for forgiveness for his captors as He said, "They know not what they do." Only the perpetrators acquired a sizable Debt for what they did.

Victims suffer even though they do not accumulate Karmic Debt. They are emotionally affected as Spirit calls to them to attend to what created their pain. They have a path to free themselves by choosing to move beyond or out of the energy of the event. When they release the lesser vibration of the event, to forgive, they are allowing their own healing. If they open their energy up they are able to free the vibration of the event and forgive from a place of empathy and compassion. If they hang on to the anger, loss or pain, they can remain affected by the lesser vibrations for as long as it takes them to let go. The perpetrator in contrast will walk a very difficult and rocky road. They do not expect to pay for their Debt or that they must learn a lesson they have yet to acknowledge. By design, this is Cause and Effect and how the Universe maintains the energy ledger called Karma. We may not witness the perpetrator's future struggle, but struggle they will until they balance the Debt they caused.

Do unto others as you would have others do unto you.

Were you taught this rule as a child? Did you fully understand its meaning? Can you view this from your Spiritual sense, from above all else and apart from old beliefs? Can you see it as a candle you've never seen before? There is an entire universe of Cause and Effect tucked neatly inside this sentence when we take a Spiritual eye to see it. This rule is about far more than just getting back what I give out. If my intentions come from a lesser energy, if I fail my purpose, fail to serve the greater good, I will fail to fuel the fire of wholeness and joy in my existence. I will be alone in my suffering; aware or not of why. This sentence begins with how I am to others, and this is a crucial part because it is what will determine the joy. Jesus knew the truth of this and maintained His purpose above all else.

We have all been programmed. We are domesticated and taught to obey from day one. We are conditioned to be fearful because fear has always served an important purpose - to keep the masses controlled, in civil obedience and abiding the law, or so the story goes. We are forced into what we fear; will we be caught or will we have to pay? What do others expect? What will we lose? Will we be safe, will we fail or will we be included or counted. The list of what we fear is long and growing.

Life is complex. The busier we become, the more unaware we are of how conditioned and habitual we are. I hadn't asked myself the right questions and I hadn't been able to see how fear had played a role either - all along. My best guess is that no one is teaching you about fear. When we operate on auto pilot from within a deep sleep, when we're complacent or apathetic, accept the status quo and allow our brains to be washed, our Energy Signature will be much lower than our potential. And reality responds in kind. We easily increase our Karmic Debt when on autopilot. And it takes time, energy and attention to rebalance it every time, aware or not.

In Spirit's Design, we have all that we need to exist in a safer zone. We have fully developed our physical senses and the host of hormones and emotions to keep us safe. If these senses can be manipulated or used against us because we're not aware, we forfeit our ability to feel safe. The Light increases our faith in the process of life itself because it decreases the impact of fear. When we realize we are meant to fly and we are certain the wind will hold us up, we no longer need to fear taking off - or flying. I had to become aware and accountable to what my energy meant personally and to the influence it had - on me and others. While this is not what we are conditioned or taught, this truth is perfectly clear from the Light.

The Bible is an amazing text. It is however an artistic expression of ethical and moral consciousness and Spiritual wisdom that was written nearly two thousand years ago. Those messages were channeled too, and many are beginning to resonate again. Each one of us progressed through those centuries through many incarnations, and we carry within us memories of the lessons from each. There are many truths held in the Bible that even today it still resonates when filtered through the Light.

We are born with an intuitive sense of right and wrong and only as we spend time here does this shift. Centuries of interpretation and many agendas of fear and control have skewed the meaning of our wisdom. So much of our inherited wisdom has been overwritten in our culture by the power of lesser energy. Fear has robbed us of our ability to see. I alone was responsible to clear away the fog and to cut through the old paradigms to see clearly again. Joining others in childish conquests was counter-productive to my own happiness and this was true for all of us. When we have lost our cause, our moral compass and meaningful purpose is when we resort to bigger and better games to resolve our frustration. And each one of us is challenged every day in the exact same way. Being conscious of what matters and what holds meaning for you is more valuable than anything.

Buck spoke one night as a storm filled the air with thunder. "Each intention, every act, word and thought has a unique vibration. Each one either serves you or takes another bite out of the music of your soul."

I would learn that life was a dance that happened inside. The Light was designed to animate and guide us forward on this physical plane. All life, in fact, is meant to dance in the Light. When we respect and honor this life and everything in it, we can sing and dance freely without fear. When we value the life Mother Earth supports, our Energy becomes fuller and higher. This alone brings music to deep within as the Light resonates like a tuning fork to the greatest of notes. Acts of honor, love, service, compassion, kindness and respect become their own reward ... every time as they fuel the music of our soul. I would learn that there was divine order in the chaos if I knew where to look and what to look for.

My Point of View

My point of view creates a pattern
from which I weave a sacred tapestry,
the craft and art and work that is my Life.
The more focused and gentle the weave
the greater I have honored the Life I've been given.
The finer the shapes I create in kind,
the purer the story of my journey on this plane.
At each new bend and curve I have to ask,
"Am I contributing and supportive, or do I cause harm?"
"Am I gentle and helpful, of honorable intent?"
"Am I engaged in what is truly real?"

The completed Blanket then becomes the Sacred Tapestry of my Life.
If it is to be a thing of beauty, it requires my close attention as I go.
Harmony of color, sparked with White Light, perfect shapes

that change and bend, and sometimes yield, ever stronger,
never-ending threads that knit and bind me,
accountable within.

Spirit's Voice

"There is nothing that you don't already know,
And only Spirit can slip past you unheard." **Dan White Deer**

How this book emerged had been confusing at times as there seemed to be many voices. I didn't ever have a sense that they were from just one or even a few energies, but rather from many. A Spiritual friend offered one day that they were coming from the Collective Consciousness. And at the time, I could hardly have disagreed. The true source would come over time as the Light fell upon me and calmed the world's pulse.

"We are here to share - through you and others – the truth of the Light as your world wakes up for the new dawn. We will guide many Lights to shine upon your Earthly garden that flowers bloom over weed." **Parkah**

Spirit's messages are full and kind and meant to lift us up, to help us and to guide us. It is not for Spirit to dampen the energy or confuse us with more veils or distractions. We can do that quite adequately on our own. There was no need to blame anything or anyone. There was no need to dissect the ego, charge it or the devil for disease or darkness. Blame served nothing and no one except to distract and hold us down in the sludge of lesser energy. Everything is exactly what it is because everything is in balance. It cannot be anything else until we evolve beyond where we are and until each of us ascends to the highest energy.

The messages are about inner wealth, about our human potential and our capacity to love and serve. They are about our true purpose. The world is a 'physical' place for the expression of Light and each life has a perfect share. It is not the quantity of Light that is important but the quality. There are many worlds and many realms and the Light is the integral and vital element in each. The messages added to my life and we all have access to them. Spirit offers a mighty wind which can carry us beyond the tall clouds of darkness. My role was imperative. My choices were important. My commitment was necessary. This was my life, and I was the only one who could change it and live it.

The truth added up to the energy. Everything was energy; thoughts, hopes and dreams, conflict, fear and anger. Taken in this context and from this perspective, sorting through the distractions became fairly straight forward. Dealing with conflict, chaos and trauma and solving the stressors also became clearer. The Light was suddenly softening the edges of everything. I was a single Point of Light, not one that was diffused or scattered. No one else was going to get this right and only from a place of truth would I find the clarity, grace and peace I had searched for all my life.

1986

I was 35 when we met. Robert was my soulmate. There was no doubt I had known this man in other incarnations better than I knew myself in this one. I fell in love with him the moment, the very instant he entered the room. I remember thinking however that he wouldn't quite be the dream - even as we blended like a landscape does in the fog.

I could smell the chemistry like the lilt of perfume floating across a crowded room. I stole a glance at him then consciously turned away. I had promised to never steal another woman's man, and my friend Lola, who had invited me that night, had her eyes fashioned on this friend.

A few more people arrived at his house, the neighbours from across the street, my aunt and my sister, Heather. We sat at his table and he served drinks all around. The jokes started to pile up, one on top of the other. The humor that night was infectious and although my sides were splitting, I was intoxicated by something else. I took quick side glances of his white sweatshirt, cut unceremoniously in the front to make a V-neck, the sleeves lopped off too with about as much care. He was rugged and manly with a full beard, deep brown eyes and strong muscular hands. His humor tickled my soul and while he might not have been perfect in some books, in mine he was like a rock guitar on steroids.

When we all had crowded into his truck I lucked out with the seat next to him. Unbeknownst to me until weeks later, he had asked my aunt which one of us he should dance with - and she had pointed to me. I could feel the energy between us as he drove to the fairgrounds where the dance was in full swing. It was a balmy summer night filled with the smell of dust and horses and sweet summer hay. Jumping out of the truck, I quickly parted his company and made my way into the dance and a table of my relatives. I was very consciously avoiding him, for Lola's sake, and trying to be fair.

"Can I buy you a drink?"

Robert had arrived in my life as I turned thirty-six to cause me to step into my own journey, to challenge my course, to step up to steer my ship and to commit to my journey until I reached this Spiritual shore. This alone made our story even more valuable…but there would be more, much more.

I turned to find our eyes catching each other's. I stood up as if I was on the business end of a spring. My heart stopped beating in that very moment and I wanted to stay there locked in his eyes forever. "Rum and coke…?" I watched as his face softened slightly and his lips cracked a grin, those big brown eyes never leaving mine. He turned and walked away and I followed his body as it crossed the room. My mouth had fallen open. He exuded an energy that I was clearly tethered to as he crossed the room.

"Stare any harder and he'll melt," Uncle Jack shouted just as the music stopped. I snapped back to reality. That was when I noticed everyone else at my table was watching and grinning too. I took a deep breath and sat down with a bump. My eyes found him again and he was on his way back… to me. What manner of fairy tale had I dropped into? I looked around bewildered. Where were the white horses, the carriage, the fairy dust…and damn it, where was my gown?

It was an unlikely beginning, one that they say happens when you least expect it. And then I found out he could dance. What? He had all of this and rhythm too? As he took me to the dance floor and curled his arm around my waist, he whispered in my ear, "I am not the least bit interested in Lola."

We danced, and then we danced some more. The chemistry was electric, the connection intoxicating. I was aware of him next to me and of his brown eyes talking to mine and holding me captive. The music played softly in a distant world and only lightly swirled around us. Everything else fell away as we floated above the ground …in perfect unison.

He spent the evening either in my arms or at my side, and the energy, that ethereal pulse between us was palpable. My family sent comments our way all night long but I couldn't have cared less. This was a cosmic event, and something I had never known before was unfolding. After the dance, he ferried everyone back to their cars. Then he asked if I'd like to head home too or go for a drive... with him. A thousand angels sang my response.

Robert got out of the truck at his house, came back with a quilt and we drove off into the night. It wasn't long before I could tell we were headed to Cameron Lake. Parked at the lake, in short order he found a log resting parallel to the shore. He laid the quilt over it and offered his hand to help me sit. He'd been the perfect gentleman all night, attentive, caring and seemingly smitten for some reason... with me.

I was spellbound. We talked and laughed well into the early hours. And under a dome of shiny stars, with tiny little waves licking the shoreline off in the distance, there was that silent moment; the moment when our souls touched. We were being drawn by a divine and unseen force and we were moving slowly toward the bliss of our first kiss. I could feel his breath on my face. I could already taste his words. And when time stopped altogether, we were swept off into deep space. It was the reunion of two energies that had been connected since forever and had just found each other again.

His voice was deep and kind. **Parkah** stepped forward. "You are spiritual first. All are born whole, valuable and worthy through Perfect Light. Nothing will change this, only the veils of life that hide the purest water."

Only I can decide to direct my course. As is often the case, life had distracted me and caused veil after veil to lie over the Light and to keep me from seeing the truth even though we are destined to find the Light. It had always been there – a testament to its wonder. Think of the magic of knowing that within you is the glory of the Love that comes directly from The Source. If I could have faith in this, if I had been taught how to tap into it, or if I knew it was even there at all, could I ever go back into the sleep that had sucked me down into the abyss? No matter what else fuels our fire during this incarnation, we are here... and we are here for this reason. It is solely ours to ask, "What will be the weave and quality of this tapestry and what will be my role in its making?"

People everywhere and from all walks of life, all religions, races, genders, status and age want the same thing: to be safe and happy. When we trudge off to war, we are fighting for the same happiness and safety as is the soldier on the other side of the fence. How better would it be to use these resources to ensure everyone is safe and happy instead of killing them for wanting what we all want? We begin at the beginning and as with any journey some will arrive first and others will be last. We are meant to pull each other along. We are not meant to trudge through the mud alone or to judge others as they fight for their lives just as we do. Cooperation, instead of competition, peace versus war will build a better world, a happier and safer place, no matter the challenge or the Tribe.

"You decide and invest in what you want to experience." **Little Reign**

Ultimately we make choices that express who we are through acts, reactions, and responses. Nelson Mandela invested in peace of mind while held in prison for twenty years, and when released, he became the president of his country. This is what is meant by living from the Light within. During his incarceration, he chose Spiritual sanity over anger and resentment. He walked away from prison a peaceful man who was so respected he would be chosen to rule an entire nation. It is called Free Will and inner freedom. One day, I would choose the Light over its absence where I would learn of its reward too.

$$HQ = LC \times IF$$

[Happiness Quotient = Light Connection x Inner Focus]

The Happiness Quotient is basically a measure of the degree of connection to the Light; the quality of the Connection to the Light multiplied by the focus upon it. At its most fundamental, happiness is not the result of anything outside of us. While we may experience happiness from some things of the world, it is rarely long lasting. Lasting happiness doesn't come to us but rather from us as it is born within.

Everyone must also find their own Light as there is only one way to it. Each of us must earn our spiritual wings. No one fully arrives at the Light without serving, without having felt love and compassion and kindness. People can say many things, but the proof of a connection is in the quality of their Energy Signature which is the sum of their intention and actions. They cannot ever fake the truth they express.

Parkah explained that the Light is safely tucked away inside all of us and it can never be extinguished, altered or changed by anything. Looking back upon the history of my life, I could see now that Spirit had been present …when I had no conscious awareness for decades. Though I enjoy this wisdom, I prove to myself all the time I am still human and tethered by the physical. The difference now is that I am aware, and when I fall into old habits or patterns, I am able to consciously return back to the Light before I do too much damage!

I had made many mistakes and skipped in and out of the abyss for 30 years. As my less than stellar experiences added up, one on top of the other the veils had too. I hadn't been taught about the power of the Light, my right to it or the benefits of it. I hadn't known how each veil could keep the brightness of the Light from my awareness. No one was teaching that the Light was the best guide, the best resource, the clearest wisdom or the grace I could never find anywhere else. Though I had missed it on my way, the Light had been there regardless, gently nudging me forward and whispering in my ear that there was something better. I now know the one purpose for this incarnation was to reconnect with the Light. It was a single lesson, perhaps the biggest challenge and yet the greatest reward.

Learning of the First Nation heritage of our family would add incredible value and a new understanding as I re-evaluated the past through this new filter. It had been a very important filter I had used for decades without ever knowing it. This was going to color the search and paint a new picture of my entire life once everything was where it was meant to be.

Chapter 4

Spiritual Dynamics

A T THE MOMENT of conception, Light touches down in the very first cells. The Light is a vital part of each being. It is only from living a physical life that you begin to softly fall asleep." **Kimtah**

We spend a lifetime learning how to live in this physical space. The more we tether to it, the more veils and the greater our disconnection from our true nature. We are easily trained and manipulated to forget the value of being connected. How can we work toward our truth to meet the challenges of our physical existence if we are not aware? Life itself is the greatest distraction. Keeping our eye on the bouncing ball of gain and greed and material pursuits is when every trauma, challenge, conflict, disease and loss can take a silent toll. When we are not aware of the resources of the Light, we chance falling further and further away from it. It even makes sense that we would feel an emotional grief in the center of the chest when something so vital to our wellbeing is missing. Depression can happen too when we are repeatedly unable to find something of value that will fill us, help or soothe us when the going gets tough. Yet we may have no idea what that emotion is about or what it is trying to tell us. It can and may very well arrive as a mere response which we cannot identify or which seems to have no apparent cause. Understanding that our emotions are the bridge between us and Spirit can be challenging to learn …if we're not tuned in. Emotions however open up a vast wealth of wisdom on how life really works from within the truth of a Spiritual Being.

"Spirit's voice is subtle." **Little Reign**

Once reconnected, I knew that becoming separated again from the Light would show up in some way. It would be that unexplainable emptiness again, a longing or yearning for something I couldn't quite put my finger on. I would experience other emotions to confuse the issue; loneliness, confusion or just plain exhaustion. And when the disconnection continued, I chanced obscuring the Light with more and more veils. The more veils, the less I was likely to see or sense the Light anyway. In all of my history, I can recall many times when I was at a total loss for what to do, where to start or how to fix things. Can you remember what it's like to be in the middle of a crisis and have no plan? What can you do but take a chance and make a wish? How many times did you have to clean up that mess too?

Decision Day

The day after I met Robert, I drove to my favorite beach, sat upon a giant rock and stared out at the ocean as a light rain dampened the moment. I had to clear my head and I had something to decide. I knew I was in love with him already, but something was telling me that all was not as it appeared. Could he possibly love me back? I was guessing he had his share of women vying for his attention. He was a commercial fisherman, so he travelled a lot. Did he have a woman in every port, perhaps? Would this be a good idea? Could I be the one? Could he even settle for just one woman? I was wary and insecure because I hadn't been 'the one' yet.

I was thirty-six and he was forty-one. Both of us had the experience and knew what this would take. I was trying desperately to find a reason why I shouldn't pursue this any further. How could I protect my heart? In deep conversation with myself ...I had to believe however that love would win over all else. I had to believe that love does conquer all, especially one that felt so deep already. I knew he was my soulmate. As I tried to convince myself that love would triumph, it wouldn't be common sense that would make my decision. It would solely be my heart. Looking back on the decision, knowing what I know today, there was no other choice. Robert was to bring to me what I would not find anywhere else.

> "The Light is the vital energy of purpose, meaning,
> identity, self-wisdom and fulfillment." **Kimtah**

I am here in this physical world. I must survive the physical challenges and stay safe first and I must learn to be successful at it. Yet remove the physical dynamics and it is solely the Light which provides warmth and which fills this life with happiness and reward. Without this connection, the deeper I sunk into the darkness, the more the outside world fell in upon me and the greater the fear, loss and pain became. I was walking proof.

The Elders would teach that our existence is cyclical. We are the cause for each physical incarnation from birth to death. We come here specifically to progress and to move through each challenge for a reason. Learning our lessons we should find fewer and fewer bumps in the future. Upon our death, we do not cease to exist. The Light within is released to recycle through another incarnation to continue to progress.

This Light doesn't dissipate. It remains coherent, bundled in a beam like a fiber optic strand and it lingers close to those who were loved and the places cared about. After death, our Light has no body and likewise no physical senses. It doesn't see, feel, touch, taste or hear the world as it did in the physical. In all realms, here and on the other side, these beams are influenced by spiritual energies around and near them. They are influenced and have conversations via energy sentences. And these form memories too which will be recorded in each respective beam. Everything is recorded in our beam over many lifetimes; knowledge, experience, wisdom, hope, connection, love, anger, joy and Karmic Debt.

Humans are social beings, and so we have an innate need to connect with others, to fit in and to belong. This places pressure on us as we attempt to find comfort and a place to belong somewhere. We have lost faith in government, institutions, healthcare and education as everything is held captive in cold economic cement. More and more of us are seeking something that brings meaning back, that feels real or resonates. Today, people are leaving the church in search of something else as religious controversy makes them question and doubt. There are a growing number of indicators of the shift in the Earth's Energy too as more are standing up to be counted against the blight of greed and crime.

There are other shifts too. More young people today are lost or being stolen from their purpose and inner power than any other generation to date. Men and teens are committing suicide in record numbers as they lose their emotional connection and knowledge of their Spiritual value. Men have long been denied this emotional connection altogether while young people have no idea how valuable emotion can be or what it is even for. They are taught to stay tapped into lifeless technology where they are conditioned to deny everything. It is no longer a mystery why anxiety and depression stats are increasing as minds are being rewritten by technology and divisiveness, greed and fear. Very few are feeling the love as technology doesn't have a heart.

Joseph Campbell, renowned 20th Century author and expert on Myths, stated there is a need for religious institutions to come forward into the modern world or suffer more loss of the faithful. Even decades ago he could see a kind of stagnation causing an exodus from religious doctrine. He also acknowledged humanity needs to be connected to Spirituality of some sort. By divine design, we yearn for and search lifetimes for a Spiritual connection, even when we are not aware. How many dynamics in life are we not aware of today that have powerful influences over us?

As the Light is where we came from, we only need return to it. This won't be a new connection but a short journey back to where we began. We are coming back home to reconnect to our Source, to what is familiar and to what animated us in the first place. I found it ironic that I spent the first fifty years searching the world out there for what I could only find inside of me. It is true the diamonds in life are often right beneath our feet.

> "The unfulfilled space and the emptiness you feel within
> exists in proportion to your disconnection from the Light.
> To disconnect is to be lost." **Sarah**

The greater my disconnection, the greater was the emotional reaction that followed. Emotional pain results more from being disconnected than anything else. Many of us today have developed a *healthy intolerance* for the pain in the violence, greed, war, injustice and the like. Others are turning off their hearts and shutting down their emotion in order to cope. And that's the good news.

"It is healthy to be intolerant of lesser vibration." **Kimtah**

We are not always aware of what is really happening when we experience emotional pain. Veils that lie over our inner Light cause an empty, hungry feeling that makes us yearn for just about anything to fill it up. It became clear that I nearly spent an entire lifetime looking for something to fill that void because I didn't know what it was. Those who have all the material trappings, who are wealthy and famous claim they're just as lost, sad or unfulfilled. Money and fame and all this provides are not sufficient to fill up the empty space or address emotional pain.

"The empty feeling is caused by separation from the Light."
Wahwaskenah

The Greatest Meaning

Spirit always shone a light on what meant something to me. I had to learn how to read the messages and the Spiritual emotion and what they meant. And I only needed one of them to validate they were there. My inner voice came from the Light and it spoke to my true nature, my gifts and my purpose. My entire being was connected to the vibration of my internal Light, and it was always there to respond and guide me to the right path. But first I needed to tap in and stay conscious. The Light was as vital and available as oxygen and was a powerful guide second to none.

Many times over we fail to negotiate as we press forward hungry for our fair share. We are way too busy, always rushing off to the next task, the next appointment, the next job and doing the things we need to mark off our endless lists. We are becoming islands as we run against a relentless wind. As such, many of the fundamentals that helped us survive or get by for so long have fallen to the wayside. We have become angry when the God we learned of as a child doesn't show up when needed most. The circle was no longer intact and common sense had become the new oxymoron. We weren't caring for others in our tribe as we once did and we no longer listen to Mother Nature either. Humanity, at least in North America, needs a spiritual reboot.

His Mom

When Robert introduced me to his mother, a mere month after we met, she scanned me briefly then said, "It takes one to know one." Robert explained later that she had sensed the First Nation blood within me.

I had struggled through decades of abuse, trauma, fear and chaos. Thankfully I emerged on the other side through the grace of Spirit. Today, those events have morphed and changed me more than anything else. As hard as they were, they provided the clues of what I needed to learn and understand. We all have to check our ego at the door, look straight into the mirror and take stock. Today it is upon each of us to share the hope and the practical steps with each other to achieve a reconnection with the Light in this lifetime. This phase in the evolution of life on Earth could not happen at a better time, proving everything is moving along ... as required. To progress is our destiny.

Still there is a power that hinders our best attempts. We are conditioned to be good little sheep. The establishment has found many effective ways to isolate us, to silence our voices and to keep us under the whitewash of complacency. And so, we follow. Can we still become a Light in the darkened places of the world? Can our combined energy influence or change the status quo? Look to the past for the truth. Many times over we have witnessed that it only takes one person to set the world on fire. One person started the Women's March in 2017. One person stood up for human rights, another for the rights of women. Landing on the moon took one person to dream it. Even asleep, we push toward destiny. We might as well get on board and help paddle.

"Life is naturally drawn to the high energy of Unity." **Lucy**

Life Sparks

Every life form arrives with its own magic. The magic is Sacred Light: the source power and animator. Light is the Ultimate Force and the highest spectrum of white energy. This energy is many things: love, peace, grace, happiness and wisdom, to name a few.

"The Light sparks life. What greater love can one know?" **Parkah**

In this life, our attention has been directed by beliefs, perspectives, knowledge and experiences. We are fed many mistaken ideologies passed unceremoniously down to each generation. As the power shifted from the church to Science, many began to seek evidence: not only what we see, touch, hear, taste and feel but what we can prove, qualify and quantify. We had not been as able to prove the Spiritual ...until recently. Science is uncovering evidence of the energy in which we swim which offers evidence of mystical too. As an example, studying Spirituality led me to books that touched on physics and the sciences. It was so interesting that the deeper I dug into physics, the more evidence pointed to the Divine.

Great stories and doctrines have been injected into our attempts to understand higher energy. Whole subjects had fallen into confusion and conflict for centuries in our attempt to describe the indescribable. Suddenly science is diving deep into the microcosm of energy not with the intention of proving the Light, but proving it nonetheless. Many have felt there was something greater yet they couldn't seem to complete the puzzle with any degree of certainty. We want to know when something isn't whole or right. When tragedy happens, even believers tend to wonder where God is and why He didn't intervene. They often feel as if they have done something wrong when prayers are unanswered. We ask, "What's wrong with me" instead of "what's wrong with my understanding?" When God ignores us, we feel lesser-than, bad or unimportant. Is this really what God wants?

Peak Experience: Gabriela

In 1979, in a twist of fate, I was led to work in a doctor's office at a rare time in my life when I didn't have to work. I remember wondering what was wrong with my head that I would seek out work when it was such a joy to just be a mother and wife for a change. Shortly after beginning the job, I befriended one of the staff, a nurse by the name of Gabriela. We connected easily and built an instant friendship.

A mere four months later, when Gabriela had been away on what I thought was a vacation, the doctors informed the staff that she had been diagnosed with terminal cancer. The moment they told me, something happened. I felt a surge transmit through me like a bolt of lightning. The message arrived deep within me, "She will survive." No one else at work, the doctors or nurses believed my insistence that she would be alright, however. After all, they had read the clinical reports, and they were envisioning a very different fate. What had been the spark that touched me that day, and where had it come from?

To fully validate the source of the message and how it had arrived wouldn't happen until long after I had started my Spiritual journey nearly twenty years later. I would come to forsake the mirage of this physical plane and see the truth beneath it. Physicists have long said that our reality is far different from how it appears. The trick is to question our perspectives, our outdated paradigms and the automated beliefs so we can take a look at reality in the buff.

Why had we already associated Spirit and God with Light? How much do we already know of the Light, naturally and intuitively? How much have we been convinced toward something entirely different? How is it that we have been kept from the Light for so long? Happiness becomes less possible the more we are distracted by life, old paradigms and old beliefs that we can't possibly see the truth anymore. Where were our leaders, our faith-healers, our Angel guides? Surely I should have had at least one angel to count.

I was exactly where I was... and this was the only place I could be. It would become more and more important to take a pause on a regular basis no matter where I was or what was happening. I would learn to look for the wisdom that was hidden in my own story, safely tucked between the chapters of trial and error, sadness and joy. We are all on the same path, each at a different point. The wisdom I was to gain was determined by my capacity to receive, to adjust, to evolve and to unlearn what no longer served me. If you were to step into my life right now, the outcome of this life would change completely simply because I have my capacity which is unique to me, and you have yours. We cannot do each other as we are made of different frequencies.

> "You can only be who you are based on your capacity to be who you are." **Blew Like Sage**

Our own capacity to deal with life is developed over our entire lifetime. Some of this capacity comes from DNA, as with natural ability and talent. Some capacity comes from life events and experiences and others from what we're taught and what we learn. Our capacity is malleable but it always results from a personal process that is unique to each one of us. I cannot borrow or even purchase someone else's capacity to use as my own. I only have what I have within me at any given time. The more curious I become, the more I want learn. The more I question, the more I am open and the more I can receive. The less I seek of the outer world, the better I am able to know the world within.

> "Close your eyes ...and pretend you can see." **Parkah**

Parkah explained further. "To rely only on what your eyes see is to be captured by the worldly illusions that will trick you into believing what isn't important or real. There are many who are building illusions that trap and enslave them and others. When you close your eyes, and notice, the Light will place gifts before you instead of illusions. Take nothing of this world seriously for nothing will remain after you are gone."

Humanity is destined to progress toward the Light as nothing is stagnant or stays the same. Our destiny is forward as we ride happily along or even as we go kicking and screaming in protest! While we can consciously develop a greater capacity to deal with life over time, progress is constantly knocking at the door. I am on this journey, like it or not, believe it or not, call it whatever I might. I can choose to move along or linger here to think it over. No great lesson in *my* life depends on anyone except *me*.

For decades, even though I had been searching, even though I could connect unrelated dots and had witnessed miracles of a sort, I had missed the Light. I always believed in a Higher Power, righteousness, morals and principles and certainly fairness. Still I had never understood that these come from me versus to me. After fifty plus years I learned my answers were not to be found searching the outer world.

G. F. Thornton

I never thought to question having an intimate or personal connection to God. Instead this belief would become the fuel that kept me moving forward. Even with each miracle that should have made me realize the magic was internal - I had never looked within me for anything. Our societal conditioning does not encourage us to look inside as we might just find our power. It's like putting solar panels on your roof. Why would the hydro company ever want you to do that? This is an underlying manipulation in the world that favors so few at the expense of so many. We are stuck by unbelievable agendas when we fall asleep and allow ourselves to be unknowingly manipulated.

Knowing

It had been at that very instant that I felt a pure strength, a resonance that rose up inside of me and I just knew Gabriela would be okay. I tried to convince them as they hung their heads and mumbled over the medical reports, picking out each terrible detail. I could feel their sadness. Months they said, she only had months left. She would not be around to raise her teenage daughter for much longer. They would not have any part of what I was saying. Nothing of what was happening in the room that day mattered. I still knew. The knowing was very different from wishful thinking or hoping or simply saying what seemed to be the right thing to say at the time. This was an internal knowing, a strength and pure truth that filled me up. I would even recognize it at the time as a special message because it resonated to the depth of me.

The importance of where I was right then cannot be stressed enough. I was moving along in a giant ball of humanity rolling down a gentle slope toward a common destiny. I had just received a message, a gut feeling and a pure instinct that this person, this friend of mine, would survive this daunting prognosis. What could bring me closer to the Light within if not such a miracle? Each of us will arrive in our own time and obviously I wasn't ready to appreciate this message or its origin just yet. I would learn many years later that no matter what I was doing or where I was, I would gain some ground in one day and more the next. It was true: nothing remains stagnant for long, and it takes far more energy to stay stuck in one place than to go with the flow.

"You are meant to take a meaningful pause from time to time
to allow new wisdom to sink in and
meet up with your soul." **Simi**.

Each meaningful pause helps to integrate new information into a deeper level of understanding. In our busy lives we can forget to take the time to be still and reflect. When we pause is when we build an understanding of the value and meaning of life as a whole. In Nature, all life takes a pause each year as winter sets things to rest. Each night when the sun falls below the horizon, life rests. Life is cyclical, as are we; daily, weekly and yearly. When we are conscious of what a pause can offer, we realize what we can catch of the wisdom within each one. Knowing what to look for is a key.

As I look back at the acres of my own life laid out behind me, regardless of what was going on, Spirit's path had always been there. Staying the course, and giving myself permission to be where I was at any time and to stand firm in the knowledge that I would move forward was validation of the journey. Offering myself permission to be in my life as I was and to know I would be safe seemed to empower me even more. There was no need to meet the world's expectations as I began to trust that I was accountable to the Light and that I would take care of this tiny bit of the world which would then add to the whole. The timely and purposeful messages from the Elders would reshape my life. I was okay with going first.

"Give yourself permission to change - when you are ready." **Kimtah**

In this simple sentence was the freedom to see and hear exactly what was and what could be. I found strength and freedom in giving myself permission to just be. Being critical served no purpose for it hindered forward movement like tar on a wool blanket. It was best to understand that mistakes made on the physical plane can open up the mysteries of the Universe – when we gain the eyes to see them. Nothing will ever damage the truth written in the Light. When we are ready to look within to where we'll find it, the truth will be there ...totally intact and waiting. When I became tired of running the material marathon, it had always been possible to stop for sustenance from the Light. One day I would see that the journey to Spirit had actually been a pretty short trip from out there to in here.

Real Simple

I had heard many Spiritual and religious talks in my day, and many times would come away a little more bewildered than when I arrived. How very capable these apparent sages were to say such a great deal and yet not say much at all. It was quite a skill. Was I simply not able to hear or did they really not have much to impart? At church, I questioned the rules that seemed to have no sensible basis. I questioned the interpretations. Something inside of me rejected hyperbole and pretense like fingernails scraping on a blackboard. When something didn't resonate, it was just as much a message as something that did. There was big doubt from time to time if I would ever be able to straighten out all the nuances.

"Spirit Energy is straight forward and simple." **SoSo**

It seemed that I didn't have to sit upon a mountain in a faraway land, read a library or seek wisdom from others, some of whom sat upon those mountains! My Spiritual progress happened with little outside assistance, except from the messages. This made the experience very real and very convincing. Yet, as I stared back at my history, Spirit had always been there. When I turned to look within to understand better, I would find Spirit buried beneath no less than 50 years of veils!

"Time is not the essence – love is. If time takes too
much of you, know that you have not loved enough." **Parkah**

Sitting at the bottom of the abyss in a dark little corner all alone with my anger and sadness, nursing my most recent wounds, I caught a glimpse of Light. It happened in 1999 with my Bubble of Peace. When I stopped shaking, when I let go of the outer world the door opened and I could actually entertain something else. While it isn't necessary to reach a desperate place to find a glimmer of Light, the Bubble captured me and made me look beyond the usual. My journey to the Light would begin with a single door and a rather short trip - to the core of myself.

The Hospital

I had to tell Gabriela about the message. I drove 3 hours to see her in the hospital the day before she was scheduled for a surgical procedure. When I walked into her room, several people were sitting with her. They immediately got up and left even as I insisted they didn't have to leave, and that I could come back later.

I told her about how certain I was about the message. I explained that I had absolutely no doubt that she would be alright. I said that this was not my heart simply wishing for a good outcome nor was it just the proper thing to say. I told her I had never been so sure of anything before. I expressed the feeling of loving energy that happened inside of me as the message arrived. Her eyes grew big and sparkled with tears and there was a glint in them as she nodded. I was certain she wanted to believe too. After a short ten-minute visit, we said a prayer in gratitude, and I left.

As I exited her room, I wasn't walking. I literally could not feel my feet falling upon the floor yet I was clearly moving. I was floating above the ground as if I was inside a bubble that was also melting away the noise of the busy hallway. I remember the powdery softness of the moment; the gentle light, the muted voices and the sense of lightness.

Two weeks later, we were called to a meeting at work to be informed that Gabriela had experienced a spontaneous remission. The specialist couldn't explain it. Although everyone was over-the-moon happy for her, none of my co-workers seemed to understand the full meaning of this news. Not one of them acknowledged the message. A mere month later, I left the job when my husband was transferred. Had the whole thing been planned in cyberspace? I would visit Gabriela several years later to find she was still happy and healthy and raising her daughter.

Today, in hindsight, the bubble in the hall that day was almost identical to my Bubble of Peace some twenty years later. I only started to appreciate all the messages received throughout my life after 1999 however. To connect with Spirit meant to consciously open up and allow it. It turned out to not be a question of praying the right way to the right God in the right place but rather of making a conscious choice to find what had been hiding inside all along. When I had reached the very bottom of the abyss, the day I decided to let go of my grip on all the material trappings and the only direction to go was up, was the day the crack in my armor opened up just enough to let in the Light. This became vital evidence that when our Earthly attachments are gone, we have no need to cling to the illusions.

Death

Death is the process responsible for the tunnel of Light and for the movie-like review of the memories of an individual life as the energy moves out of the body and back toward the Source. As if travelling back through a fiber optic cable, the consciousness experiences the memories of the physical life it is leaving. As our Light Energy remains coherent, each beam will return to another incarnation at a later time complete with the Energy Signature, memories, knowledge and karma from the last life. It becomes the gathered knowledge of each incarnation. This is when and how our Consciousness becomes aware of its own recorded history.

If anyone has witnessed someone days prior to death, it can be quite clear what is happening. Here are two examples from my own experiences.

A Friend's Death

As a friend was on her death bed, I offered to assist her and her family. Just a day before her passing, lying on her bed, one eye was wide open and the other closed. I fully expected as she faded in and out of consciousness, that she was decisively visiting the other side while keeping a watchful eye on this side. Once everyone had visited and had said their goodbyes, she consciously let go and crossed over.

In another circumstance, it was quite clear that the Light had left a dying man just two days before his body died. It was easy to sense the lack of his essence as I sat beside him. Even as his consciousness returned momentarily over two days and he even spoke with family, one could tell his essence would be missing at times. His Light was getting ready, testing the path to the other side, before his body died.

Some people will often be waiting until just the right day or time before they let go of this physical plane, like my mother who died on Mother's Day. I am convinced she died on this day so we would never forget our mother. The choices we can make around our death can be a symbolic gesture or a way to say something without speaking. Even though their

Energy Signature can remain near the body for days, often loved ones are so focused on the body that they can miss the Spirit even as it tries to comfort them.

Love for family doesn't change after death. It becomes stronger as the departed Spirit lingers just on the other side to protect and help as loved ones grieve. They wish they could explain they're alright and safe and that they will wait to welcome others one day. Some Spirits stay close at hand for years to guide and protect those that are left behind. My son is convinced that my mother is always with him, protecting and guiding and has 'saved his butt on many occasions!'

Enlightenment, incarnation and reincarnation are the effects and Karma is keeping score. As each individual Energy beam evolves, humanity is also moving forward as a macro beam of all life on Earth. We no longer have a population that thinks as we had in medieval times, the Renaissance or even the in Great Depression. Each generation gains and accumulates a body of knowledge. Just as my Light progresses, all Lights are progressing and accumulating knowledge as time moves past us.

The Test

Just recently and in three short months, I tore the cartilage in my knee, my partner would be laid off, our landlords had sold our place, I had a car accident and the insurance company would write off my car and my boss informed me my job and my hours were going to change. This would have been devastating if it had happened several years prior. I would have been in a state of dread, worry, anger, panic and likely depression where I would bemoan life's unfairness and injustice – as usual.

I dropped into automated fix-it mode at first. I was anxious for two days and started running through possible solutions for how we'd manage and stay sane. The next day however I returned to the book to remember I had to drop the fear, open up and allow the Universe in and return to trusting the Light – not always an easy thing, but this was Spirit's test. Could I employ what Spirit had taught me to my own life? Could I walk the walk? What I needed to do was to allow the windows and doors to close that needed to so new ones could open. I would spread my wings and rest on the thermals with faith and trust. I had faith that Spirit would hold me up and soften the blows of the outer world, and that peace would move back in. And it did.

To let go of everything I had clung to for so many years was scary at first – much like taking that first plunge off the high diving board. Once I realized I could do it safely, the next jump wasn't near as scary. We are not taught to have faith in the process of living, to have great faith in life or to trust unconditionally that we'll be fine. Instead we have been convinced there is a devil just waiting for us to mess up …then BAM! I was taught to be careful, to worry about what's coming, to plan and focus on what's next and to control what's out there as much as I could. To sit back and be comfortable in the armchair of my life had to take full-on courage.

Next was finding the clarity of what I had been missing and what underlies all the distractions. When I had fallen, when I gave up the fight was when the voice of Spirit could finally reach me. When the cacophony of the outer world was no longer my focus Spirit's little bell was ringing in my ear. It had been a time when many might turn to God and prayer in a last attempt to save something in their fight to stay afloat. Yet without all the noise, obligation and expectation and at the end of my rope there was Spirit; plain and simple. I was open to listen without any interference. When all the distractions were on hold at the bottom of that abyss I could finally hear Spirit's subtle little voice over the din.

"Allow the Light to offer new solutions – it is allowed." **SoSo**

It seemed I wasn't in need of a facilitator. What I did need was reason enough to let go in the darkness, to let go of the material world to look for peace and happiness somewhere I'd never looked before. This in itself was contrary to the outgoing, get-it-on, in-your-face, you-can-do-anything attitude expected in the West. Westerners also believe that doing personal work quietly or privately is sneaky, weak or inhibited. We are taught to be bold and confident about what's happening and what we're doing about it, and it didn't matter if we believed it, or not. Just applaud when told to.

Those who process their world within are actually closer to the emotional bridge to Spirit. Sometimes this can be confusing. We have all been made to feel that we are flawed, wrong or unusual if we don't obey a social standard. It's common to be confused or frustrated when we don't measure up with what others or the world expects. Internal processing, or introverts, is closer by proximity at least to the emotional clues of Spirit.

Our social standard toward individualism, independence, material pursuit and disregard for inner reflection has us seeking answers in all the wrong places. To focus on the outer world as if diligence alone would allow me to find happiness was a huge fantasy. Nothing could have been further from the truth. **Sarah** would offer another; "Everything that will fulfill your life is written within you and you need only seek its expression and allow it." Spirit was about to show me where to look and how to open up. All I had to do was get out of the way and let it happen.

Skeptical and not trusting much, once I started this journey toward Spirit, I made a conscious decision to protect it from as many outside influences as possible. This journey was mine and I had ample reason to be cautious of how others might influence it. There would be sufficient evidence along the way that there was no need to seek an interpreter or a guide for the Spiritual to be accessible, possible or effective. I had a sense I was to go it alone. I needed to be cautious of any possible interference and to not let anything change what seemed to be happening naturally and on its own. If I could knock on the door and access the peace and happiness of my Bubble again, then why couldn't everyone? So when I dug deeper, information on light certainly made me sit up and take notice. I had to test everything too, to pay attention to each nuance, to satiate my mistrust – at first.

> Seek and ye shall find. Ask and it shall be given.
> Knock and the door shall open.   **Matthew 7:7**

This quote implies that we are all one and equal and that no life form has any greater access or better path to Spirit than any other. It instructs us that when we seek, we will find, and when we ask, it will be given. When we knock on that Spiritual door, it will open. It doesn't say that you have to go through someone or that you have to knock on certain doors or be a perfect Christian or a faithful Catholic in order to be *granted* access. Regardless of my religion, my belief system or my lot in life, it was clear; the path to receiving the truth begins with seeking.

The Light is a very high vibration and it is our greatest resource. Nothing can alter its purity. We have been convinced that in order to understand or benefit from the Highest Power, we had to have help. We have been convinced we lack purity and are so full of sin that we are incapable of connecting with God or being in His favour. In the past, the lowly peasants were not intelligent or Spiritual enough to arrive at something so sacred and holy and wise on their own. And yet for me, it made no sense that some could receive while others couldn't and some would go to heaven while others wouldn't. This didn't feel like Divine Design but rather reward and punishment and a basis for the hierarchy. When my mother was on her death bed in 1989, I simply could not believe she was going to hell because she had not accepted Jesus. She had been far too good a person to be denied heaven, if it existed at all. We must be taking the rules too literally.

There is no purpose in trying to control another's journey for it will make little difference. Each person will travel their path and will take their time to arrive at their own cornerstone based on their ability or capacity to learn what they came here to learn. Past lessons are written within us, and no one can take us to the boat if we're not ready to sail. Life is full of details and yet the meaning of all of it is the only truth there is. Evidence of someone who has a strong connection to their Light is clear, even to a non-believer. Those who are connected exude something different; an undeniable energy, a softness and a gentle energy. We sense this energy, the simple grace, the internal peace and self-wisdom. Spirit has said many times over that we should go in faith of the Light and to not be fooled by pretense or the illusions and trappings of the world.

"The greatest Spirit in a crowded room will be the quietest." **Parkah**

Learning of Spirit changed the meaning of everything. Coming from an inner reality, there is no longer a need to fight or defend what happens out in the world. This was how to navigate life and it should matter to no one but me - for only I can account for the direction taken. I am the creator of the storm or the calm in my ocean. I could find peace where the outer world no longer held power over me or I could wallow in fear. The world was a landscape for the seeds of my destiny to bloom, and I would choose when and how to plant them.

The Light addressed everything. It was a silent, coherent beam. It was made of Sacred Energy that had captured and recorded all incarnations, all lessons, challenges and triumphs. It was the capacity of my soul, of achievement through past lives and it remembered the wounds and counted the scars. It contained the seeds of good intention, of kindness, compassion and love, and I could choose to plant and care for them, or deny their existence. The garden could only bloom after it was planted. Living from the Source, I was accountable to the Source. The greatest Spirit in a crowded room is in simple observation of the outer world to move around in and silently be apart from. It was like pulling the weeds and watering the flowers in the garden – and remaining untouched by the world as it whirled around the spectacle. The greatest Spirits have divorced the physical and blend into the nature of Mother Earth. They do not fight, argue or show off their garden for it matters not if others are watching.

The Mayan Calendar

There were many expectations at the end of the Mayan calendar in 2012. Speculation included the apocalypse. We were well aware of the extraordinary knowledge and wisdom of the Mayan people. And so, when their calendar was due to end, we were expecting various catastrophes as we questioned what the event could possibly mean. Is it our dreadful history that we would expect the worst instead of the best? What if the end of the Mayan calendar meant that the suffering naïve stage of human evolution was coming to a close? What if it meant that our accumulated knowledge would now afford greater progress in all areas for all life on Earth and a new calendar was meant to mark our next step to enlightenment? What if this would become the era of the feminine energy simply because centuries of male dominance and conflict had run its course? Just as a child must first learn of their physical world and how to survive in it, our history was clearly the childhood years of humanity on Earth. We are now setting off into the young adult stage where the teen in us will start to rebel, when we'll stomp our feet and shout out about the inhumanity and unfairness – just in time. We will pay attention to creating a lifestyle that is softer, more pleasing and peaceful and effective. The calendar will now herald that the evolution of life is reaching a new phase of gentle, feminine Spiritual Energy.

G. F. Thornton

Indigo, Crystals, Rainbows & Stars

There has been more and more information about 'special children' being born in the past twenty or so years. These children would be named based on the decades into which they were born. Each title somewhat identifies their uniqueness. The Indigo Children, they say, are highly sensitive, have mental challenges and are often misunderstood and difficult. The Star Children are super sensitive, highly intuitive and have developed strong and eccentric strategies and perspectives. History will eventually record these definitions as errors that were based on out-of-date paradigms however. And one day we will come to learn about the profound insight and wisdom inherent in these budding forms of humanity. Spirit doesn't mess around.

Society has focused on a small portion of this population who we are starting to identify today in the new generations. That there is an identified population that has already declared their uniqueness does not mean they are the only ones who are present. There are many children who are here and who will be reincarnations of Old Spirits. Of these, there are millions who are quietly or secretly living behind closed doors, perhaps out of caution, until they are ready or the time is right. They are silently wise and gaining in knowledge all the time as they wait for the perfect moment to fulfill their purpose. They will rise to do great things in the future for they are the progress of humanity. There will be the lack of acceptance from those who are still devoted to old paradigms and even older beliefs while their united purpose is perfectly on point and timely.

The babies being born today come from a Light that has gathered more knowledge than any other in history. To say these children have come here to expand the consciousness and the state of the world for the better makes perfect sense when viewed from the Light. And we are seeing such incredible gifts and talents in these new generations. Just as has been said before, we cannot go backwards to another era of thought as wisdom is always increasing from one generation to the next. And this wisdom does not unravel or dissipate. It remains coherent.

While these children are misunderstood, misdiagnosed and set apart from others more from society's fear than wisdom, they are the next step in our evolution from what is today to what will be tomorrow. There is a natural evolution with each generation that is likely to not be understood by previous ones. These new generations will reset standards, change governments and economics and redesign thinking on an unprecedented scale. The 60s and 70s had the Flower Children and the Boomers, and the 2000's will have the Stars and Rainbows. These children will open up the pathway toward even greater and more enlightened beings than any other we have known to date.

Two Spirited

There is a new class of children; Two-Spirited Beings, those who have a balance of male and female energy. Society treats these people as if they are aberrations. Actually Two-Spirited people are not new nor are they aberrations. If anything they are a natural balanced human and we need many more of them to fix what's broken.

Wahwaskenah brought this forward, "Two Spirit people are highly revered in some cultures. Families that include them are considered lucky. Your First Peoples believe that a person who is able to see the world through the eyes of both energies is a gift from The Creator."

Today, they are bold, determined and neither deterred nor insecure about their blended yin/yang energy. Theirs is a timely arrival. As humanity learns of these people and begins to accept them, Nature will open up to more. These special Beings are pushing forward in recognition of their blended energy which could well be critical to the survival of the human race in the future. While there have always been Two Spirit beings, their numbers place them on a new human map. Male aggressiveness, anger, violence and greed will be quelled as these balanced spirits move to their full expression that sits gently in the middle. This could not have happened at a better time. Bless these Two Spirits as they brave the ignorance of limited minds that misunderstand and fear such gifts.

Peter

In the spring of 1984, Peter and I met at work. He would become my best friend and he was a gentle giant and a kind and funny person. Although he didn't admit it openly, he was Two Spirited. I loved him like a brother, and we shared nothing but laughter and good times. We just got each other and we spent untold hours laughing and enjoying each other's company.

Eventually, we went our separate ways however, not because we had to but for another reason. Peter had kept his secret from me until he announced he would move away just after Christmas one year. I knew I would miss my dear friend, but I told him I understood even when I didn't want to. About a year later, he called to tell me he was in the hospital. When I visited him there, he spoke of his most intimate secrets. He told me how embarrassed and broken he had felt when he admitted to the world that he was gay. He told me that one short relationship with another man had brought about AIDS. It caused him to run away from his truth to the little town where we would meet.

As he lay in the hospital bed, his face and body nearly unrecognizable with disease, he talked about what it was like to live with profound sadness in his soul as he felt like a victim of the greatest challenge life could have given him. When he died a few weeks later, he was only 35 years old.

I mourned the wounds he felt in light of his beautiful Two Spirited soul. He had felt broken and sick and wrong when in fact he was kind and whole and wondrous. Peter had focused heavily on what others thought instead of the beauty he expressed in his balance and kindness. Shame and guilt had taken his life long before he actually died.

I am the Light

Sarah whispered, "You are not your body. The biology will return to the Earth at its death while the Light within it will be released to fuse again with the Source."

There are opposites in all things. There is an opposite of the physical which is the Spiritual. There is the absence of Light and its opposite is Perfect Light. Perfect Light is found in the future while the darkness is only found in the past. Each beam remains the same coherent beam for as long as it returns to this physical plane to add to its energy. One lifetime could hardly be sufficient to achieve insight, let alone enlightenment.

My journey is guided by my perspective, and your journey will be guided by yours. I could have been 100% stuck believing that my wandering and unsettled pursuits was all there was to find. I had seen myself as flawed and felt anxious and scared, while deep within me was a constant knowing that there was something better. From where do you suppose this came?

And so it was. I seemed to be honed into something that was compelling me to continue to question and seek. There was a voice of Spirit whispering in my ear. I was destined to arrive at a single point on this journey were I to listen, a place where stillness and silence would transmit the greatest voice. I would come to meet myself, deep within, where this Energy would be found – an Energy I would no longer deny.

At first, the energy of the Light was subtle, and yet today I understand the depth of my pain was Spirit trying to get me to turn around and look within - all along. Spirit was practical and consistent. The tears and the pain had been the voice of Spirit all along. Spirit worked with exactly who I was and what I needed, what I valued and what had meaning to me at each and every moment. How could I be anything other than who I was? And the Light always shone on the best route back to home! My mother wrote this on every birthday card;

No matter where you roam, you will always have a home.

Learning to hear the unique voice of Spirit was a key, and it took some practice. Still, Spirit had always been accessible and had travelled with me no matter where I had been or what I had gotten wrong. Spirit held the clues to my happiness - and I never found such clues in any other place or through any other form. Spirit spoke from within and made me aware in small and simple ways and in grand and profound ways too. I had to learn its language and how to tell when it was Spirit's voice and when it was just the chatter in my head. Learning how to focus away from the noise of the outside world made it easier to hear that little voice within. Meditation was a tool to stop the chatter so my Mind could connect with the voice I had never heard before but meditation wasn't needed either, just open arms.

My search had been driven somehow. It was never la-la-la wonderful and all was well. The past had been brutal at times. It had been rough and barbed, hard and made of stone. At times it was painful and angry, and at other times it was hopeful and happy. Joy and love would be missing one day but would fill the next only to cycle back around again. I recall likening my trip to a roller coaster ride of extreme highs and lows. Life often flung so much at me that at times it was best to shut my eyes and not even watch until everything could be filed into the past. I had lost hope that my life could be anything else many times, and I often struggled to stay just above depression. Thankfully, I never stopped seeking something better.

If there is something really important to share with you here, it would be that Spirit is simple. It seems to be human nature to dissect and disassemble everything to understand how it works. Spirituality, God, the Ethereal and the like have been subjects we have taken apart, dissected time and time again and put back together, not always in the same form as they had been received. We do so with the hope of a greater understanding and of unearthing the clues to discover more. Spirit and Spirituality were two of those on-the-outskirt words. Both had been used a great deal but neither quite fit for some reason. Spirit had been linked to Pagans, Witches and Mystics, to ghosts and alcohol and evil which had been forbidden in the past. How could Spirit suddenly be good news? As soon as the word Spirit is uttered, a wide range of definitions and paradigms pop up. It was interesting to watch their faces when I asked people what Spirit meant to them. While Spiritual energy can be explained with the Light, my own understanding was just starting to fall into place. The word Spirit needed a new definition. The Light would then make a real simple space.

"Spirit is Conscious Inner Light Intelligence." **Lucy**

We never lose our connection to the energy of those with whom we travel these incarnations. The veils and the busy world may filter them from our consciousness but they are always with us. Some travel with us on this plane as guardian angels and others become guides or protectors who pop up from time to time out of all manner of dimensions just to help. Spirit is not as mysterious as we think – it is actually real simple.

In Search

I had spent over fifty years in search of something. As if a little angel had a hand upon my shoulder nudging me along, I remember an insatiable need to keep looking even though I had no idea what I was looking for. The urge was subtle, like a gentle breeze blowing upon my back that I could easily have missed. Whenever my lot in life was just too painful or went wrong in some way, I remember saying over and over again, "there must be something better than this." In my heart of hearts, somehow I knew life was more than just how it appeared. All the while, it was a whisper in my ear for as many years and it was the little voice of Spirit talking to me, calling me and encouraging me to seek. Yet the voice wouldn't be identified until years later. I mistook all the chatter and the messages as the same useless stuff. I would continue to leave one relationship after another, one job after another, one industry after another and I would move more times than seemed physically possible. And it grew to be apparent that I was definitely looking for something, even if I couldn't quite name it.

Nothing is ever created or destroyed. It is merely changed. I was the same beam of Light in past lives as I am in this one, just a bit smarter from the trials and challenges, shining a little brighter today than yesterday perhaps. The Light which shines within today is the same information that will shine through my next incarnation and the next. When I am feeling inspired, happy energy on this Earthly plane is when I am living with that Light.

"Experience physically. Feel emotionally.
Know intuitively. Soar Spiritually."
Rose Fuller, M.Ed. RCC

You may already know your purpose even if you haven't recognized the Light either. Many people find their purpose early on, like a child prodigy or someone whose gifts are found effortlessly because they can be easily identified. Many people who come to their gift early find out years later that it was the gift that connected them to their Spirit Energy. Even if we haven't acknowledged this connection or why it happens, the benefits can still be there. It isn't the acknowledgement of the Light that makes it what it is. Harnessing the Light however has given me a different perspective on everything. It has planted the seeds of wonder inside where at one time only anger lived. And that was enough.

Many Junctures

There have been many junctures over the years. With determination and work and sometimes plenty of perseverance, I have been able to stay on course long enough to hear the orchestra of Spirit. I would find my home. I would find a soft pillow, gentleness, some kindness and a welcoming hug that touched me deeply and made me sit up and take notice. Many things have become what they were meant to be, like intolerance for unfairness and love for beautiful, innocent animals. Regardless of where I am, how I am or what befalls me from this day forward, there will always be purpose and personal wisdom available in every event. There were the clues to be found in each experience when seen with courage and open eyes. This would be how happiness could happen.

"The higher one soars, the fewer there are, even though moving toward this greater energy engages and assures us. Life from this Sacred Energy will change your understanding of everything else." **Parkah**

I thought about how many times I had been called to Spirit in the past. This has happened to us all. We are naturally drawn to the Light just as a moth, and the Light shines everywhere. We have all seen the Light and have known the presence of Spirit and likely didn't recognize it. You may have witnessed its miracles and have known its angels, but missed the meaning because the experience was a fleeting moment inserted between chores and dancing and hangnails. Events and life's distractions can easily slow our progress. And they are cumulative. The more drastic our reactions, the greater are the barriers that hide us away from the good news. My honesty and awareness would be a solitary path to this self-wisdom.

Spirit took every opportunity to speak, to fill me up and guide me. Within each life event would be the clues. In hindsight, the cascade that took me to my inner truth had begun in one simple moment as if I had finally slipped over the crest of a waterfall. When I finally fell into the warm pool below the pain, the truth was there, safely hidden and protected. A single moment, a simple decision, or merely the desire to find a better way to do this life had opened a door. The only thing left to do was walk through it.

Little Bird

Night was settling in as I was returning some equipment to the pool shack while on vacation in Mexico. I noticed something on the tiled floor of the breezeway. As I got closer I could see that it was a small bird. I wondered if it was injured and whether it would let me help. I put the equipment down carefully and slowly approached her. She didn't fly away. In fact, she let me pick her up. I cupped her in my hands, held her close to my chest as I spoke softly that everything would be alright. It wasn't possible to tell if this little bird had been injured or not but I shared some healing energy anyway. I didn't quite know what to do next. I watched as another bird flew into the breezeway and could barely find its way out. Ah, so that's what happened. The breezeway had obscured their path to freedom.

I walked down the breezeway to another open-air hallway where there was a planter filled with tropical plants. I wondered if this little bird might feel safe tucked in there for a time. I stroked her wee head, and while I couldn't see anything wrong, the tiny bird stayed in my hands for about fifteen minutes as I talked to her. My hands could feel her tiny heart and I could feel when it eventually slowed. I sat her down beneath a plant and told her again she'd be alright. She waited for a time then tried her wings, lifted off, made a few circles around me and flew away. She had likely been tuckered out trying to find her own way out of the breezeway when I happened upon her. I felt so privileged to be there at just the right time that tears filled my eyes and trickled into my heart. This little bird would become a reminder that I had been seeking respite from the harsh reality of the world too, and I ventured a guess the two of us were not alone.

There would be details here and there and all around that would start to resonate within me – echoing each perfect note. This little bird and its story resonated inside of my heart that night. My heart cared for her and loved her unconditionally. She made me feel something rather warm and profound in our short time together. It was a privilege to hold her in my hands. She let me feel her Spirit and we will always be connected. I could hear more when I finally let go of the noise of the world and learned how to appreciate the wisdom in the silence like with this little Spirit.

When you listen and watch closely you can catch the magic of Spirit everywhere and at any time. Watch a dog or a cat. Look for the Spirit Energy they are tapped into. They are not distracted by life and they have an innate and pure confidence in life. Animals live abundantly, even if in different ways. Cats are full of cool confidence and dogs are brilliantly joyous. They don't mope or worry about what might happen tomorrow. In fact, when you're feeling disconnected, focusing on an animal can help reconnect you to Spirit if you let their energy speak to yours. This is the key reason we feel such unconditional love for our furry little friends.

Love would become sweeter and deeper. Colors and scents and sounds would heighten. Worldly circumstances drifted softly into the background. Happiness could become joy. The sadness, anger and pain from the outer world would slip into the past where it could be forgotten bit by tiny bit over time.

Willo whispered, "Spirit is not an escape. The Light does not eliminate the pain but rather offers an alternate perspective from safety, faith and trust in what life is in the first place. You are meant to experience bliss, to have abundance and joy on the physical plane, not just now and then, but always. Abundance is not made of Earthly or material things. It is rather abundance of the sacred music of the soul, the rainbow of love and peace and a renewed faith in the process and trust in life."

The old questions that had haunted me no longer needed answers. Spiritual energy was pulling my attention away from the pull of the outer world. Suddenly from Spirit - everything was exactly how it was supposed to be. There was no longer any place for the truth to hide. I could attest to this on a personal level because I knew the darkness all too well. No greater gift could I have imagined than the new warmth and comfort of Spirit.

"The only thing that can fill you up is a higher vibration." **Little Reign**

Happiness had been just an elusive word for many years, a word that merely tempted me from time to time, and one I felt would never describe my life. For decades the distractions had filled my days with fear and anger because I had been stuck and focused on the world. Happiness would not be found there. The material things, the career successes, the new car or the right house on the right block had not been the stuff of happiness in the past. This I already knew. They had been the trappings of the physical world that took me further into captivity. It had all happened whether I tried to control it or not, whether I was Spiritual or religious or not, and whether or not I had caused the events that tied me to the world. The best thing I ever did was to go from the false outer landscape to the true inner treasures. The firm commitment I made to find a better way to do this life was the single most important of my life.

The Tantrum

I actually stood in the middle of the room and stomped my feet like a child in a tantrum and yelled, "I will not take another step until I find a better way to do this life!" I was tired of feeling like a ship with no rudder.

I would start by getting to know what I was really all about for the very first time. I worked on identifying my values and what had meaning to me. I took stock of how I showed up in my life and what strategies I had adopted as a child that no longer served me. I could see many others who were so focused on the outside world that they had never found their inner wealth either, and now I could see their confusion and pain too. And I learned that lasting happiness would not be found out there – by anyone.

I stated looking at other things too; the afterlife, karma, reincarnation and even the ability to communicate with those on the other side. I would become a philosopher and a pseudo-scientist always appreciating the empirical evidence, the scientific discoveries alongside the ancient wisdom and modern tenets. It became now clear that everything has within it a touch of magic and every experience brings an understanding if we're curious and open enough to see the truth under the illusions.

"Life is a series of experiences that offer opportunities
to make you whole." **Dan White Deer**

I could no longer ignore the meaning of my experiences. I started finding clues in the past that opened doors in the present. Looking back, there were many times the Light had been shining on my path. During my 30 Years of Darkness, I would never have said the pain and the tears would someday become a testament to the Light. I would never have believed that my tears had been Spirit nudging me to turn inward. I would never have said that the loneliness, grief, loss and fear would be the most valuable clues of all. Yet it was true. Not only had the rocky road of the past polished me, it had quietly encouraged my search every day for decades. I doubt I could have known the peace in the Light if I hadn't known the pain in the darkness.

It would turn out that my emotions were not the enemy. Each emotion was insight. Each one led me toward the best that I had. Each one taught me of my deepest hopes and each one was designed to guide me toward my best achievements. Emotions were the connector from the physical world to Spiritual wisdom and they directed me to the secret of fulfillment. **Sarah** spoke again, "Emotions speak to you about what you value and what is valuable, to what has meaning, what hurts you and scares you. Emotions identify what will fulfill your life." When something resonates emotionally within, it is a clue you have found something that touches your soul ...and it is meant to speak to you. Each message was another clue too. It seemed that it would be very wise to take notice of all of them.

Dream Meeting

Robert was a commercial diver with a crew and his own boat called The West Wind. The summer we met, he went away fishing for months, and I missed him terribly.

I remember the first time it happened. It was a warm summer night, and I had gone to bed early. I dropped into a deep sleep quickly and into a dream that felt so real, every detail was clear and every emotion was ripe. I was perfectly suspended in the night.

Suddenly, I saw him across the room. I could smell him, that musky maleness that always pushed me over the moon. I came close and touched him, the sparks zinging from my hand to my heart. I could feel his embrace. We were at a restaurant and dinner was on the table and I could smell the smoky steak. Even from within the dream, I wondered how my senses could be so alive. The next day the phone rang. Robert was calling me ship-to-shore. He asked how I enjoyed last night. I was shocked! We started to discuss the details of the dream as if we were simply reminiscing about a recent vacation. We talked about the setting, the dinner and we even rehashed our conversation. Amazing as it seemed, I never questioned our ability to connect with each other as if we'd been together in the ether for as long as forever.

We walked and talked and danced in several dreams after that. We could connect beyond the physical and beyond the reality of the humdrum and the drudgery in several ways. We could finish each other's sentences and I knew when he was home from fishing even before he called. Our connection was other-worldly. He was my soulmate, no question.

During that time, I hadn't connected all the dots on a Spiritual level. My focus had been totally on Robert. Years later, after the BoP in 1999 however, I looked very consciously and honestly at everything that had happened. And my relationship with Robert would prove to have a very different meaning and purpose than what I had remembered - indeed.

About ten years ago I started to see flashes of brightness each time Spirit brought messages to me at night when my eyes were closing in on sleep. The flashes started as shadows then bright dots. Over many months they developed into bursts of light, then to the shape beings and finally to several beings at the same time. Every time they appeared, they signalled a new message. Spirit was gaining my trust as it offered these Lights to release me from the darkness that still was holding me back. There were definitely a few forces at play.

I had plenty of work to do as I set out to clean my closet filled with dust and trauma and bad memories. This would draw me into the Light more and more with each new clue. Spirit was sending messages and I was focused on picking up on them. The more I grew to trust the Light, the easier it was to focus on it. Over time, this book became governed more and more by Spirit and the Elders. I could not, for any reason, rush its writing for the Elders would only work from the level I was on at each moment. I often felt they were tapping their toe - patiently waiting for me to catch up. These Spiritual experiences were becoming touchingly personal. I was happy to work on me and dig through the sand of every beach I had ever walked. Once I could hear Spirit's voice above the noise of the waves, I felt the freedom of its vast and open ocean.

"There is great wisdom in your life story." Rose Fuller, M.Ed. RCC

We should come to our own conclusions and decisions, separate and apart from those of others. It is essential that we contemplate and test from our truth before we accept something. We have the wisdom and we can stop being sheep. We can own our journey and the lessons we need to find within it. They are presented to move us forward and to help us grow and evolve from where we are today to where we will be tomorrow. No longer worry over what someone may have said about you – for their opinion has no bearing on who you really are. No one can define you. Only you define who and what you are, and no one else. Grow confidence in whom and what you are within for there is no greater wealth or higher truth.

When you can recognize just one experience through Spirit, either now or from the past, it can transform you. The wisdom in the Light changed my temperament and patience. My faith and trust would grow in the process and I would begin to see the ills of the world from a very different perspective. Watch for it, wait for it …and then take notes!

"The Light will keep you from the ills of the physical world." **Parkah**

What are you doing when you feel fulfilled inside, when there's one of those perpetual smiles on your face or you lose all track of time because you're so engrossed in something? When you are creating and inspired you will slip silently into the Light. We drop in and out of this 'zone' all the time but do we recognize it as the Light?

Be in the moment and take stock. What are you feeling? How did you get there? Separate the emotions and begin to learn how to get back to the zone any time you want to. When life would knock me off my Spiritual track, I worked diligently at marking my path and getting back. I had to be aware first and sometimes it took a while to notice I'd fallen off. I didn't always realize when I had let go of the Light until the darkness started filling up my world again. I had to learn how to be conscious and aware at all times for this very reason.

It seems our world is split in two. On one side are the compassionate, the kind, the empathetic, the caregivers and the philanthropists, and on the other side are the rebels, criminals, the angry, the prejudicial, the haters and the terrorists. The only way to bridge this gap, to heal those who on the far right is to reach them and help them, educate and heal them.

Rather than go to the Light, can we begin to come from it? Can we learn how to live in peace? Can we have good intentions and be kind, compassionate and caring? Do we realize the many rewards of such a way to do this life? Are we capable and can we all reach within ourselves to touch this magic and bring it into everyone's life?

The answer is yes.

Chapter 5

30 Years of Darkness

WHILE THIS BOOK is not about saving women from abusive relationships, I would be remiss, personally, if I didn't include some of the information I learned about abuse, about what abusers do, and how and why their victims can and should escape. Some of my stories included in this book are graphic and scary for a reason. They are meant to show you that no one is alone and others have suffered too. They are meant to shine a light on what far too many women have endured. The 'Me Too' movement is opening closed doors and windows into the secret and frightening lives of far too many women living in peril at the hands of partners and others. And it appears this sad story happens far more often than any of us could have imagined. The truth is finally being revealed. People, both men and women, the world over are beginning to take a stand to stop those who believe that women are property and can be forced to be submissive like a slave, treated like a commodity, seen as lesser than or on this Earth solely for their pleasure. It is time to call a spade a spade.

G. F. Thornton

The following story happened in March 1999, roughly three weeks before the Bubble of Peace event.

The Final Straw

I had excused myself from his office where we had been sitting in simple conversation with a glass of wine at the end of a busy day. I announced I was tired and heading to bed. I entered the kitchen, selected a dinner knife and a tin of cat food to feed Tilly.

Tom rounded the corner, grabbed me by the throat and proceeded to choke me and throw me around the room. I thought of the knife in my hand. I remember the pain of the counter, the wall and the floor several times while my mind was in a hurry to understand. What did I do? Will he kill me this time? Could I use this knife? I quickly decided I could not and dropped it in the sink as he slammed me into it. I would use my brain and my nails before I could use a knife. I screamed as loud as I could every chance I had but I knew the neighbors were too far away. I remember planning what to do next as if I was watching a movie in slow motion from the couch. I decided to slam my knee into his groin. This did nothing but make him mad. Lesson learned.

Tom and I had been living together for six years and had built a successful business. This however was the second incident. The first attack happened in our first year. Thankfully, my son had arrived at the door with a two by four and a warning. I didn't report him but left him immediately at great expense. Once he found me, he begged me for months to come back. And after several months of pleading his case, I did return.

To this day I don't recall how long the attack lasted as it was clear my psyche had been protecting me. I endured, taking each second one at a time, screaming when I could, fighting back when I had to and understanding that if I had to fight for my last breath, I likely would not win. I don't recall how it ended. I just remember finding myself alone in the master bedroom. I was sitting in the bed, shoes and all, and had drawn the blankets around me as shock and fear shook the room. My eyes were wide open and my mind was a blur of more questions. Should I report him? Would he open that door for another round? Would the authorities believe me? Could I leave him? Where would I go? What would I do? Would I lose everything? How would I support myself? Would he do this again? Would I survive?

I reported him to police. There was no other round. The authorities believed me and would arrest him. I left him. I found a place to hide. I would learn how to heal. I lost everything. I got a job. I never gave him another shot at me. And I survived. He would be charged with a criminal offense and would be given probation for six months, even though I had found out I hadn't been his only victim.

I had sufficient reason to become laser-focused as I picked myself up from the bottom of this abyss. A month or so later was when I experienced the Bubble of Peace and I went from living outside of me, out in the scary world, from continuing to be trapped by abusive partners and the chaos of life distractions, to turning toward my inner sanctum. It would be a time when I would discover more than I could have imagined. It would also be a time when I worked really hard at getting to know why this happened at all. I began living moment to moment, wary and afraid of what could be next. I was finally awake and in each moment from then on I knew I would fight to find a better way.

They say that doing things the same way over and over again, expecting different results is the definition of insanity. And this was what I had been doing. I kept ending up in bad relationships and yet I didn't think I could change how or why I fell into them. I thought it was all about them. When I started to reflect in 1999, right in front of me in decades of my own history, were the very things I needed to open my eyes to see. I would find wisdom in my story. I intuitively knew I had to wake up from the deep sleep if I ever wanted to create a different story. The deep sleep and that familiar abyss had been an all-too-common master.

Larger Truths

I had lived six decades and in all that history, I could look back and actually see how the world was changing. Working for 52 years, I had learned a thing or two about 'the system.' We have slowly become the birds, the silly little birds of no importance, existing on huge institutional ranches built solely for thoroughbreds. We work for massive companies that have infiltrated our lives and now control every aspect. Their web, made of greed, control and deceit feels impersonal and impenetrable. They clip our wings, tether us, hold us down, abuse our loyalty and now expect more and more for less and less. They make our cages small then smaller again and won't even allow personal touches because 'we don't own the cage!' They keep wages low and hopes high while the little birds are stuck in dead-end jobs with no future. And we let them because **we have been conditioned to let them.** Corporations have learned how to stagnate the economy, transfer massive wealth in their direction [2008 Crash], and raise profits to become powerful enough to take over entire countries. The elite have grown drunk with power and wealth beyond imagination. They hide behind corporate identities making greed the plague of the 21st Century, and only they are immune.

And in many homes a similar game is taking place. In our intimate relationships women find partners who are incapable of being responsible, who have never quite grown up and who use and abuse in all manner of ways. I would learn that abusers don't have to be physically violent to be abusive. Some women have become violent but it must be said that men are historically the abusers and women and children are their victims.

I learned some things about abusers. They look for responsible, accountable women who were disciplined, successful or vulnerable, who love to take care of others and who commit. Abusers know to be on their best behavior just until they find a woman who will invest in them. Then they relax into who they really are and start to show their true colors. If you are doing all the work in a relationship, with anyone, think about it because valuable relationships are fair and equal and should feel good.

After the Attack

When faced with being caught after he had beaten me up in 1999, Tom gathered as many allies as he could while I went away from town for a few days to regroup. By the time I returned, our friends and associates were all on his side and weren't about to believe me at all. He had done a masterful job of convincing them that he had been my victim. He was such a master in fact that even a few in my own family believed him over me. After I had reported him and the police suggested a restraining order, he remained vigilant and showed up at meetings and events he knew I'd be attending. Tom would terrorize me for nearly a year.

Suddenly his tone changed and he became a slobbering, apologetic mess swearing he would never touch me again. Interestingly, this was shortly before his court case. He started begging me to let him come back. When I continued to say no, he tried creating self-doubt in me by saying that no one would ever love me again. On and on he went. I finally told the police he was regularly violating the restraining order. That was when they asked me if I wanted them to arrest him! I replied, "Isn't he violating 'your' restraining order?"

The event itself and a full year of trauma until the court case, the restraining order and his incessant stalking and terrorizing by a cocky young lawyer took the music out of my soul. I persevered and I stayed hidden. A short time after the attack however was when my Bubble of Peace shored me up and gave me something else to focus on - as if right on cue.

Many men in my life came from circumstances in their past that taught them how to survive against all odds. Most of them had suffered abuse and crazy environments where they were supposed to feel safe, but couldn't. Most of them had confessed of abuse and neglect, and every time I was appalled at their stories. Rather than why their parents had failed to excel in their own lives, their stories played to my compassion and empathy. I had to learn they could only give back what they had been given. How could they be balanced, compassionate and loving when they had only known the opposite? They had been lost, forced to develop some awful or crazy strategies to stay out of harm's way. And they brought these strategies into their adult lives - to show up one day in mine. When they were faced with opposition, accusations or sometimes the law, they knew how and when to play victim. They could instantly turn on the strategies to deflect their own responsibility. And they had learned how to duck and weave through the chaos. Best of all, by the time I met them they had learned exactly what would work.

Ralph

We had connected at work and for several months he had been charming and attentive. I was driving Ralph home after work and we were on a stretch of country road without a house to be seen. Suddenly he started bad-mouthing my mother whom he'd never met. There could be no reason for the tirade. I ignored him while I wondered what had happened that he was suddenly behaving this way. He lifted a paper bag from his right pocket, reached in, unscrewed a cap and took a sip. It wasn't pop. He continued with the insults. I knew this kind of behavior all too well.

In the next moment, I pulled over to the side of the road and told him if he didn't stop bad-mouthing my mother, he could walk. As he opened the passenger door, he grabbed the keys from the ignition, something you could do in my car while it was running, slammed the door and ran off into the bush. I sat there a moment, my mind buzzing. "Now what do I do? I can't shut my car off and I don't have another key. I need my car," blah, blah, blah, I went on. "It won't be smart to follow him – but I have to!"

I entered the bush and found him standing on top of a hill about 50 yards in. Our eyes met. Then he turned away. Against everything that made sense, I started climbing the hill. As I neared him, he raised his arm and threw the keys into the air. I scrambled to the top to watch as they rolled through the air and landed in the thick underbrush below. I was sweating by this time just as the thought occurred that if he had a mind to, he could kill me right then and there, and no one would likely find me.

I kept my eyes trained on the spot where I saw the keys fall as I made my way slowly down the other side of the hill. In the corner of my eye, I could see he was following me. To my surprise he started looking in the underbrush too. I made my way over to where I saw the keys fall and checked once more to see what he was doing. He was bent over about twenty feet away searching the thick brush. I looked down for a while then saw the metal shining back at me. I checked him again, then gently cradled all the keys in my hand and picked them up quietly. I pretended to continue the search as I started to make my way back up the hill. Checking over my shoulder, I could tell he was duly focused. I stood up and ran like the wind, jumped in the car and sped off in a flurry of dust and rocks.

I shook and cried all the way back to town suddenly aware of my stupidity. I saw a police car in the parking lot of the bank and pulled up beside him to cry out the details. I begged him to follow me to the house so I could pack and get out of town. Dusk was settling in as I hid my car around the back of the house and the police car pulled into the front driveway. I thanked him profusely and said I would only be twenty minutes. Inside, I took a look in the mirror and saw black mascara had run down both sides of my face and my hair looked like someone had drug me backwards through that underbrush. I stripped quickly and hit the shower. Two minutes later, while I was drying off, I checked outside to find the police car had left. While I was throwing things into a suitcase, headlights panned across the front window. Thank God, the police were back.

The headlights never went out however and then I heard the car leave. I heard that voice again. "I know you're in there, bitch! And I think I'll come in and rough you up a bit for that little stunt!" I grabbed a stiletto to use if he followed through on his threat. My eyes had grown large, my mind continued to search for solutions and my body was gearing up to fight.

I hunkered down silently in the corner of the bedroom and my eyes stared at the ground-level window as the tree outside created eerie nighttime shadows. I held my hand over my mouth to stifle any sound as I tried to breathe silently. I could hear him outside in his drunken stupor as he threatened me again, louder this time. "I can come in and get you whenever I want, you know!" A quick elbow through the single-paned window and I would be his victim. The police had obviously left so I was a sitting duck. With a case of beer, he sat against the front door to taunt me and drink himself into an even bigger rage. All I could do was wait to find out my fate. I tried the phone and called the police. I quietly begged for them to send an officer because someone was outside of my house threatening to come in.

Minutes later another set of headlights flashed across the wall of the bedroom. I heard voices, a car door slam and then a knock at my door. My heart jumped into my mouth. The police had returned. They told me they were taking him to jail to sleep it off, but that he'd be released in the morning. I explained I was on my way to the nearest hotel as I had an out-of-town interview the next day. I said that I hoped to escape for good.

I left the hotel the next day for the airport and the interview far, far away. After a grueling four-day interview, the company hired me and flew me to their Corporate Headquarters on the West Coast. I never returned to my rented house or that town, not even to retrieve my belongings. A friend would drive everything out that would fit in my car the following month. Settled into a new apartment and my new job, one quiet spring day there was a knock at my door.

Ralph would torment me again for another two months. I played puppet really well and long enough that he agreed to let me buy him a one-way ticket home. After two attempts to successfully get him on the plane, I ran away again, leaving the best job I'd ever had, to escape him for good.

While dire fear of him had filled me then, sadness for the loss of this life in this way fills me now. He had not known the gifts of Spirit for it was imperative he continue to place all of his attention on the dangerous world he believed he was in at every moment. What he learned as a child came forward with him into his adult life. How would someone learn the grace of Spirit when there was no one around to teach it? Ralph would remain lost in the spiritual desert of the physical and material world; asleep and distanced from his Light until he was ready to change. He was left to live on this level, fearful and sick, poised and waiting for the next shoe to drop. Even alcohol played a role as it dampened his pain and allowed him to release his anger. He had become a puppet on a string as old triggers would snap him back to old strategies. Each one of his victims would pay the price, including me.

Not to excuse him, it is important to understand how easily an abuser can be created in a toxic environment. Once I was connected to Spirit, the entire world looked different - even Ralph. My journey to the Light meant I could see him from a different angle. I could mourn the loss of his soul, his lost potential and his sad and painful reality. Today I feel compassion for those, who like Ralph grow up in such spiritual deserts.

Let's be clear: when you leave him or report him, when there's a piece of paper that says he's not supposed to be within a mile of you, when you think you are done or you have moved far enough away, do not let go of your safety. This kind of person will wait for you to make the slightest mistake so he can make his way in again. He chose you because you believed him once – and he thinks you will again. Remember that these people have very long memories. When you start to relax is when they believe they can take advantage of you again. To get back in, he may threaten you, say he'll just be around the corner, or perhaps he'll threaten to harm those you love. The individual threats may be different, but the basic dynamics of these strategies will always be the same at their core. Here are some of the red flags to watch for:

- What did he learn as a child: compassion or intolerance, balance or fear, kindness or anger, responsibility or complacency?
- Does he want to know your every move or does he insist you report to him?
- Does he ever let up on what he expects of you?
- Does he create doubt in you about yourself?
- Does he manage your money and/or your time?
- Does he try to isolate you from friends or stop you from doing things on your own or without him?
- Does he say things that make you feel lesser than, bad, ashamed or solely responsible?
- Does he threaten you: with leaving, cutting off your money, taking the kids, hurting someone or abusing your beloved pet?
- How many things in your life are so important to you they can be used as leverage to keep you where you are?
- Does he play victim when you catch him at something (saying things like, "I would never do/say that; you know that's not what I meant; you are taking this too seriously.")
- Does he gather allies to support him and go against you?
- Does he make it about two or more of them - against one of you?
- Does he suddenly do something really nice out of the blue that throws you off track? Does he play to your compassion or sense of responsibility?
- Does he ask you to do things for him that he is never satisfied with because 'you did it all wrong?'
- Does he physically threaten you? Is he intimidating or just plain incapable on his own?
- Does he behave really nicely when others are around to witness his apparent love for you? Would they believe he was abusive?
- And once he has attacked or pressured you, he will do it again - regardless of what he might say or promise.

G. F. Thornton

Mel

We were living in a motor home in the park where he worked. It was 1982. We had been married for two years and I was working hard at our relationship because I had made a vow. Yet he had become a master manipulator. When we'd 'discuss' matters of importance, I would come away from our conversation wondering how I could have forgotten my perspective. Mel was a salesman and at work he was a Star. At home he used the same tactics to confuse and manipulate his unsuspecting wife into seeing his side of things and forgetting her own ideas ...every time. At one point, I even thought I needed a psychiatrist because I felt I was becoming more and more confused with every day. What he had learned to do at his job had become the way he would manipulate me at home.

They don't have to be physical to be abusive. Abuse can be psychological, emotional, intellectual and/or spiritual. Some people are just incapable of being normal or fair. Parents and friends can be critical instead of supportive because they don't know how to solve their own problems let alone yours. Sometimes people cannot give back what you give them. Sometimes others are incapable of being sensitive, honoring, kind or helpful. And when you have someone like this in your life, you must remember that they will not change because you want them to or someone thinks they should. When you know exactly what you have always gotten from someone, you cannot expect to get anything else. Protect yourself and remember who they are and how they are, and save yourself the pain. Ask yourself who is the calm in the storm, the rose in the middle of the weeds or the ray of sun in a darkened room. Is it him, or you? He is not your fault.

These are some of the strategies corporations are using too. Creating fear and maintaining self-doubt, holding us down and keeping employees stuck. When you feel like a piece of gum on the bottom of someone's shoe, you know you're in an environment that will never care about you. The skill at hiding their agenda and moving it forward is amazing and sad. Their ability to divide and conquer all the little birds is glaringly apparent. It's called an **Employer's Market** where staff members are afraid to move up, down or laterally and will hang on with a death grip to their job out of fear. Historically we cycle between and Employer's Market and an Employee's Market every 8 to 10 years. Yet we have been stuck in an Employer's

Market for well over 15 now. We are in a giant game of control. More and more people I talk to speak of this dynamic in their workplaces today.

Healing

To all the men who traipsed through my life with their cork boots - Ta Da! There was a reason for that madness. Had I known I was to remember I am Spirit first, I could have saved myself a lot of grief and a really soggy pillow. That I eventually arrived at Spirit regardless, even if it took me fifty years, would become a testament to the truth of the path - call it destiny, fate, Karma or just dumb luck.

"Ponder what the world will be like when everyone wakes up." **Simi**

Time

Healing from the attack took time. Weeks and months slipped away, one second at a time as I learned how to remain awake and focused. The move away from him was a huge burden, physically and financially, and it was more hard work than I ever could have imagined. I borrowed a couch from a friend far away, and she and I walked and talked a thousand miles over the next year. Luckily for me she was a counselor so we had many evenings in deep conversation where she helped me sort out, not only this event but many of the traumatic relationships from the past 30 Years too.

Little did I know I would begin a journey to take a closer look at my own truth. Who was I? What did I stand for? What were my values? What was I really doing here, and why had I fallen so far off track from the confidence and strength I had felt as a younger person? Why did I feel like the monster when clearly I was the victim? Was my capacity for caring and being responsible what I sacrificed to allow abusers to live in their own toxic game of dominance, complacency, control and abuse?

One night in a dream, **Little Reign** took my breath away as she spoke honestly. "Life is beautiful but it is sad that this beauty is so easy to forget. Instead of embracing the joy and the miracles, bad news is sought and celebrated. Humanity focuses on hate instead of love, anger instead of happiness, catastrophe instead of triumph and war and crime instead of peace. Your kind is captivated by broken hearts and bodies instead of health and love and the miracle of healing. Many seek to hear of those who die instead of those who live. You chase evil instead of angels and are fascinated with the horrors of life when life is a superb symphony that can only happen in very special places in the Universe. Each life, in fact, is a bright photonic angel in a giant Universe filled with Perfect Light, and still there are those who deny the spectacle. Who or what has championed such madness? How or why does your world accept this?"

These were questions I would not soon forget because they touched and validated what lived inside my own history. Looking back from the safety of the world I have created for myself now, I could see how and why people could manipulate others for their own benefit. It was clear we live in a world of survivors. Eat, or be eaten.

Healing Hands

I healed an arm burned by scalding hot water and a leg that had slid on the gravel into home plate. My hands had calmed a child's fever in minutes so I had evidence that my hands could focus energy that could change physical properties.

My sister and I had the privilege of being with our mother during her final months. She had been sick for many years with Lupus. For weeks before her death, I spent each night applying white healing energy to her entire body. Yet I felt I had failed when she died anyway on Mother's Day, May 12th, 1989. It was reason enough to deny the healing hands as I believed that if they couldn't heal my mother, how could they heal anyone?

A short time ago, upon discussing Mom's death with Heather, she said that I hadn't failed Mom. She reminded me that we knew Mom had decided years before her death that she had wanted to leave this incarnation. She reminded me that no amount of Light Energy can heal someone who does not want to heal. My heart knew she was right and that it was time to finally accept the truth. I could reconsider the healing hands after more than twenty five years of unfounded doubt.

Who was I to think I could channel messages or heal? Surely crystal shoes or boiled frogs would have to be involved. Having never acknowledged psychic or healing gifts, three quarters of the way into writing this book, with the Elders grinning down upon its pages and constantly tapping me on the shoulder, I would have to reconsider. There were messages that were morphing and progressing in depth and the subjects were starting to connect and make sense when not much else in the world seemed to. Like the perils of driving while texting, I knew I had to pay more attention to where I was going and spend less time crying over where I'd been.

Psychic skills were not accepted then as they are today. I didn't see auras or hear actual voices so it was fairly easy to dismiss. In truth, my denial had mounted to an excuse to not take a more difficult road but to remain safe within a self-induced coma for another thirty years. This served a point: not everyone readily accepts their life's purpose or their gifts, especially if they are what will make things difficult. I was certain I had to earn my wings and work really hard before I could fly! Many more years would bring the evidence needed to believe - in me - first. Certainly greater acceptance of psychic abilities helped but part of this lesson had to do with taking this road and not worrying about what others were thinking. Only I was to decide – and for my own purpose only.

> I believe you understand what you think I said but I am not sure
> you realize that what you heard is not what I meant.

Identifying a Message

How did the chatter sound? How had it arrived and how had it felt? I also had to be conscious when receiving a message. This took patience, living in the moment and real honesty.

The differences were:

- The chatter was nonsensical or every day conversation.
- The chatter was familiar with familiar words, ideas and thoughts.
- There was seldom anything of importance in the chatter.
- The chatter was often worrisome, challenging or the usual negative rhetoric.
- The messages were about important things: Light, love, ethics, joy, happiness, etc.
- The chatter was always happening; not so with the messages.

- The messages weren't there all the time; only at moments when the chatter was less intrusive or when I was focused and able to identify one like during a meditation.
- The messages weren't linear conversations: they arrived in one fell swoop – like a ball of information: I called them onions, because ...
- When I captured one, I could peel away the layers and expose more depth and meaning.
- There was always the emotion of gratitude or wonder surrounding a message.
- And the clearest sign was that messages were always good news – and this was very unlike the chatter too.

The next revelation was that if I hoped others would learn from these messages, I should at least go first. In a familiar cliché, I knew I had to walk the walk to talk the talk. I processed the material, first because it inspired me and second because it was helpful for what I was trying to sort out for myself. I was reconsidering everything I thought I knew! I had to open up and stretch my mind to embrace new thoughts because - these messages were different.

The messages were coming together as if everything had been planned. Still, I could no more know what was to come next than I could fly. I could see Spirit was teaching me in ever-increasing levels of complexity. And at times there would be signs like two owls on the same night, an angel in the clouds, a feather on the ground in front of my car or hearing a bold proclamation from a friend. I was invited over and over again to witness as the world morphed and changed before my own eyes until I believed.

Chapters would disappear and appear. Words would be there one moment, erased the next, and the title – well, there was nothing static about it either. Each day when closing the computer I could feel the material sinking into me. Naps helped. I began to smile again. The information was helping me to see my own world in an upside down way that tickled my mind and kick started my heart again. Some serious reframes were happening.

There would come a time when I felt strong enough to step out into the world again to see what was happening for others in their circus. I decided to go back to school. This part would serve to validate many other things. The messages along with the shift in the Earth's energy and many responses to it would be validated. The research would take me out into the Universe and the Matrix in a wide circle and bring me back to this Energy inside, to the Light and the quantum magic every time. Others were writing and talking about the same stuff and yet it was all new too.

The Atom

When I was in my thirties and after I had spent considerable time searching for answers to the purpose for this life, I came up with something that might seem a little crazy. I had considered the structures and the vastness of the Universe. I considered the details of electrons in an atom: the space between them and the nucleus. I pondered what time meant; akin to our few years on planet Earth being but a blip in the big picture of the Universe. What was a minute to an elephant and what was it to an ant? I wondered about the speed the Earth was travelling and wondered why we hardly seemed to be moving at all. I thought about the elliptical shape of galaxies and planets on their disc-like orbits around a sun. I considered these and other phenomena, and what I came up with seemed to make as much sense as anything else. 'Earth is simply an atom in someone else's coffee table.'

I could not afford to slip back into old paradigms if I was to embrace new information or was being called to write about it. I started to work at integrating the messages into my history first as my own life would be the test. My personal journey was about to lead the way. I would have to take time to define some things for this purpose, like God and Spirit. While the Elders were using words like Spirit, I had to take a closer look. This word hinted of the Higher Self and Consciousness, as in Spiritual. Then again it also defined the human spirit, ghosts and even liquor. The word 'Energy' would become a more appropriate, all-around word. I would find ample evidence that this word was suitable for this purpose too simply because it didn't come with a lot of baggage. A unique language was developing as I took time for messages to resonate with the right words. I needed to be ready to receive and knowing the best words to use would be important.

LIGHT: the essence within each life form which is a stream or coherent beam of energy; the Source, the Force and the energy of the Matrix of the Universe; unique vibrations and frequencies which animate life.

About six years ago, I struck out of my research fog to start a Sacred Circle. I wanted to bring like-minded people together to talk about Spirit. At our first meeting, I asked the group what 'Spirit' meant to them. Some pretty blank faces stared back as I waited several minutes for a response. Then after grinding away, someone finally said, "Well, that's hard to explain." Ah, yes, you too? We continued meeting for several months and while I heard some amazing stories of Spiritual events and even a few miracles, I wasn't any closer to what this word would bring or if it would be perceived in the right way. In some arenas it was as though Spirit was a great and magical secret, a taboo or at least something that only a few had ever fully embraced. Time would change all that as the words needed for this book would begin to arrive out of necessity, if nothing else. Together we would create a new language that would at least help us to think about the energy of the Universe in a different way.

Connecting with another much larger Metaphysical group, I joined. They used the terms 'Spirit' and 'Spiritual' quite liberally. They were focused on energy healing, alternative therapies like Reiki, crystals and psychic connections to the dearly departed on the other side. I believed in the other side and wondered if I had stumbled upon a group that would be helpful. I would study Reiki and attend Readings and Channeling workshops and various other events and shows. I learned some things but I was frequently surprised at my own understanding in comparison. Returning to the outer world validated the Spiritual changes that had taken place already in mine. Gratitude rose in my heart.

Once I was untethered from the world, the knowledge from channeling this book would take me to beyond my own expectations. The Light had changed me without help or guidance. I was beginning to see the distance my journey had taken me spiritually and how much I had been able to adjust. It seemed the Elders had given me a considerable leg up.

I watched others as they worked with and talked about crystals and healing energy, guides, and so on. It seemed hard to understand why a persona would change if someone was channeling a Spirit, or why their voice or their posture would suddenly change. I was wondering why this sort of anomaly hadn't happened for me too. And in the very next moment, **Sarah** whispered, "Years ago, when you were writing down words in order to get to sleep at night, your handwriting often changed one page to the next, and sometimes even within the same sentence." I had to bite my tongue and hold back my paradigms - again. I hadn't even been aware of what auto-writing was at the time, so the changes in the handwriting hadn't happened on a conscious level. If these writings had just been offloading, they would have been in my hand. That they were penned with various hands had to validate their ethereal origin.

This reminded me to keep an open mind. I believed more and more in Spirit as I was amassing some compelling evidence. Intuitively, I had to give myself more time to understand. I had always sensed there was more to life than just what met the eye. I needed to stay open to all possibilities and some patience would be required; a rare commodity in my energy economics. As I tripped through my past, I found many challenges had been met with a resolve that had saved me over and over again.

First Kiss

I would spend every summer vacationing with grandparents until I was twelve. I would spend a month with Dad's parents and a month with Mom's. I'd visit my Dad's parents first. Gramps was lots of fun driving me and my best friend to the Dairy Queen in the back of his pick-up, taking us to the pool and hiding dimes inside the brick wall in his workshop for, as he said, whatever I needed from the store. He had told me I could have those dimes and that he put them there just for me. It was our secret. For some reason however, I never went to his workshop. Even then I had sensed something was not quite right.

Nan and Gramps would regularly drop in on their way back east to visit relatives. Gramps would want me to sit with him in the back seat of the car as we drove them to the airport. I remember the first French kiss he laid on me and how it had shocked me. He whispered, "That's a secret just between me and you." I was ten.

We intuitively know when something is right or wrong. We are born with this knowing and we respond accordingly. I was shocked at the kiss. My Spirit responded with an emotion that told me something was wrong. Emotional energy like this is meant to alert us and keep us safe. How many of us are confident enough that we trust this wisdom when it shows up?

As the energy connection developed, I began to notice a deep emotional response as those dearly departed from this world drew near in Spirit. There would be a wave of love enough to make me stop in my tracks when Spirit was near. Memories would flood in, and often a tear would tip out of my eye as a zing moved through my heart. Auto-writing would start up again which would open up another door. There was energy all around me that was trying to get my attention.

Rehashing my history I could identify many other experiences to which I had given little attention. Some had been so striking that I must have been in a coma to have missed them. Others were subtle little rainbows that had appeared in my sky when I least expected them.

At one point a few years ago while I was looking at the past, I was thinking about why I hadn't been stuck in a bad relationship like some women. My resolve to move on and to not give an abuser another shot at me was clearly solid. I had walked away too many times to not wonder where I had gained that resolve or why I had been so bold and adamant to not stay in unsafe places. I started to think that perhaps this next story, something that had happened over and over again each year I visited Dad's parents in the summer, might have had something to do with it.

My Resolve

Gramps was a functioning alcoholic. He had worked at the mill for forty years and had rarely missed a shift. Once or twice a week however he'd head straight for the pub after work. Sometime past midnight he'd call Nan to come and get him. When they'd get home, she would sit at the stove and cook him a hot meal while he would berate her for everything that was wrong in his world. His tirade always woke me up. I would be tucked in bed in the spare room, blankets cuddled tight beneath my chin and tears flowing down my face. A huge conflict would rage inside my head, "Why do you let him talk to you that way? Why don't you stand up for yourself?" She never did.

Today I realize how trapped she had been and why she never wanted to make waves. She was partially disabled and would never have been able to fend for herself if she'd left him, or at least that must have been what she thought. I felt sad when I realized what it meant for her to have to sleep with him when I visited. The bedroom I would sleep in every summer for a full month – was her respite. More than anything else, these experiences taught me a valuable resolve that would never allow me to feel as trapped - as she had been.

I was seeking! Standing in one place for any length of time was not my custom. I had meandered through 68+ jobs, 32 addresses and 8 provinces. I had traversed 3 continents and far too many cities and relationships to count. This roving and wandering would come to an immediate halt in 1999 at my Bubble of Peace. Apparently I was ready to come face to face with myself. Being in that safe, warm bubble suddenly protected from the intrusive outside world, the experience moved me so much I would spend the next eighteen years planning my return so I could eventually move in and stay. To be in life without Spirit had been such a stark contrast to what life was like with Spirit, that I wouldn't wish a Spiritual desert on anyone. I had found my mission.

In the end, I would connect not only to the Light and the Elders, but to those I knew who had gone before me. So touching and loving were these connections, I would be drawn again and again to seek them out. When this incarnation ends I know they will be there to welcome me to the other side. What role, if any, they might play in the direction of this life now is yet to unfold but I know we are interconnected forever. There was no doubt of the ancient wisdom that had coalesced along this path or in the blood of my ancestors, Spiritual all, of which I was becoming ever so grateful. I would honor the road that stretched out of the darkness into the Light, for me and for everyone; no matter the race, color, age, gender or address. My hope was that Spirit could open a window so many others could see the rainbow just beyond their doubt and pain too.

Please understand one thing: few, if any, of us are in our lives in a way that we have chosen. We are molded and conditioned and taught to be in this world in the way those who have the hidden power decide they want us to be and it will always be to their advantage. We call it the status quo, and it is anything but new. These attitudes and viewpoints have been growing and influencing us through social and cultural trends for many years.

As we are so interconnected through technology today, those who wish to control something now have some powerful tools to assist. Massive data silos now exist on everything we do and think. This information is being used to enact and conceal an ever-widening net of control. As such, the masses are being divided, conquered and brainwashed with amazing efficiency. This keeps us under the control of those in power, whoever they may be. While the masses are continually being convinced they have little or no power, they actually still have all of it. When everything is attached to money, anyone who spends money actually controls the market. It only takes the masses uniting toward a cause and controlling how they spend their money to change it.

If we knew one tenth of what goes on in boardrooms around the world, we'd book a seat on the first cargo ship to Mars. There are plenty of current examples of the kind of powerful agendas that are possible and the effects they can have, especially when no one seems to be watching. And these are being maintained by very questionable people with very questionable agendas in very powerful positions …politicians, leaders, corporate giants included.

It may seem like quite the challenge to topple these giants, but I hear that a simple sling shot and a rock aimed precisely at the right place will do the trick.

Chapter 6

Light Changes Everything

"You already are the dream." **Parkah**

LIFE IS NOT ABOUT FIGHTING, striving for or becoming your dream. It is not about being whoever or whatever you want to be in the future. When you are connected to the Light you will see that your dream has always been inside you. All you need to do is open the window within and let the dream out. It isn't a fight or a chore and you don't need anyone to validate you or your dream – because you are the dream! Connecting to your Light is how you discover what your dream is, and when you can see it, you become it. I will finish this book and send it out into the world because I am this dream.

We are all a product of where we've been and what we've bumped into. Each road is unique and lessons learned, or not, are the catalysts and the details that make us who we are. I learned how to sit back and view my life as an Observer as if I was watching a show on television, and the star of the show was a stranger. This allowed me to take stock of the past without any emotional attachment. I could look at the story and be honest about what I saw. If I ever expected to adjust or change how my world felt, I must be able to recognize and challenge anything that no longer served it. To be an Observer was a great tool to help with exactly that.

Most of us are not able to see how we are in our own lives. We complain about the mistakes others are making while we go about making the same ones. Some will accuse others of being negative while they complain all the time. Some see the insecurity in others but they can't see their own. Why are we not able to see how we show up in our own lives or how we impact others? It happens when we are asleep, unwilling to see the truth or insist on denying our role or mistakes. It is this blindness that can be used against us and it is becoming dangerous to our health.

We use our senses to navigate the world, and they're always on alert. Over time, we can be crippled by a lack of awareness and honesty. We might identify when something is wrong, but not know why. We can feel justified to blame others for the pain we feel, even when we are secretly the cause. We often project the emotion we're feeling inside out into the world! I had to learn how to recognize the strategies and old habits that had come forward in time to taint my world. I had often transferred how Dad was with Mom into how I thought my life partner should be, not because it was right, but because it was all I knew. I never expected to be abused, yelled at or betrayed because I had never witnessed or learned of it. I was taught mutual respect, responsibility and negotiation versus conflict and control. When what I got was conflict and abuse, I simply walked away. Obviously these guys weren't like my father because they'd come after me!

When I blamed someone else for something, I'd end up finding it within myself one day. It all started within. So, I vowed to open up and change because the past was becoming a sad reminder of the alternative. I had to learn to trust my self-wisdom, to look within for answers and to be brutally honest about how I had fashioned my own world ...because I had.

Spirit Stepped In

Only when I was tuned in to my internal vibration and stopped chasing the material fantasy was I able to hear the symphony. Crossing the fine line from the edge of darkness into the Light would be a surprisingly short trip.

Still it wasn't possible to fake this journey. I was connected or I wasn't. And it was not anyone's place to judge my failure or success as the only way to arrive was under my own steam anyway. If I thought I could fudge my way through this part, I would only create bigger mountains.

Home is in the Light. We arrived here 'from' it. When we finally awaken and are ready, we do not set out on a new journey but rather we return to the one from which we came. We learn how to survive in this physical world and we are meant to recapture this for each journey.

When I was ready, Spirit would step right up to the door and walk in. There was no fanfare, not even a tiny note from a cherub. There was no choir, no white cloud or thundering solo and no doctrine or guru attached. I hadn't flown off to a mountain top. I hadn't been on my knees or bowed down to a symbol, Capitalized Name or entity of any kind. I hadn't been pleading to God or other spiritual being, angel or entity. After many years and many messages, my spiritual journey was destined to unfold just as it had. I had been taught that being spiritual was very difficult, almost impossible, and I believed it would take years and years. How was it then that the Light could slip in under the noise and chaos with such grace?

I had been vulnerable and innocent, yet hopeful and excited too. What I would learn began to resonate as if I had always known this stuff. I had connected with something organic and deep that felt like magic. It was new and it would never get old! There was a resonance chiming along with an internal something I still could not name.

Could this be God? This question had come up before but had always lasted only a short time as life's chaos would quickly fall in behind it. And then one day, walking down the aisle of a grocery store, I would discover that I was smiling - for absolutely no reason at all.

Safe - Loved - Heard - Belong

Every human being inherently needs certain things to exist or survive. After the basics of shelter, food, water and clothing, these needs are common to us all too: to feel safe, to be loved, to be heard and to belong. And when we don't feel we have these, we will find strategies to force, deny or avoid them altogether.

G. F. Thornton

To Be Safe

We are born into a physical world. First and foremost we must learn how to be safe. We arrive knowing we need to learn about our environment, the people in it and what might threaten our safety. As we become adults, we never stop searching for ways to feel safe: financially, emotionally, physically, intellectually and spiritually, even if we don't identify these each time. When the world feels threatening and scary, it drives us to seek safety any way we can. If we exhaust our resources, we will sometimes succumb and retreat into a quiet corner to see if being invisible will help. When we run out of strategies, we can be pushed to self-medicate or distract ourselves in an attempt to stop the mounting fear. And yet all of this goes against how everything is supposed to be. Looking fearful and failing in front of others is often more scary than the threat itself. To keep up the deception that we're alright is what exhausts us the most. It is a big job to maintain the fantasy that we hope will convince everyone that we don't need help. This can become a never ending treadmill we can't seem to escape.

The Cabin

One summer when I was twelve, Gramps secreted my friend and me away one day, saying he had a surprise to show us. He told us he had bought a cabin near our favorite beach. We innocently jumped into the back of the pick-up and he drove us to the beach. On an old dirt road, he rounded the corner, drove up a short driveway and stopped at what was certainly a cabin, its boards unpainted and weathered gray. Gramps jumped out of the truck and both of us were ready to follow when he said, "No, Faye, I want to show Juanita first. You stay here." I sat back down to wait in wonder.

A short time later Juanita ran out of the cabin with Gramps close behind. She hopped into the back of the truck and Gramps climbed in the cab and started the engine. She was crying. I was a bit shocked. Juanita told me why he took her in alone. He wanted something from her she said she wasn't going to give him. She was in tears and very afraid, and so was I. In my mind, things started to fall into place: the dimes, the truck rides, the French kisses and now the cabin. I realized what he was grooming me for too! He drove us to the park near his house and then drove home. Juanita

110

and I ran away to hide as fast as we could. What would we do now? How safe would I be at night with him in the next room? Do I tell on him? If I do, what would be the consequences?

Slinking through the bushes, Juanita and I watched the house for about an hour until he finally came out and took off in his truck. We ran home, Juanita to her house and I went inside to pack, frantic by that time. I ran into the bedroom and started packing my suitcase when Nan came in asking what I was doing. "Please call Uncle Lloyd - please call him. Tell him to come and get me right away!" I was pleading but I just couldn't bring myself to tell her what had happened. It might crush her or she might kill him. I didn't have the words anyway. A short time later, my Uncle pulled into the driveway and I snuck out the front door to his car just as Gramps was coming in the back door. I had no words or any idea of what to say to him either. In fact, I never told a soul.

For the rest of his life, I would be cautious. I would never again acknowledge him or be alone with him. In essence I had lost my grandfather that day and perhaps some of my innocence. Today, just like that day, the Light had become my safe place. The Light had centered me even though I wasn't aware. I would realize that whatever was going on out there, nothing could steal what lived inside of me. Looking at my past, I began to see the Light was mightier than trying to find shelter in the world. The strength belonged to me and I could nurture what was inside. I could decide what I thought, how I felt and what was safe as I exercised this Light. While the world spun around me in crazy circles, I would eventually find peace in this one. Check #1.

My Resolve

Nan called me a few days later and begged me to come back. She said Gramps wouldn't touch me or talk to me. I didn't know what she knew and I wasn't about to ask. I felt sorry for her because I could just imagine that he had blamed her again for everything. I went back to Nan's. The first word he said to me, I grabbed him by his shirt and backed him into a corner and told him what I thought of him. I said that if he ever so much as looked sideways at me, that I'd kill him on the spot. Then I remember saying, "I'm your grand- daughter, for Pete's sake!"

G. F. Thornton

I may have been only twelve at the time, but on that day - we were the exact same height.

To Be Loved

Humans are social beings. We instinctively need to connect with others. We become stronger when we work together than when we compete. Our world is such that human interaction is also necessary. We travel in packs, learn in classes, shop in groups and live in families and communities. We identify strongly with our people and our place. And the relationships we develop are tied to our ability to form strong, caring and loving bonds. When our closest relationships are turbulent or imbalanced however, it affects everything else including our safety, being heard and belonging. Doctor Lissa Rankin alludes to the fact that we are naturally healthier and stronger when we are surrounded by our Tribe, by people who love and support us. The energy of a single strong relationship increases our vibration which enhances our overall health and wellbeing. This connection, due solely to its energy, is the important part of the world that does make an impact. We are naturally social but being so will always increase the complexity too.

Gary

In all my years, only one man had truly loved me. I dated him for a short time when I was nineteen. After I told him that I couldn't love him back he never really went away. I introduced him to a co-worker, whom he would marry and build a nice family with. He became like a brother – adopting my parents and spending untold hours in the shop with my father and in the kitchen with my mother. My parents would become grandparents to his kids. My Dad finally had the son he always wanted and Gary finally had a family. To this day, he still feels he is a member of my whole family!

If my heart kept saying no, I cannot be sad when someone knocked and I didn't answer.

My head would be down and I would be pushing against the tide for decades. Yet now as I look at the dynamics of my life closer, I could see that nothing would have deterred me from this moment, this task, finding and then writing this book. You see, it is never about the details and it is always about the meaning. What something meant to me and my capacity to respond would drive me toward my destiny regardless of any of the details or decisions. I was exactly as I could only be and I would always be exactly how I was until I made a change. Spirit on the other hand never changed location. If I was to be loved, I needed to begin within myself where Spirit's love was unconditional. Robert, the only love of my life, would spur me toward many things, and the love of Spirit was just one. Check #2.

To Be Heard

Everyone needs to be heard. We're taught to be independent and when we are, we still need to have a voice to speak our concerns, our beliefs and opinions to fulfill our needs and live in our own lives. In each relationship, we want to be equal partners, valued, respected and heard. This also means being taken seriously. When this doesn't happen, it can be a consistent reminder that something very fundamental is missing from the relationship. Often we will get to the point where we respond in one of two ways: we shut up and become silent, or we become loud enough someone has no other option than to HEAR US! Either way, it is a primal need to be heard as we have come here specifically to express Light into the world.

Laughter

I grew up in a very funny family and we laughed all the time. We used humor when we needed to be heard so we must have had a lot to say.

One Christmas, ten of us started at the dinner table at 4pm and we were all still sitting there twelve hours later, our sides splitting from the stories, the tall tales and the jokes. I loved those days. Boo, in his mid-seventies by then, had been cautioned about walking home the icy December night. There were no street lights in Dashwood, and when it was dark, it was dangerous to walk the length of my aunt's property down a steep hill to the log cabin. Boo said he'd have no problem as he opened the front door and stepped out into the night air. Reaching the top of the grassy hill, he laid down on the lawn perpendicular to the hill and simply rolled home - quite safely and happily to the amusement of all who were cheering him on.

This was what my family did! And when we wanted to be heard, we told a great joke or did something totally out of the ordinary to take others by surprise. Yet in relationships, being heard on a serious note was important too. I loved to listen but I was rarely listened to. This often was the fuel for an argument, which I would rarely take part in. I believed that an argument was two people with different opinions, and arguing was as useless as cement flippers; they would only take us down. Talking, negotiating and coming to a compromise were far more effective. It didn't take long to realize that this would take two people however. In a perfect world two could work it out. In my relationships, I rarely counted to two. Check #3.

To Belong

We are social beings and we have an innate need to feel that we belong. This becomes most evident as we enter school. Becoming part of a group is often a goal, and we can be dashed when we aren't invited or feel as though we don't fit or belong in some way. In elementary school, I had sometimes been the last one to be picked for the team. With my view of the world coming from the mixed First Nation and Mainstream mud meant I knew what it was like to not belong. It never bothered me because I didn't like the Mainstream song anyway. Still the drive didn't diminish. I was looking for where I did belong versus trying to belong where I knew I didn't fit. We all strive to belong - somewhere, even if it's on a bowling team with Mom!

Slic Chics

In Grade 7, my friend Wendy and I started a club. We called it the Slic Chics. Enrollment in the club was by invitation only and so we began by inviting our friends. We held goofy initiations where we'd dress pledges up in weird costumes and send them down to the local Soda Shop Drive In. They'd have to pull in and park in the lot as if they were driving a car and then they'd have to order lunch. We collected weekly fees and had a meeting once a month, each time at a different house.

One meeting at my place turned out to be the talk of the club. Mom adorned my room in Japanese decor. We sat cross-legged on the floor and were served lunch with chopsticks instead of cutlery. Japanese music played in the distance. Mom wore an official looking kimono and sandals and had her hair pulled up in a knot that was adorned with beads. Our glasses of soda were topped off with colorful paper umbrellas. Mom was a hit.

We belonged in our little group, and while it didn't last beyond elementary school, this small effort made a big difference as we all started to realize if nowhere else, we belonged here.

As for belonging to my First Nation roots, I had no idea how their philosophy was playing a role. These needs were not exclusive to Mainstreamers but held an important and special meaning in the First Nation community too. In First Nation tenets, inclusivity and belonging were paramount. All members of the Tribe were honored and important as each person had a vital role that added to the security and wellness of the whole. In Japan as well, there is great respect and honor within their culture. In busy places like airports, terminals and malls these spaces are void of the cacophony of loud and intrusive conversation. One only hears the footsteps. Entering a place of business, one is greeted with folded hands and a respectful bow. The energy in Japan filled me with silent reverence.

> "You always seek to connect with
> the Light from which you have come." **Lucy**

In the bush, cooperation was not random but imperative. Each person; male, female, Elder, Shaman, Chief, 2-Spirited and child was valuable. Each person was heard, each one belonged and the Tribal community caused bonds that ensured safety and survival. While these cultural dynamics are centuries old, they have been sacrificed, lost or misplaced due to the ongoing assimilation agenda of Mainstream to this day.

Wahwaskenah would bring something forward that would chill my bones. "One tribe knew nothing of the other, yet one would rule the other. The same thing is happening now. This time, instead of knowing nothing, the ruling class knows everything. And they are using this information to manipulate for their own purpose *because they can.*"

Many struggle with their identity, mourn lost languages, ceremonies and culture the world over. Assimilation and oppression are not exclusive to First Nation people. Refugees, immigrants and displaced people are all mourning such losses. The best values from each culture however are still written within their Light just as they were deep in the past. There are still ancient beliefs in the Light of all people that can never be removed or assimilated. When you learn a culture, you will belong to it. The strength and insight of Spirit, First Nation Spirit included, was what allowed me to turn and face this life with renewed faith and hope. Check #4.

Spirit's Voice

Parkah returned, "Hear the Voice that fills the wind. Each Light is meant to be a Voice which places wisdom upon the pages of life that teach something, that inspire and bring hope and love. Spirit Wind sings the music until you hear the messages and embrace each gift. Tuck them in your pocket and take them wherever you go to inspire others. This is the wisdom that can raise you up to float above the heaviest, wettest sand."

I was falling for Parkah.

Little Reign sang too, "You are the expression of Light Energy. Perfect Love is the Light's completed design. All love is Light. All Light is love."

Anita Moorjani wrote about the totality of the Perfect Love as she wrote of her impending physical death. Her book describes the profound and insightful wisdom of the Perfect Love she found on the other side. She came to understand that God is not a being as much as a state of being. She learned that we are Love. We are to be ourselves, to live our truth and be that Love.

> "Many are convinced of their country's reason for war.
> From the Light there is no reason.
> Peace cannot come from war.
> Love cannot come from hate." **Simi**

Peak Experience: March Winter

In the depth of a cold grey and snowy March and in a state of depression, a friend took me on a trip to the Baha'i Temple in Wilmette, Illinois. Its ceiling was a massive dome that was made of stone lattice which allowed bits and pieces of the sky to be seen from inside. After being greeted at the entrance, I selected a single chair out of hundreds in the rotunda where I would sit to contemplate and pray. I was sitting motionless in my sadness for some time. My head was bowed. My hands were folded in my lap and my eyes were closed tightly as I basked in the gentleness, the peace, the silence and comfort of that place.

After a time, I opened my eyes, and there it was. I looked up to the dome above me for a source. Even with hundreds of crevices in the lattice that the sun could have shone through and three hundred chairs I could have chosen, a single yellow sunbeam had fallen upon my hands as though the angels were touching my prayers. It took my breath away.

As we were leaving, I was waiting near the entrance to say goodbye to the woman who had greeted us on the way in. My friend standing behind me kept tapping me on my shoulder as I silently wished he'd just go away and let me stay inside the peace I had found. He continued to insist on interrupting my moment and I finally turned to ask what he wanted. He merely pointed and said, "Look." There in all its glory, upon a massive green bush was my favorite flower, a single white gardenia blossom, showing its beautiful face in the depth of winter. Tears filled my eyes and got caught in my throat as the message that I would be alright and that I was not alone surfaced in this little white face. An angel had clearly been there that day, watching over me ...and I felt the Light. I count this as one of my miracles.

Paradigms & Perspectives

More than anything else, paradigms and perspectives are responsible for the shape of our personal world. This is an example of one paradigm from my own life I had accepted in Grade 2. It would help me to see why being cautious about what I know and questioning everything regardless is a good thing. This is also an example of some simple wisdom in my own story.

My Elementary Tree

In second grade, I quickly and effectively learned how to draw a tree. I remember being so excited about this basic design and how to color it that I would come to use it over and over again for many years.

Shown here, this drawing is undeniably a tree; the top is green the trunk is brown. Even though I accepted this as a representation, it would be years before I realized there was something quite wrong with it. Thirty years later as I was taking lessons in oil painting, I noticed it was near impossible to locate a tree in nature that had a brown trunk! Given this information, I seriously had to adjust my belief that I had the perfect tree. Although this scenario was inconsequential in the big picture, it was a valuable lesson about what I believed, why I believed it and how it could affect everything else. The next time you are outside, look at some tree trunks and count the ones that are actually brown.

No one can know everything because there is just far too much to learn. We have to choose what we invest our time and energy in because we can't possibly do it all. A policeman does not need to study the stars, nor does a doctor need to learn about baking bread. And as a result we live in a world of an ever-increasing number of specialists. And all of us readily accept information from these specialists on the subjects we do not have time to research for ourselves. We pick up bits and pieces on a wide variety of subjects but rarely, if ever, do we question what we receive. What we end up with becomes the truth, a belief or what can be called a paradigm, just like my tree. Minor in scope, the picture of that tree was not real or true, but I had believed it was for thirty-five years. This paradigm fell easily, but those that surround our deepest and most important beliefs fall much harder and some become road blocks on the path toward personal growth.

"Releasing the past frees you up to touch the future." **Parkah**

Move the Bus

My mother had opened a retail shop in the mid-70s that sold baby clothes. At one point she took on a partner, a co-worker and friend of mine, Maryanne. Twice a year the two of them would drive deep into downtown Vancouver on a buying trip. My mother hated driving in the city and would often go well out of her way to dodge making a left-hand turn. She also avoided driving behind a bus or truck because she needed to see ahead.

On this particular day, Mom suddenly found herself behind a bus. She commented in no uncertain terms to Maryanne about how she hated driving behind something so big. Maryanne looked over at Mom perplexed, and simply said, "Why don't you just move the bus?"

Her words flitted around Mom's mind as she tried to sort out the meaning. When nothing surfaced, she asked Maryanne what on earth she meant. Maryanne, still perplexed, returned, "You know ...just focus your eyes and move the bus."

Maryanne had extremely bad eyes and had to wear coke-bottle glasses all her life. When she focused her eyes a certain way, she could move objects in front of her enough to see around them. As she had never been in a situation like this before, she didn't realize that this was a very unique ability. To Maryanne this was normal. To my mother and millions of others it was anything but.

We all have our own 'normal' like Maryanne. There can be things you do that others can't. And if you never have the opportunity to talk about it, you can easily believe your skill is not exclusive. For me it is an ability to connect dots or bits of information from somewhere in the past to something in the present.

Sarah came back again to add, "Your Light is unique to you. It plays your very own song. It is a guide to meaning and true value, to how you identify, what your purpose is, and what is written just for you."

We do not like to challenge our paradigms. It took centuries for the world to accept that the Earth was not the center of the Universe or that the Earth was not flat. We hang on to what we believe, very tightly, even in the light of new or proven facts. As science is plowing along at breakneck speed these days, we no longer have the luxury of a couple of hundred years to adjust to new evidence or to topple old and out-of-date paradigms. And being stuck in the past will seriously thwart our progress. Can you identify your individual paradigms and consider whether or not they still serve you? And if they don't, are you able to let them fall?

Changing the Picture

Suffice to say we each take our paradigms very seriously. It is imperative as technology speeds the world along that we learn about new discoveries and can adjust quickly. One day, it seems we may need to quickly save the

Earth and life upon it, including our own. How much will we be forced to set aside to save ourselves? School text books are slow to keep up due to the cost of reprinting. The internet and computers can maintain near instant updates which is making this medium better than printing. Yet technology is the new addiction as it steals our brains and encourages us to live in a fantasy, separated from reality by a screen. Standing in one place and looking all around it is hard to recognize the truth. However, we must be willing to question the information we have just to keep up.

Here is a list of some dominant paradigms followed by more up-to-date information;

- Our physical reality is more about the stuff, or the matter.
    - Energy is 99.999% of everything and matter doesn't really matter all that much.
- Survival of the Fittest, the Law of the Jungle and Darwin's laws of Evolution determine if and how we survive.
    - Our cells respond to the environment and so does each life form. We adjust to everything as we go.
- Genes are our determinant biological inheritance and the most we can hope for is that science can correct the flaws.
    - Genes are not the only determinants. Energy, frequency and Light, color, words, thoughts, relationships and our environment have profound effects on whom and what we are.
    - There is Light stored in every cell and every DNA strand in the human body. In this Light are written many things; our lessons, purposes, values, capacities and needs.
- Everything is basically random and purposeless; an organic compound of chance and coincidence intertwined with chaos.
    - Everything is what it is according to our destiny.
- Everything is chance while some things happen due to our individual capacity to choose.
    - We come with a destiny and there is order in all chaos.
- We are separate and unique individuals, and we are on our own.
    - We are highly interconnected with everything in the Universe, and we do not, ever, nor should we stand or operate alone.

- In the West, we live in a democracy where we elect our representatives in a government designed for the people and by the people.
    - Governments are controlled by corporate executives who are not elected. Any corporation with big profits can change policy and political will.

Wahwaskenah and I shared a dream one night. As it isn't possible to repeat all his words, so I take literary license to offer what he was getting at. Spirit speaks to us all the time. The heart of Spirit is always coursing through us as a mix of emotions. When my emotions make me cry with heart-felt pain Spirit is calling to me to pay attention to what caused the pain! Spirit was never dormant or sleeping on the job. It seemed so simple all of a sudden. The deeper my pain and the greater my cry, the louder Spirit was calling. When I was crippled with emotional pain was when Spirit was shouting at me. How could I not have known?

It is always a good idea to question and contemplate anything that might impact your life. We need to prepare for the task of adjusting as quickly as we can as the world speeds forward. Even though we are Spirit first, we live on a physical plane that is still full of dangerous stuff and some of it is hidden and secret. Life is the consistent and impending distraction. As all science, and certainly physics and quantum physics challenge our understanding of this reality, we need to be mindful of these facts and let in the sunshine from what is new. Fighting for old out-of-date paradigms can trap us in a lazy ignorance which we can no longer afford. Believe in global warming or not, humanity needs to seriously adjust to how it supports our only home - Mother Earth. We must make less of an impact as Mars doesn't look like the best place for your couch.

For those who are already connected to their Light, this book is about the fine tuning. It is a reminder to check in, to assess where you are in time and space. It will validate that when you are connected, you are absolutely in the right place even though it may feel like you're all alone on the path. You are never alone. The Light within is a far greater and more noble companion than any other. Renew and have faith in the Mind's intuitive energy and remember there is a grander and more purposeful reason behind it than what you might see at the time.

Parkah remarked that I was already the dream. He would go on to explain that everything within me, everything that made me who I am today was designed to fulfill my purpose for this life. If that purpose had been something other than channeling this book, I would not be who I am. Every trait, characteristic, skill, mood, emotion, energy, cell, ability and talent, and my own capacity, circumstance, passion, motivation and past was all there specifically to fulfill this dream. Yes, I had to open the window and let the dream out, but everything in my life was a single step that took me closer to the window.

You already are the dream too. What is it?

Chapter 7

The Presence of Spirit

THERE IS A SECRET within the secret. There are many powers in the Universe we don't understand, and there are laws we have no idea about either. Still, many people are talking about the shift in Earth's Energy. Some say we are no longer approaching the Age of Aquarius but are finally inside of it. Others believe the axis of the Earth is actually shifting and still others believe God, Mother Nature or aliens from Sirius have something to do with this sense of change. Regardless of the interpretations or the perspectives, there has been a shift in Earth's energy and it is palpable.

What Love Does

The summer was filled with fishing from Robert's boat, campfires, love and wonder-making. Love had moved in to roost in my heart unlike any I'd ever known before. I was finding more and more things about him that were very familiar. We melded like a hand that fits a favorite glove.

All of this, but he kept a wee distance too. A year or more after we had met he told me the story of how his wife of eighteen years had left him. I thought this might explain that invisible and impenetrable wall he seemed to be hiding behind. He worked hard and made a good living and he felt he didn't deserve what had been served up when she left.

I attributed the final wee distance he kept between us to those battle scars. Although he didn't seem sensitive quite like that, perhaps he had been at one time and had vowed to never be again. Pain could do that.

It would take nearly 30 years to fully understand the dynamics of our relationship. And even so, nothing could have prepared me for what would be learned in the end. We will look closer at some very interesting scientific discoveries later so prepare to challenge yourself and what you believe too along this path. Dig in with your heart and allow your mind to open up to some wonderful new thoughts and insights, the least of which could change everything ...for the better.

There is such a thing as happiness. While the world isn't all pink daisies and honey, we have the capacity to make it more peaceful and safe in more ways than one. Even when everything in the world might be pointing to the contrary, my beliefs were slowly shifting because of what I was learning. One such discovery was a kind of happiness that would last longer than a cup of coffee. I would also find a host of events that would offer some serious validation too. The beauty of Spiritual Happiness was that it won't rub off or dissipate into the atmosphere tomorrow, next week or even next year. It won't abandon me or change the color of the tree trunks. Spiritual happiness came from something sunny, energized and fundamental that had always been there. It was the true and complete expression of love that could only come from Divine Energy. And if I could find this insight, this resource and this peace, anyone could.

Love Has a Way

Summer slipped into autumn more beautifully than it ever had before. What was it that filled my head with fluff and rainbows; that touched my heart with joy and my eyes with sunshine? Was it really only dopamine, or was there something else that coursed through me as this man captured my heart? It had to be love.

Love brings us into the present and opens up our eyes so we see the vibrant colors and full beauty of life. Our heart awakens to the Light. It has a way of turning the music on where each day becomes another symphony. And every day I would find something else I loved about him that would make me shine even brighter. I could barely believe the depth of the love I felt so easily, so quickly and so completely. I escaped my own life to join his as often as I possibly could. I surrendered to him completely and selflessly.

Then one day I would wake up to see that if I allowed someone else to steer my ship, I wasn't allowed to complain about where I ended up.

This is the Energy we are all hungry for as we try to grasp love and the Light in each incarnation. Like a magnet to metal or a moth to a lamp, we are naturally attracted to the Light. This is where we came from, what we're made of and to what we will all return. Like coming home to my favorite log cabin in Dashwood where life was happy and safe, I was drawn to him.

Oh - God

So far the key subject in this book has been the Light. The book would be unfinished however if a few key subjects were omitted or left undefined for its purpose. This is one.

God is a word. God is a concept, an idea, a name, a model and a reminder of Divine Energy. It is the most controversial subject of all. God is the most talked about, the most focused-upon subject ever and still the least understood. It would be foolish to deny or validate God as you know Him. No one else has been successful at that task to date and I rather doubt I could be the first. The concept of God has served very influential roles for millennia. Doctrines are human endeavors of the eras in which they were created, likely with and without the hand of God. It is not the purpose of this book to suggest that Divine Intervention doesn't happen, as I believe it does. And since writing this book and being connected to the Elders, I have come to believe it even more. Still our understanding of The Source has been bounced around for centuries. Only those who have had a Near Death Experience have tasted the slightest evidence of what Perfect Energy, or God, really is. As not one of us can know for certain, God is speculative, interpreted and all about individually defining faith.

We are still intricately connected to the same Light that shone at the very beginning of the Universe - call it what you will. Humanity has always had experiences of Divine Energy from the very beginning and we have always needed to express them. Interpretations, perspectives and misconceptions would mold and change the meaning of God many times. Our own beliefs range from ones we feel are true all the way to those that couldn't possibly be true. In my own life, I had found many reasons why I could never fully accept nor deny the idea of a higher power.

Even though my search had included a number of churches, I never considered myself to be religious. Let me be clear: it is not a mission to follow, promote or deny any religion through this book. Since I discovered the Light, there has no longer been the need to wonder, fight for or believe anything. Beliefs are individual, and the weight they hold should remain individual too. Adherence to any ethical code or moral standard is supposed to show through our acts and intentions; religious or not, spiritual or not. Whatever helps us to be better, happier and kinder beings is a good thing. If religion had brought me to lasting and honest happiness, to peace or wisdom, it would have served a noble purpose. Whatever adds to us will raise our purpose and ideals to a higher level. Whatever segregates or causes us to be critical, fearful or prejudicial is not of the Light or Divine Energy.

We can protect the amount and kind of energy in our own lives by being aware and consciously choosing only what adds to us. However, because I wasn't aware of how certain energies influenced me, my life had been left to chance. Chance was exactly what I had done for the first fifty years and I no longer wanted to dance to such a crazy song. And too, somehow, somewhere in my inner self I had always felt there was a better way. I had attended church for the lack of something else - five times.

Fire in the Sky

Robert took me fishing on his boat. Near the end of that beautiful salty day in question, we were standing on the deck watching the sun set. Across the entire expanse of sky were clouds that looked like the ripples on a sandy beach. They were wispy and light and they covered every inch of sky between us and the horizon. We watched in awe as the setting sun lit up those clouds in the most vibrant red we had ever seen. And as the clouds turned the color of bright red flames, the spectacle was reflected perfectly in the lightly rippled water below. The whole landscape was ablaze. I had never seen anything like it before, and I have yet to see it since. I remember wondering what kind of magic it was, and what love was doing to me.

God is a name, a Being, a concept that is well embedded as the only omnipotent and powerful Being - out there. We even have pictures of Him as if artists had actually seen His face. God is the greatest of mysteries. A host of interpretations have been put forth. We call this force God, with a capital 'G' for emphasis. We revere the one power that had created it all. Still many of us wonder why this world is such a mess and His children are so sad, poor and angry. For me, there has never been a suitable response to this regardless of how we know God.

There is also no question we have always been touched by divine energy. Religion was Nike in history. Religion however failed to ensure a higher purpose or ethical behavior. Preachers at the same time would have us believe that God would never commune with such lowly sinners even though the Holy Spirit is within us or we obediently worship every Sunday.

The idea of Consciousness within was dropped around the 4th Century A.D. And in short order, God's Church would become a catalyst for hierarchies and power and control over all sinners. We would be conditioned to believe that communing with God on one's own was impossible. And to 'fear' His wrath was sufficient to keep us questioning ourselves …and God. We left Inner Consciousness in the dust so as to not interfere with the building of material kingdoms and gaining control over the populace. For centuries control was held by the powerful men of the Church while today it is in the hands of wealthy men and corporate power. We clearly continue to miss something vital in all the translations.

> "God is not Christian, Catholic, First Nation, Jewish,
> Buddhist or Muslim …or any other."   **Sarah**

Humanity's understanding of God has morphed many times over centuries. Even God had to change the Old Testament with the New. Rarely has there been acknowledgment that their God was the same as our God; as if the persona needed to fit the doctrine instead of the other way around. Regardless of what has been assumed or believed or what this power is called there can only be a single Highest Source - call it whatever you wish. Spirit need not attack or compete with our beliefs for we certainly didn't come first. Spirit clearly aligns with the higher of the two opposing ends of the Light spectrum. In this book this energy is called Light which has no such persona, gender or skin of any color.

Understanding this power is to understand Perfect Light or the Ultimate Universal Energy. God is not beholding to one doctrine, sect or belief as so many seem to insist. Only humanity would attempt to put God in a box of any kind. Light does not have a face and has not been defined by any limiting beliefs. Light makes up the Conscious Energy Field of the Universe. Light is found everywhere from the farthest reaches and the darkest corners to within every cell and every DNA strand in every living thing, deep inside each atom to the quantum levels and likely even beyond that. Light is energy, and it is the key fundamental force of all and everything. If you wish to call it God, so be it. A name will not and cannot change anything.

> "Light resides within your body.
> Remove the physical to find the Divine." **Orella**

The ancient stories gave God a face, white hair, a body and even a gender. At the time the world would best associate with a male but this would prove to be a tall order for some. The male gender was a given as women were lesser than men, most notably by the church. The bible validated and enhanced the male prowess which also seemed to set women as far less-than and subservient-to, a tag that is still maintained in many circles today even beyond the church. Gender and the hierarchy paved the way for prejudice and power politics. Even today women are given to be less than men, not only in the house of God but in life too. How would that be possible of God? If it hadn't been for men and women equally, humanity wouldn't be here. Yet many religions have a long way to go before God is held above their out-of-date paradigms.

In ancient First Nation history, women were revered as the keepers of the sacred circle and the fire. They were equal partners and their wisdom was respected and sought. As well, the warriors were the embodiment of strength and courage. Each gender, including Two Spirits, were respected and honoured for what they brought and how they added to the wholeness of the Tribe. God was the Great Spirit of all and everything. They honored and recognized the Great Spirit in everything when they hold out their hands and say, "All my relations." Everything in their world is about relationships with this sacred energy. Their philosophy doesn't focus on what is wrong, but what is right. **SoSo** tells us that humanity needs to understand that the Highest Power is not male or female, human or animal, white or brown, but rather straight up Pure and Sacred Energy.

As they come from another realm of higher energy, the concept of God was used sparingly, if at all, by the Elders. Not only does their expression exist in another realm, they have a greater understanding of the Source Energy and how it could be beyond our comprehension. A whole book could be used to define the word God and it would still not suffice. It is folly to attempt what no one else has ever achieved. Spirit prefers to meet everyone right where they stand. The word God belongs to you and is yours alone to consider and decide. The beauty of God will be found in the mindfulness of your truth, in your service, kindness and compassion and is not dependent upon a building, a book or someone else's interpretation or belief.

Personally, God constitutes all of the laws of the Universe that make everything possible just as it is. It is not my desire or the Elder's to detract from a belief in anything; God, sects, doctrine or religion. Spirit's messages are clear that whatever these mean for you is exactly what they mean. Remember the relationship you have with the Divine is personal and intimate. No one can take you to God or the Light any more than they can remove you once you're there. I hope you feel the inclusivity for this is the ultimate truth given to us through the Elders.

Jesus - Was Not Christian

Blew Like Sage was clear; "Jesus was the personification of Perfect Light in human form. Jesus was the old soul who lived on Earth. He spoke and taught and believed as claimed in the Bible. Jesus was inclusive; wise, accepting and fully compassionate to all. He loved the lesser amongst us just as he did king or queen. He chose no one as greater than any other and His teachings were truths, not debates. He spoke of how all of you are created equal. He was the keeper and teacher of moral and ethical character and of good intention. He knew of the Divine Light. Disciples of many a sage would wander off track to become manipulated and confused by others after the death of their teacher.

Christianity has always challenged us to denounce the material things of this world and to stay centered and true to one God. At no time would He instruct us to splinter into many sects, go to war or kill, to disagree or compete with each other or to build material kingdoms in His name. Rather, He taught of love and compassion for each other, of caring for the sick and vulnerable, of helping and healing the poor and taking care of everyone. Not only is this a right equally for all, it is also the only way. Why and how we are so off track is humanity's sad story.

Heaven or Hell

Is there a Heaven or Hell? **Sarah** reassures us that the Light is an abundant energy that fills the entire Universe. Perfect Light is what we realign with once the biological body dies and our Light is set free. Near Death Experiences bring us to describe this incredible place on the other side, heaven if you must, regardless of religion or belief. There is a place filled with brilliant White Light and Perfect Love, real or imagined, mere chemical response or atomic reality. The Other Side is overwhelming to our simple human senses. Those who have been there tell us their heart felt as if it would explode with love when suddenly in the presence of the Light.

I had a hard time believing in the devil even when I attended church. I was taught the devil was sitting right over my shoulder just waiting for a chance to corrupt me. **Sarah** explained that the concept of the devil served no purpose other than to scare people to submit and give us really good reasons to abide by the church. This is a questionable way of getting us onto the side of love. Love is something we all naturally strive for, not what we should seek because we're afraid not to. Fear has no place in Love.

The West Wind

Robert's boat, The West Wind, had a sliding wooden door into the wheel-house, and on one of my trips with Robert I managed to get my finger caught just as the door was slamming shut. After I did a little dance and uttered a few choice words, we took a look. He just shook his head. We could both see the signs of a very painful bruise seeping in under the nail and we all knew what that meant. Either it was true that a fisherman should never have a woman on board a working boat, or I was about to show them what I was really made of.

"I have to find a needle and poke a hole in my nail ...and now!" I looked to Robert for an idea of what to use. He was shaking his head slowly back and forth. "I don't have a needle! This is a fishing boat, not a quilting circle." He paused and looked around. "All I have is an electric drill."

I nodded my head, "Yup. A drill will work. What bits do you have?"

He scrunched up his eyebrows and continued to shake his head, "Are you crazy woman?"

I asked him to get out the drill and to install the smallest bit. I asked him to steady the drill on the dash facing me and run it slowly. He complied. I held my finger and firmly pressed it against the drill bit until I could feel it break through the nail. The chance I had just taken and my internal fear was worth it as the boys broke out in a cheer. It was the day I earned my boots!

We all experience a decrease in our Energy Signature from time to time. I know you have felt the zing of wrong-doing in your chest, that tingle of guilt, when you realize you've done something you shouldn't. Doing wrong decreases the Energy Signature and creates Karmic Debt. This becomes a dip in your Energy which is something to tend to and rebalance. When someone's Light has been covered over with veils of anger, hate, greed and the like, the veils brings the darkness. This is not because an evil entity has hold. Life itself lays the veils between us and our Light which imbalances our Energy Signature. Rebalancing is the only remedy.

G. F. Thornton

Jerry

I was nineteen. Jerry was twenty two. A good friend of mine had introduced us, so I felt as though he came with a recommendation. He was one of twenty kids in his French Catholic family from Quebec. He was visiting British Columbia to find work. He seemed to have a good sense of humor and we enjoyed each other's company - in the beginning. If everything was going his way, he was fine. As soon as I started to be suspicious of him, he changed into something else. Breaking free suddenly wasn't possible. He threatened to drive his car through the plate glass display window where I worked if I wouldn't go outside to talk with him during my shift. He always drove my car when we went out, and he had no idea what speed limits were. I recall hanging onto the seat as he raced at 100 miles an hour through the streets of Vancouver paying no attention to traffic or traffic lights. That I lived to tell this story is another miracle.

I had tried several times to back out of this relationship, but he wasn't about to let me go. One night, while I was at his place, I tried again. As I was putting on my coat, he jumped up and grabbed a large glass tumbler, smashed it on the edge of the counter and before I could escape, the giant shard was at my throat. "You're not going anywhere - for a very long time" he growled at me, his eyes burning into mine, his voice menacing and mean. He would hold me captive for days and taunt me with threats about how dangerous he would be if I ever thought about leaving again.

I knew this wasn't right. Yet, I was naïve at nineteen and was just starting to make my way in the world. What I did know was that I didn't have the resources to escape Jerry without some help.

I became a hermit, sleeping and hiding at home whenever I could. I lost interest in work and just about everything else too. When Jerry would call, I'd just ask Mom to say I was sick. I had no idea how long I could keep him at bay, but at least I felt safe at home. The respite didn't last long. I started working on the words I'd use to tell Mom what was really happening. One afternoon as I lay in bed, the curtains tightly closed, Mom knocked on my bedroom door and asked what was going on. I told her about the threats, how I had tried to get rid of him without much luck. Then I told her about those days he held me hostage as I apologized for the lie that I had been at a friend's. I told her about the chard of glass held to my throat that had kept me hostage against my will.

She instantly stood up and said, "Get your coat." She hurried me to the car and asked for directions to his place. When we arrived, she knocked on the door, and as soon as he answered, she grabbed him by his shirt, told him who she was, and that he needed to get his suitcase packed really quickly unless he wanted the police to lock him up. He complied. She drove him to the Bus Depot and bought him a one way ticket out of town. Her last words to him were, "If I ever see you in this city again, it will be your last day on earth!"

I was too young to understand the implications of what had really happened, why Jerry was the way he was and why I had been his victim. Jerry was only the first in a long line of men who would take advantage. Unbeknownst to me at the time, my life would be filled with abusers.

At one end of the spectrum God exercises His wrath and rules all and at the other answers prayers and sends miracles. Human interpretation of God however often seems to serve up more fear and divisiveness than hope and love. We can't seem to have one without the other. Some believers use interpretation to validate their own agenda. This book will be thus accused by some, I'm sure. Those who claim they are to war in God's name for instance offer their own interpretations. Yet they are merely striking out at a world they cannot control, tolerate or change. Their fear and their focus on the outside world and what others convince them of have become a demise of fear and power. Rest assured Karma will be keeping score whether we witness the retribution or not.

> "Light is everywhere, all the time.
> It is a constant chore to remain blind to it."
> **Blew Like Sage**

Religion

Our devotion and penance to a higher power has always been served one way or another. Most of us do not yet know the answers to why we're here or what life is really all about. We see the incredible Universe of stars above our heads and we can only wonder. It will be many more millennia before we can comprehend even the vastness or the deepest mysteries of the Universe. We can feel insignificant as if life is merely a quirk or coincidence while others will be paying great homage to whatever they believe is the power that runs it all. Acceptance that there must be such a power is more common than not. We are all drawn to a higher power, authentic self or sacred energy. Yet we have quite the time sorting out what this power is, where it is, what to call it, how to describe it and what will entice it to our advantage. Such is the making of religion.

"Light lives in all life including the greedy and the sinner. Being unaware, denying or refusing it does not change its existence, but speaks to the quality of your connection with it." **Lucy**

I was to refrain from using a wide brush as rarely would I find simple black or white, but instead, an ever-changing palate of gray. The concept of God or a higher power need not be human in form to be powerful or valuable. The concept of the Light held no such physical form and I found it to be both powerful and of value. The Light is contained within, and each life has a full, equal and individual share. There is no purpose for conflict for responsibility remains in the only place that makes any sense – within each of us.

Testing the Light in my life, I found the calm in the storm and a safe harbor. The Light didn't use fear to convert me. There was no need for a threatening devil or wielding the wrath. And the Light answered questions I could never answer before.

Each new message would bring more depth into the book and each editing session brought another level of resonance and understanding. Spirit was teaching me in levels and phases. I couldn't learn the end until I knew the beginning. There was a growing responsibility to the task I had been given as I wondered how it would all wrap up. As the book advanced, the lesson became one of patience and trust in the process as one year turned into five.

Religion's intention was to provide a moral code to keep us connected to a Divine Compass. Jesus didn't seek a church to be built in his name. He wanted us to know goodness and kindness and to perpetuate the truth of what he taught for many generations. The Bible was meant to cast His teachings forward instead of entrusting them to each new generation of interpretation. Many preachers however would become fallible interpreters and purveyors of the very sin of which they were to warn the masses. They themselves would become too tarnished to be the keepers of any sacred compass.

… your body is a temple… **1 Corinthians 6:19-20**

The goal of early Christianity was to revere and connect with God, to achieve mental stillness through meditation and to establish unification with the Radiant Light – personally, just as Jesus taught! Conversely, the goal of the clergy was the instillation of fear and an unquestionable loyalty to those who seemed to control the Word. With fear on their side the clergy gained the power to control the masses. Followers succumbed to the fear yet revered the church as the keepers of knowledge mostly because at the time there was no other choice. On the other hand, the faster down the road to politics and economics that the clergy ran, the faster corruption and power replaced the appeasing of God. Kingdoms and power became more important than truth and faith. Some in this century seem even further distanced from sanctity and sacredness. In nearly every institution, we are being influenced more each day by that which the church ardently warns their flocks against; greed, crime, dominance and fear. Corruption has been perpetuated and has tunneled deep into secret corners of all society, even the church.

More Rocks!

I signed up for a two-day creative writing class at the University many years ago. The instructor gave us a task right up front. We were to go out into the yard and select a rock and bring it back to class. We complied, all the time wondering what we could possibly be doing with a lump of granite. The instructor directed us to get to know our rock. Study the colors, the shape and size. Feel the weight in your hand and rub your fingers over the surface and feel the temperature, the bumps and nuances. Notice the things that have been trapped inside the granite that have become speckles and spots and think about what they are and why they're there. Place it under your arm and warm it up. Give it a name, a birthday and a history. At the end of the day we were instructed to write a story about our little rock that we would read to the class the next day.

Most of us took the rock home on Saturday night. Some painted faces on them while others made them a house or at least a bed. We added ears for hearing, eyes for seeing and wands for the magic. It was all quite interesting. We spent considerable time writing and then reading our creative rock stories on Sunday. Our rocks had taken quite an animated and personal turn. At the end of the day, in closing the instructor commented that we could return our rocks to the yard. I picked up my rock and papers, pens and coat and went outside to do just that. I could not, however, find a suitable place for this rock, and neither could anyone else. Standing in the yard, we watched each other as we all had the same thought: we had to take our new friends home.

The purpose for this exercise was to be creative. Many of us found something very different however. If we could build such a caring relationship with a rock over 24 hours, imagine what is possible when we take our neighbor out for coffee! I will never forget standing in the yard not wanting to leave this little friend behind to live in the weather, to be kicked around and walked on. This story would become one of a powerful and spiritual connection - with a rock. Spirit has a way of speaking to us - even when we have no intention of hearing anything.

Some of my stories, like this one, are simple little events, but they all made an indelible mark. You too will be able to find such stories in your past. In retrospect when viewed from Spirit each will take on a different meaning as your understanding morphs and changes. Even the painful, scary or abusive memories hold meaningful clues to direct you, hopefully sooner than I allowed them to direct me.

Interpretation of the Bible would become a skill. The more the church reinforced or preferred certain verses, the more skewed the meanings would become. Over time, it grew easier and easier for the clergy to promote the passages that served their purposes and supported their cause. The Bible would be changed from a sacred text that could not be rewritten to a test of interpretative license and questionable agenda.

Corruption and greed have been the undoing of emperors and kings, civilizations and cultures the world over. Religion has been no exception. Today, the tarnished reputation of the church for example is giving followers a great deal more to consider. And the fact that women to this day have barely gained status of any kind in any Church points directly to the inherent ignorance of the sleep from which many have yet to awaken. Ask any religion of the world if they have created their own perspectives and set of paradigms from which they are unwilling to be released.

We are all a product of where we come from. Those raised with a specific doctrine are at the mercy of their lessons. Each person has a choice as to whether or not, or even how much the agenda of the Church will affect their path. There are those for whom religion has brought great solace and love. When anything, religious or otherwise, brings you to true faith and love, it has served the grandest purpose. What needs to become evident today is what the Light would shine upon for all instead of only some; compassion, caring, kindness and love.

When viewed from Spirit, there are no reasons for poverty or starvation and everyone should have access to clean water, a home, education and food. These are basic necessities of life. Who can claim the right to deny these to their equal? We have at our disposal all we need for the entire population of the planet to live safe, healthy and prosperous lives. In the past, we could easily blame geography for any disparity. Today, we cannot as technology has joined us globally. Why then is quality of life reserved for only the few? Why do millions suffer or die and why are children left to starve? This isn't God not showing up or letting us down. It is only about us not showing up. Why haven't the teachings of Jesus been expressed through all His believers? The reason appears to be the very same thing which Jesus warned of in the courtyard; money. Those who have money are safe and those who do not are on the treadmill of striving and starving. How can we not have moved even an inch forward toward greater equality, peace or happiness if 4 billion people claim to follow God?

What would have happened had the Church remained as one sect, had followed the teachings of Jesus and continued toward Inner Consciousness? What would the world look like if we knew the strength, the resources and the guidance found in the Light within? Indeed, what would civilization be if personal moral and ethical foundations supported meaning, values, identity, purpose and equality? How would the world look if we were all connected to the wisdom of the Source? How would our health, community and family look if everyone understood their wealth comes solely from the

Light within? Such answers were about to lead me into the future... for this was certainly my destiny.

Religion as a whole is not at fault. There is no fault. Each life on the physical plane must find their personal wisdom. I must crawl before I can walk and bruising my knee caps will be involved. I cannot travel to the Light without being willing and able to navigate the path there. Each one of us needs to progress and cast off the things of this physical world to uncover the truth. It is the task of everyone to earn passage; no matter the path. No one will go forth before they are fully prepared to rid their focus on the material cares and woes or anything else that will stall their progress. This is what it is. Make no mistake that Karma will keep score of every thought, intention and act regardless.

The Ultimate Love

One of the most fascinating subjects is love. When humans hear the word, it is natural to go directly to our human experiences and what we know; love for someone, for a partner or spouse, intimate love, love for a child, family member, parents, pets, and so on. Human love is subject to influence from other energies on the physical plane; fidelity, perspectives, paradigms, sex and procreation, to name a few. Perfect Love is filled with Perfected Energy and Perfected Intention. Perfect Love is Spirit-filled, something we all unknowingly strive for in some way and which we will find for certain only on the other side.

Love: A chaste intention; a true and high vibration which is felt deeply as compassion, honor, respect, grace, trust and wisdom. The greatest Love on the physical plane is Spirit to Spirit.

Perfect Love: The Ultimate Ascended Energy of Perfect Light

Soul Mates

Robert and I talked about being soul mates, about our unique connection, the familiar knowing, the truth we both felt about each other and that instant bond that defied logic and reason and psychology books. We talked about everything. He taught me about his world, the wilderness, the ocean, fishing and nature. I would often sit back and just watch him in awe. I watched him sleep and work with his hands or just fishing on a golden day. There was little that lessened this love, except one small thing …there was a tiny distance he kept between us. It was as if he would never cross that final divide or the last wee bridge to inside his heart. It confounded and taunted me. Only once did I feel him fully surrender, and when this happened it took me across the Universe and back. In the beginning I accepted this distance as a clever technique to keep me wanting more. After a year however, that theory had outgrown itself. There was something, a little niggling thing that would keep him just on the verge of falling.

For those like Anita Moorjani, who wrote Dying to Be Me and who experienced Perfect Love during her Near Death Experience, there is no return from the awe. There is a full spectrum of love somewhere. Perfect Love is at one end of this spectrum where the Ultimate Energy resides - the one we are all drawn to. For Anita, this Perfect Love was found on the other side and it would save her human body from the fear that had diseased it with cancer. Her realization of what this love felt like, of what was possible and real was life-changing; physically. In fact, after her Near Death Experience, Anita returned with a new vision of love's brilliance and purity – a trip that literally saved her from death.

I would find many such stories as I journeyed toward the Light that would validate steps along the way. What happened as I set my own foot upon this path? Where were the messages coming from, whom or what was sending them, how and why was I receiving them became my curiosities? I prayed regularly that I was up to the task and had a clear and intentional honesty toward that direction.

It's in the Light

The human body holds the power to heal itself, not only the biology but the psyche as well. In a future chapter you will learn about the power of the Light in healing. Written within each cell and each DNA strand are specific details for the physical like the color of eyes and hair and height and other traits. And in this Light is given the true purpose of this lifetime and the lessons which will take you there.

My life lessons would be determined for this incarnation based on what I had gained in past incarnations. My Light holds intimate messages of what will have the greatest meaning on this trip. My health, power, resources and greatest strengths would come from within me, not from the outside. This book was written in my own Light, as it is in yours. What an incredible place to hide our truth - safely tucked away inside each of us.

The Garter Snake

We were sitting on the ground in the garden, pulling up and eating baby carrots. Boo was always thinking about something. I could tell. I looked up to see his giant outline backlit by the summer sun. He spoke to me, "I have a pet garter snake, you know." A picture of a giant snake skipped through my mind. "You do?"

"Yup. Want to see him?" I nodded up and down slowly, not quite sure if I did or not. He did, after all, say it was a snake.

Boo took a cursory look across the carrot tops and down the row of lettuce then whistled softly. I waited, afraid to breathe. He whistled again. Within a minute a foot-long garter snake slithered out from under the carrots. Boo placed his hand face up on the ground and the garter snake slid up his fingers and coiled up inside his palm. My eyes were as big as saucers and my mouth hung open. "I didn't know snakes had ears!"

In the grassroots movement today the meek are rising up to inherit the Earth just as they are meant to. Such is the next step and the simple insight of the Higher Power. It is the flower within your garden, the greatest love you can ever know on Earth and it brings the wisdom, grace and happiness you seek. Light is the symphony, the sunrise and sunset, a good heart and a walk through the rainbow that lives forever across the sky.

"Light spurs you forward to great things." **Parkah**

Superior

Fifty years ago, I had heard it said that Earth is the only inhabited planet in the Universe. Something inside of me knew it couldn't be true. Today, such wide-brush statements come from limited vision. We simply cannot know if we are the only inhabited planet because the Universe will always be just too huge. I fully expect, especially given new discoveries of more than a thousand planets that could be inhabited in just our little corner that we are not even close to being alone. If life is here, life is there. Today Scientists report there are billions of possibilities just in the Milky Way. That we could even think we are the only life speaks to paradigms that are out of date like the belief that God gave us dominion and superiority over everything on Earth. Our superiority comes more from a long line of indulgence and foolhardy ideas. That we think we are superior is a fantasy when clearly our history is far too barbaric to be superior to anything.

We are a jumble of commonly held beliefs from our respective cultures. Many are now being proven untrue. Newton proposed that everything is separate from everything else, that we are separate from each other, that each one is special and individual, and that there are indeed many separate parts. Prior to Copernicus, humanity also believed Earth was the center of the galaxy, and that God had given us dominion over the Earth and all of its inhabitants. Darwin led the way for the concept that the world works by survival of the fittest and that DNA was what held the only secret of what we are and all we will become. These ultimately caused us to believe that we have all power and no power simultaneously. If we believe that our DNA determines our destiny, then we will not look to be responsive to our environment. We will roll over and die to our DNA versus changing our environment so we can heal. New evidence clearly disputes that DNA controls everything, even though the DNA paradigms will fall the hardest.

"Spirit Energy is in all things and how all is connected." **SoSo**

We now know that we are not the center of the universe and that we don't have dominion over much. Based on survival-of-the-fittest and the law of the jungle however we still seem to think we are the greatest...at everything. Yet the 20th Century was our bloodiest yet as 260 million people died from war, nearly two thirds of the population of the United States. We are embroiled and surrounded by the ultimate sins. No amount of subjective reasoning can change that. So, remind me again how it is that we are so superior.

Sin: missing the mark.

Not fully understanding the reason for my heart to pain or my eyes to leak when in the presence of First Nation Elders, the more I learned about their philosophy, the more I wanted to know. Something deep inside of me resonated with them. It seemed we were connected somehow. Even without my awareness, their philosophy had given rise to the conflict I had felt in the mud of the middle. I am only now coming to appreciate what they knew and what I missed in my Mainstream world. Being in their midst always invokes tears and deep emotion. Their presence touches and resonates with something sacred inside me – every time.

Ancient First Nation philosophy places plants and animals as more valuable than humans. All life depends on plants to balance the oxygen in the atmosphere. Lives depend on plants for food, shelter and clean water. This is no small feat. Animals provide humans with food, warmth, clothing and service. Nothing ...is dependent upon humanity ...but humanity. It can be a sobering thought when we view ourselves at the bottom of the chain and not at the top.

Measuring What?

Parkah questioned, "What is it humans measure to claim superiority?"

If intelligence is all we measure, then it might be safe to say we have the greatest capacity, which by the way does not guarantee we use it. Life is not operated solely on an intellectual level however. We exist on this physical plane through four distinct modalities: physical, intellectual, emotional and spiritual; aware or not. If we were measuring our spiritual quotient, it could be said we lag behind just about every other species. Animals are Spirit Energy. They seem, in fact, dedicated to it. They do not destroy their home or worry about tomorrow. They do not exploit the Earth or murder members of their own species. They do not follow weak or corrupt leaders, and they do not focus on being at the top or in control of much. In fact, I fully expected the sole reason we love our pets so much is because they speak the language of Spirit. They walk Spirit. They live Spirit… every day and in every way and this is the purity we are drawn to. Plants inhale and exhale Spirit. They fill themselves with Light and animate it perfectly without conflict, war or greed. **Parkah** would speak of the dependence and natural dedication plant and animal life have to the Light.

It is true those little creatures and the flora all around are the evidence of Spirit. They certainly show us the way there or the way back when we're lost. Connecting with a beautiful or powerful animal, especially those greater in stature or physical energy like elephants, horses or lions, or those we hold most dear like our pets, invite us back to Spirit instantly. It makes total sense then that if I am lacking in inspiration or Spirit, connecting with an animal will reconnect me with my Spiritual Wealth when I open up, listen and allow it. This is the resonant orchestra of the Universe. For many, to kill an innocent and majestic Spirit in the name of sport is the greatest sin and it shows a cold and empty heart. It is well to remember Karma is always keeping track of the Tribe, plants and animals included.

> **Resonance:** one energy influencing another; harmony that is
> physically felt inside of us through waves of love.

Rupert Sheldrake hypothesized morphic fields - massive and multiple fields of energy which cause shape and form and which record all and everything. Memory is cumulative and the future will be built upon this mounting intelligence. I began to notice repeating layers of Energy from the Energy that causes galaxies to form all the way to how proteins create reactions within the body to cause movement. The case for Energy in the form of frequency, sound, wave and vibration was becoming clearer. Energy creates all shape, form, movement and change. Energy is the absolute certainty of evolution within the morphic field just like the energy that causes movement and currents in the ocean.

Some physicists claim we create our reality when we observe a particle. They say the act of our observation settles electrons into a certain orbit from out of infinite possibilities. Our observation is apparently what makes a particle take one place in time and space. Thus it arrives in reality when we observe it. And here we go again. We are so very special that the entire world is here because we're watching it. This may very well be true but I have to question if it might be the other way around. Perhaps a particle

143

freezes into place to share its energy with an observer. And then we get to see it. You can see now how some skepticism is healthy and keeps us seeking the real truth until we know for sure.

Personally, I must go back to the chemistry lab and the task of describing the burning candle as if I'd never seen one before. This single event had a considerable effect because it is always difficult to settle into a belief until I have found sufficient reason for why I should. As you have likely guessed, I do not conform simply because it is expected or because everyone else has. To question the status quo is healthy and it keeps us moving forward and not standing still long enough to get stuck in the mud. To be fully aware of how easily one can be manipulated or coerced is even healthier. As you stand at the Gates of Heaven, if indeed you will have to defend your life, would it not be best to know what helped you to make your way?

So, what are we measuring? The status quo comes from many old and out of date paradigms. From Spirit, humanity is clearly not superior to much. Perhaps we should measure the inabilities, not as disabilities, but as failure to see beyond the illusions. We are failing to measure up to even animals as we rape and pillage this beautiful planet in the name of profits. No greater scourge has there been on Earth than capitalism built solely on the high and mighty drug called money.

When will we see all life as vessels containing the energy of God instead?

Chapter 8

Brutal and Brilliant

"Each event makes unique vibrations that are
captured in your Light," **Wahwaskenah**.

THIS CHAPTER brings my personal story forward to present day. The
prejudice my mother had suffered as a child had touched my life too.
And the First Nation past no one really spoke about in our family had
influenced me through Boo, Uncle Jack and Mom. They had unknowingly
given me a different way of being and thinking that was like a destiny I
could not shake. What had been showered upon them, what they had
unknowingly learned and what had been written in their blood was what
had made my own life a mystery to me.

I had created a swath of destruction with misdirected or incorrectly
considered decisions for decades. It was as if I was missing an important

foundation and a way of grounding myself to a valuable code everyone else knew but me. Nothing seemed to make any sense so I had become obsessed with finding the secrets to life I thought I didn't know. I would search the world and scour the past to find something that I couldn't even name. How does one find something when they don't know what they're looking for?

During my spiritual awakening that started in 1999, I would eventually find out what made me tick. I would be able to see how everything had been perfectly intentioned to lead me to the truth of who I was meant to be …rather than whom I had slipped into being. I was a walking, talking, breathing example of how the past can mean something very different when viewed from the truth in the future. I could see how my entire life had been laced with buffers that would keep me on track toward a predetermined conclusion. Spirit and my own Consciousness were adding substance to the Light toward a better and more evolved Energy. There would come a time when I would be of the Mind to just let it happen. My Light had been filled with lessons from past incarnations, ancient knowledge and sacred water. Even more wonderful is that this is the same for everyone. We are all a blend, a mixture of traits and race and sacred water.

My deep connection with First Nation people and the Elders had lived within me all along. The energy of their very presence was designed to fill me up and spill out of me like a river of tears. I had lived in a different place from the one that had hold of my heart …for a reason. It would be the catalyst; the pea under the mattress and the thorn in my side. It was meant to fuel the search for what was real and true. To this end, everything had its purpose. I wasn't moving toward a dream. I was the dream and I was now just waking up.

"The past is the mirror where you can see your truth." **Parkah**

In the bigger picture, I was meant to learn of and then tell a story of the Circle of Many. I was meant to feel and experience our common fears and emotions, our common needs and the unending lessons to the same. I was to reveal how we have all been betrayed and why we feel abused. I was to open the window to my own mistakes and their reasons as examples of the distractions of this physical world. I was to speak about what happens in our mind and heart when we feel we don't belong. Without realizing what had really been happening, each day had been designed to lead me to the truth of what I was meant to be …rather than what I had slipped into. And with any luck at all, Spirit's book is meant to reach out and validate everyone who lives in the mud of the middle.

Peak Experience: The Past

In 1989 I started looking for information about my ancestry. I phoned the local First Nation Band office to ask if it was possible to meet some elders. They said, "Of course." They told me the place and time, and one sunny day in April I made my way to the reserve. I was excited and hopeful inside that I would finally learn more about the people of my heritage.

I found the building, parked the car and opened the door. I stepped out onto the land and immediately fell to my knees with great sorrow coursing through my chest. I started to sob. I had no idea what on Earth was happening? I hid in the car for time until I could collect myself. All I could do was wonder what had just happened. Eventually after the sadness subsided, I entered the building and was warmly welcomed by four female Elders. They sat me in the center of their circle and wanted to know about me. They were kind and caring and curious. I marked the experience as my introduction to 'all my relations', a term used to signify the many relationships with all things on the Earth that First Nation philosophy honors. There was a presence that filled me up that day.

It wasn't until many years later that I learned the experience of stepping on the land was a common occurrence for those with First Nation blood, aware or not. I met a Chief who would tell me that I was sensitive to the pain of the many who had once lived on that land and who had gone before me. Placing my feet upon the ground connected me to them and to their pain.

"Their pain is written in your blood." **Parkah**

I would find new insight in my past as I began to uncover the greater reasons for why my journey had been what it had. In the beginning I was embarrassed to be so naked and vulnerable in my stories. Yet in the end, it was a privilege to be an example. I began to see how the book I would write one day just might make a difference, perhaps for you and maybe for others, but most certainly for me. To write and talk of experiences and what they really mean, no matter who pens the words or speaks the stories, is meant to help us grow a better world.

"The Light is an internal fire of Love." **Wahwaskenah**

First Nation Spirits had always touched my heart. The day I fell to my knees consumed by their pain, I was connecting with that past *for a reason*. How many decades had they waited for someone able to hear their story and to bring it to a bigger purpose? My energy had resonated with theirs and they were there to let me know them in a different way. Over the following years, I would collect other Elders too, and not just First Nation Elders but some from different dimensions. They were coming together with a purpose – to write their book.

All of my past has given me a clearer picture of where I am and what the road before me means. We are not perfect or ascended, and many are barely insightful. We need not be flawless on this physical plane however. In each incarnation we are to work at living as best we can and to find an inspired and more complete self that is connected to the Light. In the end we are all meant to elevate, evolve and eventually ascend one day. It hardly matters where or when we begin or what we can bring with us from previous incarnations. We accumulate regardless. And we are all naturally drawn to seek something to fill that empty feeling in our center, ready or not. This is by divine design …to keep us seeking the Light.

I have been a scribe and author in previous lives, and I am one in this incarnation too, so this book is a means to a very distant end. We each can claim our purpose from within the circle of billions of possibilities but we will find it only in the Light. While all energy in the Universe influences every other, your journey requires your personal intention, permission and commitment. Each one of us is in this incarnation to reach the Light *intimately and personally* which means we must each do our own work. Strangely enough, it is each unique journey that creates our bond and commonality within the Circle of Many. This Circle is powerful, not because of our numbers, but because it is round.

What goes around comes around.

The Elders ask that we rise to become the changes we want to see in the world. They ask, "Are you ready to make the world a better place, and will you start within yourself?" Everything begins with just one; one path, one gift, one step, one thank you, one person, one dream. When critical mass has taken that first step into the Light, we won't need to worry about the outer world any longer.

Parkah reminds us, "You are Light first. You are there to learn to rise above the trappings of the physical experience to soar through Spirit. It is only in the Light that you will exist for all eternity. Be wise in this."

This journey does not lend itself to being fluffy or superficial. We have a brilliant past and we have a brutal one. And it is long past time we faced both, take our measure of responsibility and stop beating each other up like kids in a sandbox. We can come together, cooperate and take on the causes that will make a difference for everyone. It is time for us to grow up and stop expecting others to fix things because clearly they're not. Take a stand. Make a choice. Be confident in the Light. Move forward.

This chapter may also validate what you are already feeling of the world around you. When you look at that world, do you see the scars that have been scratched upon its surface by greed and agenda? The Elders encouraged me to look beneath the fantasy to see the stuff that fuels the fires of destruction. Opening up to the world through the Light made me turn toward a truth that mattered most …to me and ultimately to all life.

What matters is that a small part of the population has had far too much influence, control and power and they have used it unwisely. They have abused their privilege for much too long. Equality, fairness and compassion and lessons from Buddha, Jesus, the Dali Lama and others are healing for an angry and upside down world. This Age and the shifting energy of the

Earth are meant to move us toward a greater purpose for all, not just a few. We have the ways and the means already so when do we start?

"Do you know how to make friends and honor each other?" **Parkah**

Brutal

Millions of refugees are fleeing their homes to avoid bombs and wars while the rest of us fear our own safety when called to help them. Great endangered species are being killed as a show of power and to sadly adorn beige walls in empty trophy rooms. We have destroyed great swaths of forest and have filled the oceans with radiation and plastic garbage. The Arctic is melting at record rate. Our atmosphere has been polluted with toxic gas and our minds with toxic thoughts. And unbelievably there are many who say they don't believe any of it. These two positions cannot exist at the same time and be true. Yet this is happening even though 3/4s of Earth's population claims to follow God. Something is definitely off.

Recycling, environmental and animal-rescue programs have been touted now for over seventy years. Yet we are moving at a snail's pace to make the changes we must while our fear of where we are heading continues to grow. How can these issues still exist? Animals are walking, talking, and breathing Spirit. We must ask the right questions - and put our power into the answers. We only have one Earth.

The most dangerous issue of the new century is that we are being desensitized to trauma and violence by the chaos of the world that reaches us every hour. We are being conquered and divided by ridiculous little issues so we can no longer see the big picture, even when we trip over it. More of us are tired of the violence and the drama than are not. We are tired of being manipulated, marginalized, devalued and ignored as we are maneuvered more with each passing day. The need is growing to come together to change what we seem to no longer tolerate. This systemic poison needs a treatment and some serious healing.

"Tearing down good things for lesser things guarantees you will continue to suffer the same lesson again. Each must learn their personal lessons well before becoming a virtue." **Wahwaskenah**

It is becoming clear to billions that something basic is very broken. When we follow sacred tenets and embrace the laws of the Universe, there is no basis for petty or malicious acts that are destructive; the hierarchies, the power, the greed and the violence. Brutality can be dispelled when our priorities change to honoring the sacredness of life *over all else*. Do we really need an imminent extinction to push us there? Finding our inner focus and being accountable to the Light takes the bite out of the powers that dominate. All the sacred texts are filled with this wisdom and there is much evidence that many are now seeking and finding it.

Children go to bed hungry every night in the richest countries in the world. Yet those who follow God, 4 billion of us, must be asleep for this to happen. It is up to me to value every life no matter the circumstance. Those who ignore the sick, the vulnerable and infirm, and for that matter any living thing, give cause for violence and greed. When anyone is unable, it is up to the tribe to make sure they are enabled. To deny anyone's right to life is the hallmark of ignorance and sin. Just ask Jesus or Buddha.

We are not meant to be arrogant or cruel or cause others to suffer. Life is hard enough. Why have we accepted the tenets of the law of the jungle or survival of the fittest as our model? Darwin would be sick to see how his theory has been twisted into motives for greed and apathy. The elite fear the terrorists the same as everyone else yet they deny and ignore the greed and apathy that created them. When fear fills our minds going for a walk, we must demand to know why there are people anywhere in the world who can resort to terrorism and war. Very few, if any, are born violent …yet this seems so easy to dismiss. What are our errors that led to their violence? Making money, having control over others and ignoring the value of life are not the reasons we're here. It's time to rewrite this song because it's way old. What if education that teaches equality, compassion and fairness was available to *everyone?* Enter the Internet.

"Can you foster people from love like you foster animals?" Willo

Clearly we are missing something when someone can be so lost they would take another life. We put a man on the moon nearly fifty years ago but we can't rescue a lost soul before their only solution is violence. The human condition and our inhumanity to humanity perpetuates through silence and apathy. We fear gender aberrations for instance but we dare to mention the gender that commits 90% of all crimes. We even seem to have difficulty identifying who is potentially violent – as though there are no clues.

"Everything comes from within, and is expressed through you."
Dan White Deer

Most of us live somewhere near the middle between apathy and tears, war and happiness, garbage and garden parties. We slog along through our challenges as if we know how to fix things while often our strategies are silently creating deeper wounds. We grow up, not because we are smarter or have matured but because time marches on without a care, and ready or not – BANG – we're adults. We become employees, couples, politicians, entrepreneurs, teachers, experts and keepers of the fire. Then we become parents of the next generations where we should be teaching our children what we haven't learned yet. During the formative years of a child's young life, impressions will be made by their parents at a time when those parents are the least capable of all of their parenting years.

It often takes decades to sort through all the details of our human experience. What school teaches the intricacies and complexities of our most important relationships? Who is showing us how to survive the trials and challenges and how best to navigate them? Our society imposes its judgements on all of us convincing us, for instance, that we need a degree to prove we're smart. No piece of paper I have ever seen guarantees smart. We have been convinced that the plight of another should not be put before our own. For millennia, the churches of the world were looked to for teaching values, ethics and morals. Who amongst them lived what they taught? We have grown uncertain of whom, if anyone has earned our trust to accept what they are teaching. We are each a tiny spec of sand upon a massive beach and one grain can only holler so loud. Our voices must be collective. We can come together to shout out the travesties and learn how to build good people who will build a better world.

"The Light is the seed within you, and the physical world
is the garden where it blooms." **Parkah**

We arrive with a destiny. We are Spiritual Beings on this physical plane and we are here to learn, to rise to our potential and to find and grow our gifts *to serve the whole with fairness and compassion*. This physical plane is where we are to bloom, not as unruly weeds but as Spirits with great wings. The more complex things get as we stack one year upon the next and one unsolved problem on top of another, the greater our anxiety and depression. It is no wonder we can't stop the treadmill so we can get off.

Money is how the world keeps score in the biggest game of all. And yet, I have learned the hard way that if it's about the money, it will never be about people. Our greatest challenge and the worst plague of all is that we have succumbed to being controlled by money. When money rules the game, when it is the sole reason and purpose behind everything, we can't solve poverty because poverty is the hallmark of those who have already lost the game. We believe that winning means someone becomes a loser.

There is sufficient compassion in the world to gather and focus it in one direction for the good of all life on Earth. We have all we need and we have done much greater things; many, many times. If you can't actively shout yourself, support someone who can. It is a call to everyone to champion the need instead of the greed.

"Money poisons – slowly and silently. It has no conscience and no heart
…only a master." **SoSo**

The Brilliant

Humanity also has amazing capacity, intelligence, curiosity and skill. From our trip to the moon, from technology to sustainable energy, from exploring the tips of mountains to the depths of the oceans, there seems to be very little we can't do. Our capacity to solve problems and understand our Universe is astounding. We have split atoms, grown organs in the lab, transplanted human hearts, listened to the Big Bang and even know our location in the galaxy. We have moved mountains and rivers and have mapped the Universe and the human genome. We have discovered the Higgs Boson and equations for gravity and the speed of light. How do you measure something that is travelling at 299,792,458 meters per second anyway? We can even fly through the atmosphere at 2,193.2 miles per hour and many of us have walked in space. We can communicate with anyone in the world, transfer money and view others - instantly. We have built all manner of machines that serve us and help us explore and travel further than ever before. We are brilliant.

> "Warm up your own heart well,
> then reach out to melt the hearts of others." **Simi**

We are brilliant when we are connected to the Light. Creative Energy comes directly from the Consciousness of the Universe via your Mind, ready or not. When you focus deep into something over time is when you connect to the wonders of the Cosmos. You have already experienced this many times whenever you are doing what inspires you. This is when new discoveries and brilliant ideas show up and when acting on them expresses more and more amazing things into the world. Everything we have invented and created is because of a connection to the Light. The more our world advances is the only evidence we need.

It is when someone is disconnected that they can lose their way. When a child is not shown or taught about the strength and love inherent within them, they can easily get lost. Losing that central anchor, that safe place to come back to is how we become powerless, afraid and alone. It is also when the brutality can show up as we fight to return to that critical place we cannot name or locate. Modelling and teaching about the power of the Light within is essential for this to change. Educating those who will bear the next generation is a key. Watching closely and becoming aware of those who are lost and alone, who feel powerless or worthless, and helping them to become valued members of the tribe is worthy of our time. This is how we can steal the next recruits from the likes of terrorist cells before they become so angry and lost. Each parent that bears a child should be gifted with the necessary resources to care for and nurture their inner wealth.

"Offer compassion when it is missing. Be love when love is needed. Give attention when they are alone. Find them before they are lost." **Parkah**

Dreaming

I came out from the edge of the forest and into the sunlight and suddenly felt the warmth of the sun upon my face. The path took a turn to the right and I followed it. I came upon a bench. "Hello!" Robert said as he offered his arms. I fell into them and we wrapped each other in a blanket of love.

"What is this place," I asked?

He looked around, then said, "I knew you'd come." It would be the very first time I said it. "I love you." He turned to me and said it back. A great peace spread throughout my body as every nerve relaxed.

When I awoke, I remembered the dream as if I had really been there. I could still smell the cedar and feel the sunlight. I could see his face as clearly as if he were standing in front of me that very moment. And I was still lingering in the warmth of his words. Something real had happened. Then I remembered those special words of love just as disappointment fell in upon it all. It was only a dream.

An hour later the phone rang. It was Robert calling from a tiny fishing village where he was working. "Good morning! How did you like our walk last night?"

I couldn't quite believe what I was hearing, "What?"

"You know, the forest, the bench ...you were there. It's really cool we can do that, right? Listen, I wanted to tell you this morning before you left for work that I meant what I said."

My mind was still reeling trying to connect the dots. "What? What did you say?" I needed to know if we had really been there together in that dream and whether he would know what he said.

He replied softly, "Do not doubt my love ...for I will never doubt yours."

To overcome, to change and to make the world a place without fear, war, terrorists or poverty, the responsibility begins inside each of us. Within us lays the conscience, the belonging, the value and the wisdom we are seeking from somewhere out there. It is not out there. No one, no matter how rich or wise or genius has any greater claim to this force than anyone other. This incarnation is happening because you came here to learn this. Embracing the Light, makes it possible to begin again, to make the entire world peaceful because we don't want our brutal past to become our future.

"What is it that separates kings from paupers?" **Willo**

The Hats

In 1968 my parents sent me to Europe with C.Y.O, [Catholic Youth Organization] tour group. There were 19 kids and one chaperone. It would be the trip of my life. I was 16. We started on the West Coast by train which took four days to arrive in Montreal. The next day we took a bus to New York City. Yes, the Big Apple. We were excited beyond our senses. We stayed in a hotel not far from Time Square and could see the lights of Broadway from our room.

The following day three of us set out to see some sights. We boarded an articulating bus, or one that is twice the size of a regular bus and bends in the middle. As we had always been taught, when we entered at the front of the bus, we moved on through to the back and sat down. We had never been on a bus like this before and we must have been a gaggle of giggly girls. Once we settled in, we noticed that all the people on the bus were staring at us. We had petal hats on, which were scarves that were worn like a bandana on our heads and they have fabric petals all over them. I think mine was white. We assumed everyone was staring at our hats, until we noticed something else. All the white people were at the front of the bus and all the black people were sitting with us at the back. We started nodding our heads up and down once we figured it out and yes, we smiled back and stayed right where we were. Canadians!

As a Species

Very little in this book is new. Sacred texts and equally sacred humans began calling us a very long time ago. They warned us to not put false idols or material wealth before the Highest Power. They called us to be compassionate and empathetic, to care for everyone and to be moral and principled. All of the holy books are filled with lessons of morals, good intention, compassion and love. Yet we keep finding ways to fall off the ladder as if our choices were mere options. And even today, even after centuries of lessons, there are still too many who are lost. We have an obligation to pull them back from the abyss. These are the common enemies that pull us apart when they can become the catalysts to bring us together. All the rewards in life only arrive after we do our own work.

Lucy spoke up, "Celebrate the Energy of the many voices and hearts in your human family. Physical life is a mix of a billion colors that together create the rainbows which paint the Earth in ever changing shades of beautiful. If you do not know your neighbor, how can they help you?"

Grassroots movements are cropping up all over the world. People are banding together in massive numbers and are taking to the streets to protest what they're tired of tolerating. The shift in the energy of the Earth has spurred something inside all of us and its force is moving us forward …just in time. As we search for something meaningful that resonates, remember we are naturally attracted to the energy of the Light. Each day will bring us closer to realizing we need not be trapped because of our differences and we can come together to rally over the beauty of what makes us different. We no longer have to distance from our human-ness when the energy of Spirit soothes and blends hearts everywhere. Together we can achieve everything.

United we stand. Divided we fall.

We can no longer turn a blind eye to what we're doing. When the acorn seldom falls far from the tree, we must be mindful to make sure the tree is strong and smart, compassionate and whole. There are two schools of thought; one that says we are not our brother's keeper and the other that asks us to be keepers of all. For centuries we have avoided our responsibility and we've used many arguments to do so. Something is still not working so it's time to be the keepers of all. We cannot claim to know God if we cannot accomplish this.

"You know how to never raise another lost soul and you know how to rid your world of fear and greed. That you are not is the tragedy. Turn up every Light so peace can be found everywhere." **Blew Like Sage**

Chapter 9

Consider the Truth

THE GREATEST LESSON yet was this one. For nearly five decades there was something inside of me that I knew was different. As a result I had grown jaded and confused and angry in response to life. I hadn't been able to sit comfortably in just one chair or get to a place where I felt I belonged, and so I moved every two years and searched the world. I had been missing something very fundamental in my core self that I knew nothing about. Then one day I would realize the lesson was about me; about what was written in my Light and about what I came here to do.

Everything in the past was meant to take me to within for the answers, to have me dust off the cobwebs and take a close look at what made me tick. Curiously, I started dusting at the same time I started searching for a return path to the bubble I had stumbled into 1999. These two rivers of coincidence would merge one day into a clear blue crystal that would fill that empty space inside …at long last.

From my own experiences it is imperative to find the center of your own being too. It is in your very best interest to reconnect with the self-wisdom and consciousness you arrived here with when you were born. And this information is safe and stored within each of us simply because it makes no sense for it not to be. It was because of my experiences, my research and testing everything at every step along the way that I can say without reservation that this is real. The Elders made it very clear that each journey is unique, personal and intimate and that every solution, no matter how big or small, begins within us. Being reconnected to the Sacred Essence made me a better person, a better human being and a better example, teacher and healer. It is only after my own rebirth that I was able to add value to others and to the world.

Note

Being here at this point in my life, I can see so clearly that my ancestors wrote Spiritual messages in my Light that I would find them one day. The Light has reconnected me with the truth of the ancient wisdom that has been revived and reawakened inside of me. Dare I say that the world, dangerous or safe, joyous or sad *can* make sense? The boulders upon the path that lies behind me were there for a reason; to keep me on track. And I can now see how I must venture forward if I am to remove myself from the mud of the middle and land upon a firmer ground of understanding.

In the lesson sits both the small and the huge. The small lessons concern only me, and the larger ones concern us all. This timeline began many incarnations before this one and was rooted within the span of this lifetime from my birth to today. I am but one, a single Path of One in the giant cosmic Circle of Many. My individual story resonates with every other story through common human notes. We are all searching. We all feel the pain, the loss and the joy. We have all made many mistakes and we've all cleaned up a lot of mess in our lives. We wonder and worry, fret and consider, laugh out loud and cry silently in cold empty spaces. We are the same – a single species of humanity. We arrive here and leave here in the exact same way. And all of these things unite us as equals, as the Body Human.

So where do we go wrong? Why is there such division if we're supposed to be just one? The history of my First Nation ancestry opened up my eyes and my heart to a startling revelation that I must share with you.

I had known very little about the history of my ancestors; about their station in life, their culture or their philosophy. My mother had told me a few simple things like the women of the tribe chewed cedar bark to make blankets for their babies. I had no way of verifying if it was true. I had heard comments about First Nation people not paying their way and that they should just get over the past and move on. This always spurred my anger for some reason. Then after Mom's death I started to search for information on my ancestors and I would find some startling stories.

I would also come to tears every time I entered a longhouse or watched a ceremony or sat with an Elder. I found myself in these people. I found that I thought more like they did than my Mainstream neighbours. They would take me to the center of me; to the honey in the comb, the dolphin in the spray and the color in a flower. Finding them took my breath away because there was a powerful wind that blew through me to the core when I connected with this sacred water.

Setting a Context

The history that involved First Nation people over several centuries was lengthy and difficult to fathom. It was multi-faceted and complex in the beginning and it remains so to this day. Both cultures had been born with faith, yet their faith had been raised on different continents so they didn't look the same. First Nation history is strong and spiritual and Mainstream is based on religious rule and tenet. Yet there was a huge clash between these two cultures simply because one didn't look like the other. Mainstream was not of the mind at the time to accept what was unfamiliar. They didn't speak the language so they didn't inquire. This was only one aspect of the divide that would separate them. The Europeans simply figured these people needed to be civilized.

I recently read a 600 page book on Native People in Canada written in 1986. It was about the shape of their tools, migration, what they lived in, where they hunted and what they did. It was about the gene pools, the clothing, totems and canoes. And I was shocked not one single page was about their philosophy or cultural tenets. This has clearly been a problem for centuries. Mainstreamers did not know anything about the philosophy, ethics or conduct of Native people yet they were the powerful and could sit in judgement over everything pertaining to them. The shape and fabric of their canoe isn't near as important as the depth and color of their faith. While this section points out some of the differences between their cultures, neither culture is incorrect. Consider the following before you think you can decide which one is fair.

The European conquest of the New World influenced the entire Nation of Indigenous peoples and ranged from mild to catastrophic. All cultures have suffered in different ways and each utilized their strengths, skills and resources to survive. For First Nations of North America, many didn't survive however and the reasons are anything but simple or fair.

At Home

Heather and I have very different memories of our childhood as if we had grown up in different houses. We both have very different memories and experiences of the same people and the same events. Even though there were five years between us, we still wondered how this was possible. It brought other questions to mind: What would have happened had we grown up in different communities or better still, in different countries?

Culture

Looking at different cultures is a lesson in optics, perspectives and mindsets that are conditioned. In North American Mainstream [MS] culture, we are taught how to respond. Our way of thinking is highly conditioned with what we perceive to be true *as a society*. We have federal curriculums and standards for education. Everyone is taught and trained and prepared in like fashion to the same end point. This happens in every culture. Yet there appears to be hundreds of acceptable ways to do the same thing. And this is a key. The contrast between Mainstream and First Nation cultures is a perfect example of imposing one over another as if one is better than the other. This is misinterpretation and misunderstanding and judgemental. Here are some general aspects of both cultures to show the differences and to help you consider what this could mean. Think about these aspects from the 1800s when the war first started.

MAINSTREAM Knowledge base from European diversity and pursuits	FIRST NATION Pure and consistent survival in the wilderness
Capitalism: money is the foundation	Socialism: sharing is imperative
Competitive: Law of the Jungle, Survival of the Fittest	Cooperative: working together, equality, all members are valuable
Exclusivity: Individualism	Inclusivity: Team/Group
Religion is rules and control	Spirit is foundational in all things
Individuality and individual pursuits are encouraged	Community sharing & involvement is necessary for all to survive
Written History: taught in classes	Verbal History: told in stories
Crime and Punishment: To confirm guilt in court, tried by peers, and to prison to deter future bad behavior	Dysfunction and Rehabilitation: To heal spiritual disconnection and to reintegrate back into community
Traditions: specific to European culture & Christianity	Traditions: specific to each tribe to honor the Great Spirit in all things
Ceremonies: cultural specific	Ceremonies: tribal specific
Language is exclusive	Language is Inclusive

Justice

This next table is a basic look at some of the foundations of how bad behavior, crime and offenses are dealt with differently. Think about the basics of these two cultures three hundred years ago; First Nation people are surviving in the wilderness as they have for centuries while Europeans brought their modern tools and skills from a totally different cultural backdrop. Now both cultures are on the same continent.

Mainstream	First Nation
Once found guilty, punishment is based on an eye for an eye	Crime isn't about one behavior: it's more Spirit's disfavor & message
Punishment is meant to deter future bad/criminal behavior	Rehabilitation is to appease Spirit and return victims to the community
Punishment is jail/prison time to remove offender from society	Time is spent in counsel with Elders and members to heal/appease Spirit
Court provides evidence and proof of guilt	Not about the action but rather about appeasing Spirit's disfavor
Eye to eye contact is an indicator of truth-telling and forthrightness	Looking at someone in the eye is insensitive and rude
Detailed forthright testimony under oath is expected & required	Speaking ill of another is prohibited & dangerous to survival
Criminal offenders are marked with a Record, sometimes for life	Reintegration and healing ensures continuity and the workforce
Criminals are expendable	Wrong-doers remain in the tribe
The greater the crime, the greater the punishment.	The greater the crime, the more influential the Spirits have been
Behavior based	Meaning based

The Mainstream Justice System has been built based on lawlessness. The US has the highest per capita prison population and the highest rate of gun violence in the world and with 90% of all criminals being male. A multi-trillion dollar industry, crime supports lawyers, judges, courts, jails, prisons and police rather than being a system that controls crime. To curtail criminal activities would destroy millions of livelihoods. The so-called War on Crime is fuelled and funded by crime, and so it is not likely to curtail much. And while it is often called punishment and rehabilitation, the North American Justice Systems are not about healing offenders.

In First Nation communities, often with small populations, each member brought skills and abilities that were valued and necessary to the whole. The loss of a tribal member posed a threat to the ability of the tribe to survive. Consider what would happen if the three people taken away to prison were the only experts in how to construct a canoe. Crimes happened but the crime wasn't the focus. It was far more vital to understand that the Spirits were unhappy with something or someone and therefore a crime occurred than it would be to focus on the crime. As well, to rehabilitate the wrong-doer was far more effective and helpful than to sequester them, particularly with other criminals, until they thought better of what the Spirit realm had caused in the first place. Again, both systems of justice are based on the culture they serve. Which one is right or better? It goes without saying however that one could well be more effective than the other. From the stats it doesn't seem to be the MS system.

The Gravel Pit

We were parked inside another beautiful forest when Robert poked his head inside the 5th wheel door, "It is hunting season and my boots want to run into the woods! Wanna shoot some tin cans?"

I giggled. "You mean with a gun?"

"No, your pickle fork!"

I bundled up and hopped into the truck to drive to the gravel pit and shooting practice with my man. Robert showed me how to load, hold the gun, how the safety worked and how to stand and aim. I took a shot - and killed a tin can! I took a few more shots to prove it was just beginners luck.

And while he was setting the cans up again, I took a look through the sight at some crows that were flying in circles high above us. From behind me I heard – in a deep steady voice, "You shoot it - you eat it."

First Nation philosophies were based on strong spiritual tenets: moral and ethical codes of conduct that were written in their culture for a reason. Survival in the wilderness was considerably different than surviving the Renaissance. The First Nation way of life was on point ...for them. Their skills and abilities had been acquired over centuries of observation, practice, understanding and honoring of the natural world. Mainstreamers came from a totally different landscape with totally different perspectives and goals. Neither was wrong and neither culture needed anything from the other.

For First Nation people to be assimilated into Mainstream culture meant they had to break every one of their spiritually held ethics and moral codes. I expect there are few nations that could actually accomplish this.

Faith

Whether it is a culture, a community, a person or a race, no one sees another except through their own filters. When you grow up in London and move to New Delhi you are going to notice the differences. Then how well or how much will you assimilate into their culture and leave your own behind? Here is a short comparison around the faith of both cultures from the 19th century [as it has changed considerably since].

Mainstream	First Nation
Christian Religion	Spirituality
A capitalist corporation with huge economic foundations	Deeply engrained into the entire culture through belief & ceremony
God and Jesus and the Bible	Spoken legends tell Spiritual stories of good and bad
Pray to God on high, outside of oneself	Honor the spirits which inhabit and animate all things
External	Internal
Congregations are managed by a hierarchy of male clergy	Everyone must meet their own Spiritual responsibility

In the 18th century, First Nation people were sequestered to small plots of land called Reservations. They were governed by Agents who lived on reserve, doled out supplies, managed the comings and goings of the Native people and could have been seen as their warden. Native people were required at one time to obtain a pass to leave the reserve. Many Native children were removed from the reserves and sent off to Residential Schools that were run by the church. The sole purpose of these schools was to remove the culture from the children and assimilate them into the Mainstream. They were forced to accept Christianity. They were denied their usual clothing and diet. They were forbidden to speak their language or speak of their traditions and ceremonies. They were separated from siblings and kept from family sometimes for years at a time. They were abused, made a mockery of, stripped of their clothing and flogged in front of their peers. Many died and were buried unceremoniously and uncounted in unmarked graves beside the schools, never to return home again.

"All parents have abundant love for their children. Such love is not exclusive to one population or one corner." **Willy Bear Paw**

Both of these cultures have rules of conduct, ethics and moral codes based on millennia of experiences, beliefs, needs and history. One believes in God in heaven, beyond and outside of them, and the other believes the Great Spirit is here on Earth within all things. Both of these two belief systems add value to the world, and therefore neither is wrong. First Nation people embraced Christianity, more because they had to than wanted or needed to. Even though they did, for them being faithful and honoring the Great Spirit was the essential part that mattered.

Today, Mainstream culture is a hotbed of opinions; individuals and groups. If someone or some group doesn't like your opinion, it is suitable to counter them. Individuality means you can have your own opinions, and in fact are expected to stand up to support them while at the same time it is not alright to force your opinions on others. What ends up happening is a clash of specifics, as if one opinion can determine the truth versus the subject. Argument, anger, fighting, hatred and even war never ends because there will always be a wide variety of opinions that apparently matter most.

Today, First Nation people are still all about community and cooperation, at least those who are still living on reserve. Being individual continues to not sit right with a people whose prime survival strategy has always been cooperation and community. Working and living together, especially today, fosters their sense of support and safety in a dangerous and judgmental world. While Mainstreamers give credence to the try, try again philosophy, First Nation people value being prepared and as capable as possible before taking on a task. One cannot expect to survive in the wilderness by trying to hunt or trying to fish. Mainstreamers boost themselves with adrenaline and pump people up to compete or fight. The quarterback model for instance heads up many US corporations today. In First Nation communities a sense of cooperation has historically been more effective to tackle their tasks.

I was listening to the radio just the other day. They were talking about a case that had just been tried before the court where a white farmer shot a native boy in the head for trying to steal a truck. The radio host was talking about how more Native people should want to participate in jury duty if they expect to have a fairer justice system. Most Canadians were likely nodding their heads in agreement because it sounded fair. They obviously didn't have all the information however. Native people don't talk about others and their problems in front of a room full of people, strangers or otherwise. They don't judge a person by a single act and expect that everyone makes mistakes when the Spirits are angry. Helping and healing them to bring them back into the community where everyone knows them was far more important than the offense. And it would be insensitive and thoughtless to intentionally sit and listen to others as they denigrated and insulted a member of their community.

This history began with First Nation people being Spiritual, resourceful, community-minded and observant of cooperative codes of conduct. After decades of marginalization FN people have the highest suicide and addiction rates. This is not because they are incapable but because the stripping of their culture, land and livelihoods has forced them to be dis-empowered.

Filters

There are many things that are in conflict between these two worlds. Simple and innocent things that most of Mainstream won't even recognize like farmers picking fruit very early in order to ship across the country and expand their market share. First Nation people wait until just the perfect day when the fruit is at its finest before they pick it. Both serve a purpose and neither is wrong. Individual ego is denied in First Nation communities because it poses a threat to safety and survival. One person cannot focus their energy on themselves alone. Mainstream encourages the power of the individual ego and encourages confidence and bravado to serve highly competitive social economics.

In First Nation culture, no one person gets to decide. The tribe discusses an issue and works toward consensus without ever feeling the need to state the final decision as everyone agrees to it during the round table discussion. Mainstream has protocol. They take notes, call experts, use conference calls and nominate committee members with a Chairperson to oversee the proceedings and the final decisions. Again, neither is wrong. They are very different for very different reasons.

Mainstream is a culture of strangers, accepting and relying on others without knowing them personally. MS gives credence and validity to scholars and experts and rarely find much of value from their senior citizens. First Nations know everything about the members of their tribe and they stake their survival on each one of them. Elders hold a place of respect because they hold the greatest wisdom. They are the well-known and honored experts for the entire community. Outside MS experts rarely help First Nation people because they don't understand the needs, ethics and dynamics of the community. In fact, many MS organizations have tried to counsel, mediate and rehabilitate FN people with very little, if any, success. The reasons are due to the unwritten culture and philosophy that even the FN people have difficulty explaining because not only is it so intrinsic, it is dangerous to take a stand as it is counter to cooperation.

Women are from Mars and men are from Venus in Mainstream culture. This ground-breaking book claims men's heads are essentially empty while women's heads are so full they're spilling out all over everything. Men stick to one task at a time while women are amazing multi-taskers. Men are primarily working from the physical and intellectual aspect while women are coming from the emotional and spiritual. FN people are mostly spiritual and physical then intellectual and then emotional. Intellect as far as book-learning and emotions are kept in check because tears and algebra don't work in the bush. Again, each culture has a vested interest in their specific process based on their own experience, need and survival strategies.

Mainstream value their children as possessions that belong to them and for which, for the most part, they feel responsible. Discipline is a personal decision in each family. Children are a source of joy and pain and certainly constitute the hardest job of all. Children are sent to schools that teach academics with specific social graces and status quo thrown in for good measure in independence, confidence and competition. FN families are extended to include the entire village. Children are gifts. They are taught about the Spiritual power they will honor throughout their life. They will learn Spirit has the greatest influence. Children learn from watching others and by modelling what they see. They are not sent away to learn and are always with the people who they will learn from. FN children live their lessons. Then one day they will be given the task of catching the next fish. This was exactly how Boo, Uncle Jack and Mom sprinkled First Nation into me.

Mainstream is determined to pull atoms apart to find out how they work. MS focus is on a complete understanding of the entire Universe and how every part and piece works. They are certain they can find a mathematical equation for everything. Science is at the center to quantify and qualify and prove while invention and technology race along at record speed. Artificial Intelligence is next whereby humans might live forever housed in a mainframe computer in a virtual world of bots.

First Nation people take each hour and each day as it comes. Time means very little when the sun determines when it's best to go to sleep. If you have an appointment with a FN person and something comes up in their family or community, the appointment usually plays second fiddle. People and relationships come first before appointments, clocks, the GDP or a GPA. They will hold their hands out, palm up and say, "All my relations" which I'm given to mean all relationships with the Spiritual realm. Elders are the wisest tribal members. Those who have weathered many storms are the most valuable. MS tends to feel seniors have reached the end of their usefulness at 65 when they retire and they become a burden to the society that is tasked with taking care of them. Neither is right. Neither is wrong, even if one may be better than the other.

"Do you really have enemies or are they created?" **Parkah**

Both cultures have their own traditions and ceremonies that are based on their needs, their preferences and their experiences. Again, there is nothing wrong with Mother's Day or Christmas if they add to the world. A Potlatch or a Sweat Lodge isn't wrong either because they do add something.

Sequestered on small remote plots of land, removed from their traditional hunting and gathering places, scalped, murdered and fallen to disease, sent off to Residential School or scooped up to be adopted by foster families, marginalized through the Indian Act, not allowed to vote until the 60's, to name a few, the First Nation people survived miraculously. When viewed from the depth of their philosophy, they are not savage, uncivilized, atheist or undisciplined; quite the opposite. They are different, yes. While few can admit it, the First Nation people of North America have suffered ethnocide and genocide. Yet today, they are seeking a way to help, a way to become productive and valuable members of the larger society. They have licked their wounds and are ready to move forward if only we'd untie their hands. They hold no grudge because they understand the Spirit in all things will ultimately decide everything anyway. Is Mainstream big enough to open the cage?

United Nations: Article 6: "Genocide" means any of the following acts committed with intent to destroy, in whole or in part, a national, ethnical, racial or religious group, as such:

(a) Killing members of the group;
(b) Causing serious bodily or mental harm to members of the group;
(c) Deliberately inflicting on the group conditions of life calculated to bring about its physical destruction in whole or in part;
(d) Imposing measures intended to prevent births within the group;
(e) Forcibly transferring children of the group to another group

"No one escapes the seeds they sow." **Lucy**

Vanuatu

Early in 1988, two years after we met, Robert told me he was leaving. He was going to Vanuatu for two years with CUSO to teach the people how to fish. I immediately started thinking about how I could escape my own life to go with him as I suddenly knew what it was like to be told I would die tomorrow. Then he told me he was travelling alone. My heart cracked. I scrambled for some kind of meaning, but hope faded as the reality of what was about to happen filtered in. I forced myself to hold it together because I didn't want him to know I needed him more than oxygen. My heart emptied and became silent.

He said he just needed time. He wanted to do something different at this stage in his life and he wanted to use his skills for the greater good. It felt like a death sentence at first, and then I forced myself to tell him that I understood and that I would be waiting for him when he got back. What I didn't say was that I was his and could be no one else's.

He would leave right before Christmas, and so I planned a special send off. I showered him with crazy gifts and we laughed so hard our sides hurt. It had been the pain of how hard we could laugh together that would crush me next. Yet I made certain we laughed to the very last moment before I drove him to the ferry terminal to send him on his way - alone.

Today, as mentioned previously, science and religion can no longer be separated for science is providing proof of the supernatural even though that has not been their goal.

First Nation people find greater value in silent and gentle accommodation toward healing than aggressive, punitive discipline or pursuit. FN people believe they are one of many parts in the big picture and need no dominion over much. Beholding and completely influenced by Spirit, FNs honor Spirit above all else. Respect for the Great Spirit is counter to the pursuit of material and competitive MS endeavors. Environmental disasters and the predicted extinction level events may be a catalyst toward FN wisdom and how to return the Earth to natural balance.

I have felt that being First Nation is a state of being Spiritual. The philosophies inherent in First Nation people are very different from Mainstream but they are not, and never have been wrong when viewed through a Spiritual filter. They are dedicated to intrinsically honoring a Higher Power. First Nation people still live spiritually deep in their bones. The religious might go to church every Sunday but what happens during the rest of the week?

LEGEND HAS IT Indigenous people were warned by the Great Spirit long before it happened.

"If visitors come to this shoreline and they do not remember the Sacred Handshake, your people are to run away as fast as they can. When they arrive, they will forsake the Earth, pollute its waters and create great conflict amongst your people. They will build ribbons across the land from East to West and North to South and great snakes will ride them. They will divide the land and separate tribes with invisible borders and lines. They will make white streaks across the sky too. Twice over there will be a great shaking of the Earth so fierce that structures will burn and fall. And there will not be peace for your people until you sit in the tower of glass."

To this day, Indigenous people have not been recognized as a Nation even though by UN definition, they are a Nation. Nor have they been invited to sit in the United Nations, the 'tower of glass,' in New York City.' African Americans, Indigenous and Inuit along with Spanish and Asians remain the pawns in a game of dominance, control and apathy. Even though the United nations acknowledges Human Rights, there are still many who will not admit all people have the right to a fair life. It is called Human Rights and it excludes no one.

*   *   *

In conclusion, the more I learned about First Nation people, the more I wanted to run back home to the Bus Stop and return to the time when we lived and loved and laughed together. The passage of time is bittersweet.

The conflict that roamed around inside of me for the first five decades was because I was living in the mud of the middle with my left foot in one culture and the right in another while I didn't feel I really belonged in either. To reconnect with what lives within my Light was to put my hand one more time on that old door knob and listen as it clicked then opened up to love, laughter, inclusion, cooperation and my First Nation family that blended with my Mainstream family to welcome everyone home. The truth of the two cultures was very telling and understanding both was an eye-opening lesson of great import. It is far too easy to be judgemental and not so easy to have good judgement. We need all the information before we make up our minds about another and who and what we think they are. In truth, remember, there are many, many ways to do everything.

"There is a great deal they will teach one day." **Wahwaskenah**

G. F. Thornton

PART TWO
The Science in the Magic

G. F. Thornton

Chapter 10

The Science of Light

WHAT LINKS US? What kind of energy has built a scaffold profound enough to unite this life with all else? Is this why some can see auras, hear messages from the deceased or tell of unknown futures? Does Light Energy answer all the questions I have ever asked about why I'm here and what I'm supposed to do? Are we really the evolvement of Light? And if we are, do we choose to dance with it or are we suspended in its music regardless? Is there any evidence in science that proves any of this?

Energy = Consciousness = Spirit = *God* = Light = Energy

Willo began by adding the word God and reconnecting these words with each other again as a reminder of their equality for the purpose of their book. These words are used at different times to denote various degrees, places or types of vibrational energy. **Spirit** is the pure Sacred Essence, a Coherent **Energy**, within you that is actually **Light. Consciousness** is our intelligent sentience which is expressed via that Light as it connects and communicates all things throughout the Universe. And **God** is the dynamic so many understand as the Omnipotent Power or The Source. Though the Light within us is invisible, it animates us and gives us a purpose. It also supports the sentience of the concrete reality that we call our physical experience. The physical is a small portion of our entire reality.

While we have taken a brief tour of ancient and religious philosophy, this chapter brings forward a tiny bit of the other science. We are learning that science and Spirit cannot be separated any longer for one is directly connected to the other, just as all and everything is connected. What does science have to do with spirituality? Again, I stumbled many times upon scientific information that was validating how energy is such an intricate and powerful aspect of all life. Here is some of that information.

Energy and Light

Energy is the currency of the Universe. There is energy which fills the empty space within an atom; not the vacuum we had once been taught. This energy is the fuel of life. The more research I did, the more I found science was validating the role Energy plays in just about everything. If I ever had a need to prove the presence of a higher power, science suddenly seemed to be offering the fodder.

Points of Light was what I called my theory of Light. It means that each life form is essentially a Point of Light. We are like the tiny point of Light at one end of an optic fiber that is always tethered to its Source. Science can now quantify that Light. In fact, it is stored and used in all life forms just like plants use light to produce its energy through photosynthesis.

A fiber optic lamp served as a perfect example of the concept. The base of the lamp is The Source; the Life Force. I am one of the Points of Light at the tip of a single fiber of the whole lamp, as are you another point. The lamp shows that we are always connected to the Source and that our Consciousness is a Coherent Beam which touches down on the physical realm inside a biological vessel. Each beam remains closely associated with others who were here with us in the beginning. Our quantum particles have been entangled which will keep us close throughout all eternity. Our Light, our essence, returns to The Source through the fiber when the biology on the physical plane dies. Each fiber represents one Coherent Light beam, and each one fills its own biological vessel. There are as many of them as there are lives in the Universe. The more I read, the more physical evidence I found and the more I was convinced. The only thing the fiber optic lamp didn't offer was a way to show how each fiber was intricately connected with and communicating to all others as the energy between each fiber was invisible to our eyes.

Sentience = Emotion = Meaning = Consciousness

Everything in the Universe is interconnected by a field of Energy. Everything therefore is influenced and influential. The entire Universe is a computation that is constantly exchanging energy within a certain value for each component part. Each works within the balance of the whole; the micro within the macro on an infinite number of levels. All of this is recorded in the fractal geometrics of the minute quantum thread all the way to a giant galaxy and beyond. The constant exchange of energy is the necessary balance that keeps the orbiting electrons of an atom stable and in place just as gravity is required to maintain planets in their orbits. Components therefore can never be separate or apart as each is a dynamic, albeit an individual part, of the whole. Just as one element interacts with another in a very specific way, so do all parts of the entire Universe.

Light is made up of all the colors of the rainbow. When light is bent through a prism, we see a multitude of colors. It was interesting that when I thought about it, the many colors within the macrocosm of our human family make up the White Light of humanity too.

Reading some physics and quantum mechanics bent my mind, so I didn't read much. Yet I was fascinated by the mysteries. What do they mean when they say that nothing is as it appears? I wanted to shout, "And ...!" While on this Spiritual journey, I had to keep a very open mind in order to entertain and embrace the strange, the weird and the hidden. I had to entertain new information. The more messages received from Spirit, the easier this would become as the pieces began to fit together like a giant puzzle. I would discover a multitude of layers which were being revealed one at a time - as I became more able to explore and accept each one. All would come in good time. And as Spirit had offered before - it is what it is. My belief or skepticism wasn't going to change anything; the truth included.

Niagara Falls

It was a beautiful summer day as we headed to Niagara Falls. We wanted to take the trek to the underground tunnels and view the falls from the rock face under which the water fell. In a long line up we made our way into the elevators. We walked down long stark cement hallways with neon lights lining the ceiling and the thunder of the falls echoing beyond. We filed into a cement room with a thousand lockers that held just as many yellow rain hats, boots and coats. We donned the waterproof attire, stored our stuff and made our way back to the neon hall. As this long line of yellow was walking toward the falls, another long line of yellow was walking back to the lockers on their return. We were all equally clad in the very same illuminating color.

It was an epiphany. I couldn't tell if the yellow-clad people were white, black, young, old, skinny, Christian, male or female. How wonderfully equal everyone was all of a sudden. I giggled for in that moment we were simply a long line of yellow bananas; each one the same in every way to every other, even if underneath we were all quite uniquely beautiful.

Science

In one of my favorite books, The Field, Lynn McTaggart writes of Fritz-Albert Popp, a theoretical biophysicist at the University of Marburg in Germany. He discovered that light was contained in the body and it performed incredible feats. He quantified Light inside a strand of DNA. He discovered that within empty tubules inside every cell was a quantifiable amount of light too. He discovered there is a correlation between the light and the ability of the body to do more than one thing at a time. And as it turned out, it would be light which would provide instantaneous communication for many functions like movement and healing. Light is clearly a driving force, a catalyst, an animator for our molecules, and - it has many purposes. So sensitive and vital is Light in each life form that various levels of it are now connected to health and disease and malfunction. Well! There it is in black and white.

Popp would discover that our inner light is affected by cancer-causing agents which render the healing mechanisms of the body useless. He would show that light emissions commanded and ran the entire body. And most notably he discovered there is a bioluminescence within the body; one side coordinating and working with the other in unison. This bioluminescence was also linked to time and it phased or operated in cycles or regular rhythms that repeated in one and two weeks, to one month and three months and even over a full year. He had shown that when light is shone upon living cells, they shine back. When one hand was given more light and shone more, the other hand would match it. How integrated and essential is the light when everything from communication to movement to repair and brightness dances to it?

Goodbye

The day Robert left, the light was gray and the air was dank. My fingers hung through the chain link fence as if I would plummet to the other side of the Earth if I let go. My brow was low, my heart was sick and my eyes were sad as he slowly walked away into the crowd at the ferry terminal; solitary and alone, yet so real and familiar. I loved this man. As the space between us grew, my heart felt the tug of his like a rubber band stretching to its limit. He stopped a moment and I caught my breath. He glanced back. An electric spark coursed through me. Our eyes met once more for a single, fleeting moment. Then he was gone.

Ten minutes passed, then twenty and I was still standing at the fence, waiting. The blast of the ferry horn rose up to meet the fog. I jumped. Dread was filling me up. I closed my eyes, not sure I wanted to watch. The ferry started slowly backing into the harbor and still he hadn't returned to me. He really was on that ship. He really was leaving.

"Don't stand there and watch me leave. Go home and have tea," he had said to me in the car on our way to the ferry. All I could muster was a nod as my hands clenched the wheel.

The ship backed up then turned as it churned the bay to foam. I watched it change direction and head out into open water. Then, like an iceberg caught in the current, it slipped around the corner and was gone. Giant chunks of time and an ocean of space would separate us now, and for me, I would meander along without my heart. There was nothing that could undo us; not space, not time, not even death.

After he left, I felt the empty hole inside of me. It would add to that void in my chest that I couldn't quite locate or name and still had no idea how to fill.

Science shows that the amount of Light emitted from a body is in direct proportion to the health of the internal body. The greater the Light held inside, the healthier the body, and the lesser the Light is contained, the less healthy. Popp also noted that the light emitted from a living thing correlated to a being's position on the evolutionary graph: the less complex an organism, the more Light it emitted, the more complex, the less. In complex beings therefore, more of the Light and its power is contained and used within the being.

Eventually it was discovered that all living beings, plants and animals were integrated elements of one Universal Field of Energy which communicated via frequencies, vibrations and waves. This could easily account for how schools of fish and flocks of birds are able to dance so intricately and not run into each other. As well, it is now believed that balancing levels of light energy in the body could well be the basis of our physical health and wellbeing. Things like herbs, spices, plants, sounds and even colors are being heralded as frequencies that when selected correctly support health and healing. And this also builds the basis for homeopathy and the power of water, which will be discussed later too.

Alone

Black crosses, one by one, began to fill the empty calendar. I was waiting for word; a letter from the other side of the ocean, a world away.

It was winter here, and my life was all about work, mothering, work, housework and more work. My daydreams were about turquoise waters, sandy beaches, balmy breezes and Robert. I sent little gifts like scotch tape, string, seed packets and bubble gum. Each letter took six weeks to find him, and I would wait another six for a response. When I felt really low I'd sit on the shore overlooking the ocean that separated us. I would touch a wave and know that he was touching it too. I would watch the moon and know it was the very same moon that hung in the sky above his island. This was the comfort we would share.

Awhile after Robert had left, I ran into a mutual friend of ours one cold rainy day. He invited me to coffee, which I gratefully accepted. As we sat warming our hands on the hot cups, we started talking about Robert-things. I mentioned I had been waiting for the first letter for what seemed an eternity. He tilted his head and scrunched up his eyebrows at my words. "What?" I asked him. He stumbled a bit and then said very slowly, "You know he took someone with him, right?"

I spent the next month tending to the terrible crack in my heart. I wanted to beat him up. I wanted to yell and scream at him, and I wanted to know what I had ever done to warrant this. And yet my heart defended him. For some reason, I felt this wasn't what it seemed.

When we had first met, I remembered sitting on the beach to decide if I wanted to pursue a relationship with this man. I remember a suspicious feeling that things would not work out as I had hoped. I had even contemplated how much it would hurt to lose him. And then - there I was.

Animals fascinate me. Treated by superior humans as underlings that are void of feelings, pain, intelligence and awareness they are monuments of Spirit. They are balanced and congruent. They are physical, intellectual, emotional and spiritual all rolled up into one great bundle of fir and fins and feathers. They have powers of intuition and instinct beyond our own because they are not distracted by the outer world. We on the other hand deal consistently with our own incongruence. And we only wonder what intuition and instinct really are. Humans are great at doing while animals know how to be.

Light is proving to be so instrumental that we must look seriously at all of its effects. This Energy is the glue, the computer and the conductor. Each of us is Energy. We are a collection of Energy computations which enable us to move, think, feel, create and process. We procreate and are born into a vessel, itself made of energy, which will then serve the purpose of the Light. And when the body dies, it will be replaced by a newer, better version as our Light returns to progress and accumulate more in another vessel. We 'use' everything around us to that end - collecting and fashioning other bits of Energy to serve us. Our Light is a beam of

Conscious, sentient Energy that has become Intelligent and which is able to comprehend, adjust and compute. This Conscious Energy is on an evolutionary path toward ascension over billions of years – even here on Earth and in this physical space. Today life is meant to progress and ascend and to go forth to fill the Cosmos with Intelligence.

By Friday

One month later, the first letter arrived. Robert described a little bit of the paradise he had found and spoke of the kind people and their interesting language, a form of pidgin-English, he said. He wrote about the incredible scenery, the heat, the bugs and lazy days. His task to teach them how to fish would be difficult, he wrote, as the people can find fruit just lying on the ground, and the fish are plentiful and easily caught. There was no commerce on this South Pacific Island, and no need to press toward it. At the end he mentioned that he really missed me. I would write back as if knew nothing of his roommate as I would give him time to confess.

Without so much as a hint or clue from him, the following autumn, I bounced into my manager's office to tell her of a sudden prediction. She knew the story of Robert and I, and she had been intrigued. "Mark my words! I said. "He will be here by Friday!"

That Thursday, the phone rang. It was Robert. I didn't have to ask where he was but I did anyway. I knew he was here: there wasn't a doubt in my mind. "I'm in L.A." My heart skipped a beat. "I knew it! Wait! Why are you in L.A?" There was a pause and then, "My son has been in an accident and they say he's not likely to survive, so CUSO flew me out to be with him. I'll be in Edmonton tomorrow."

I could never account for the premonition being linked to his son's accident. I could however accept that I knew the moment he would be on his way back home. I never questioned the intuitive part of our relationship, and I never dug deeper. I chalked it all up to being soulmates.

Studies show removing parts of the brain in an animal that was responsible for a certain memory did not necessarily remove that memory. Entering in the definition of holograms, Gregg Braden offers, based also on the work of Dennis Gabor in the 1940s, that the brain functions like a hologram where each part is in all parts. Here too was an intriguing concept that we have a brain that runs the biology and a Mind that connects us to the Universal Field of Conscious Energy. The hologram also facilitates simultaneous awareness of all four: body, brain, Mind and Consciousness.

The Mind

The Mind is different than the brain. The Mind is more like a Super Conductor with an antenna that connects our physical environment to the Energy Matrix which expands us to well beyond the confines of this little body. This connection can be influenced by other vibrations like the Energy of the food we eat, the air we breathe and our internal Energy Signature. Just as the cell membrane responds to the interstitial fluid which bathes each cell in our body, so too does the Mind respond to the body, the brain, the environment and the Universe. This happens via the Mind's antennae. This suggests that our Consciousness is part of a vast integrated web of Universal Energy that is Intelligent. The only quantifying denominator is how much we focus from/to the brain and how much we focus from/to the Mind.

In our physical world most of us spend far more time focusing on/from the brain. During the process of writing this book, I naturally had to focus on each subject and each lesson, sometimes for months. My connection to Universal Conscious Energy became easier and more fine-tuned the longer I spent focusing. The more time it took and the longer I focused, the more the connection developed.

Edmonton

It was 30 below in the middle of a snow storm at the Edmonton airport when my plane landed. When I finally made it inside the terminal and we spotted each other, we ran into each other's arms. Robert scooped me up and spun me around just like they do in the movies. I was home. The connection we had was unmistakable.

We spent the next four days together. He confessed about her and cried about me, and I cried over it all. She was a nurse with three kids who took advantage of her, was about all I remember. We reconnected but something was different; the bridge that had separated us was longer and wider and somehow unfamiliar. We were all about reminiscing of times gone by, of things we did and the way we were with each other, and we even talked about our soulmate connection. But we didn't make love. We just held each other as if by some magical force we would be forever linked regardless of what else happened. He professed his love for me, and I held on tight to every word.

His son recovered. Robert went back to Vanuatu and I returned to Boring, just south of Out-of-my-Mind. Our correspondence continued and as the months fell one upon the other, his discomfort of being away and of being with her began to show more and more in each letter. Whatever brand of magic linked us during those months, it never let go of me. Robert was on my mind day and night, night and day. My heart ached for him. Our letters continued and I continued to send silly little gifts like band aids, soap and popcorn to his South Pacific island far away.

Spirited beings are naturally less distracted by the fluff of life and have a brighter and clearer connection to the Matrix. The Matrix is a Field of Energy and has been called by many names: Zero Point Field, Higgs Field and the Quantum Hologram. Regardless of the name, considering this field and the kind, amount and quality of Energy it contains, what this Energy touches and how it connects information, it was easy to add these other words to its definition too: Consciousness, the Divine Energy, Life Force, The Source, Soul, Light, God, Spirit, Higher Self and so on. When you spend a little time considering the possibilities of such a power, many other things begin to drop into place too; Near Death Experience, Karma, Reincarnation and Out of Body Experiences, to name a few. And the Light speaks to them all.

Soulmates

What is the unique and special connection between soulmates? What was really happening between me and Robert? Not only did I know him better than I knew myself, our connection had been instantaneous and deep. Many years later, I would be drawn to reconsider our relationship yet again as I learned about the Energy Field and the Light. It would soon become apparent that our energies were perfectly matched. Our connection was more than just physical, emotional or intellectual. Our connection was Spiritual and our Light was in perfect unison. This would explain the affinity we had for each other, and one day I would discover a far greater purpose for our bond.

The left [logical] brain's key function is to maintain control within the biological limits of our physical-ness. This ability means that we are able to calculate time and space on our tiny scale. As Jean Bolte-Taylor observed during her stroke, once the left brain is turned off, we are no longer limited by this body. We become expansive and undefined and one with all else. Jean's consciousness didn't dissipate into the ether without containment by her left brain. Rather, her Light remained coherent and her personal consciousness, her Energy Signature, remained intact and functioning. When her left brain shut off, the right brain connected fully to the profound energy of the Universe. The task for meditation is also to shut down the left brain. It plays a role in death as the left and right brains both suddenly become uninvolved in an individual near the death of the body. The Conscious Light is released at death to reconnect completely with the Sacred Energy of the Universe. And the journey through the tunnel of Light is evidence our Consciousness can reconnect with our life story as it leaves the physical.

Chapter 11

The Energy Field

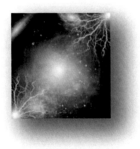

L ITERALLY BATHED in this sea of Energy, the Universe can be considered very active versus the vast vacuum of space we once thought. We are experiencing a new need to adjust, much like when we learned that the Earth wasn't flat or that we weren't the center of the Universe. We now need to see the Universe as an energetic and dynamic whole to which we are connected. Richard Feynman, one of the greatest physicists and Nobel Prize winner, claimed that in a single square meter of space is enough energy to boil all the oceans of the world. This is not only new information - it is far more substantial than ever imagined. What else would be revealed about this Field? How does it compute, what does it affect and how does it balance everything?

Peak Experience: A Miracle

It had been a spring morning in April of 1989. I had quietly slipped into Mom's bedroom to see if she was awake. She said, "Good morning." I opened the curtain to let the sun spill into the room as I asked her if she'd like to get up. Mom had been sick and in considerable pain for many years and I was home to help her. She sat on the side of the bed and told me about a strange dream. She said she was watching herself from above. She could see herself lying on a hospital bed below as if she were viewing the scene from the ceiling. She saw me and dad on one side of her bed, Heather on the other and a doctor at each end. She had called out to those around her saying "I'm not there. I'm up here. I'm the Light in the corner of the room."

A week later Mom was in ICU at the local hospital. Dad and I sat on one side of her bed and Heather on the other. A nurse came into the room, placed a flashlight on a tray in the corner and turned it on so she could add a medication to the IV. When she walked out of the room she had left the flashlight behind and it was still on. My dad asked Heather to turn out the flashlight. Suddenly recognizing the circumstances from her dream, Heather and I looked at each other and shook our heads slowly back and forth and said, "We can't right now" in unison.

A short time later Mom took her final breath. As she did the flashlight in the corner of the room suddenly glowed brighter… and then went out.

This miracle from my past is as moving today as it was then. We really didn't understand how spiritually connected Mom had been until long after her death. She was a gentle soul who lived what she believed and who treated everyone as valuable and equal. This little Light as she crossed over was her sign and a shout out to Heather and I that life is not just as it appears. Since that day, Heather and I have both grown closer to that truth, and closer to Mom's lessons through her own Light.

Dr. Richard Bartlett among many others writes about this Field of Energy he calls the Zero Point Field. He claims this field plays a role as a container and a bridge and claims that it can be seen as a mirror for the beliefs within us. This field is non-local which simply means every part of it is connected instantly to every other part and each piece or bit of the field mirrors the whole just like a hologram. The scale is never-ending. It exists within the tiniest sub-atomic particle all the way to the Universe and beyond, if beyond is even possible.

Our human Energy is dynamic, just like the Energy of the Universe. It fluctuates and changes and evolves at various times. It pulses according to cycles of other energy like the light of the sun or the pull of the moon. It fluctuates within its own range of values. We merge and sync, increase and decrease in Energy and we are constantly balancing, rebalancing and computing, being influenced and influencing, not just within our space but out into the Universe. Each life is a unique blend of multiple forces, some from others, the environment and certainly from within our own emotions, thoughts and words. They are all energy vibrations that hold our power.

Energy Signature: the total collective
energy of a coherent beam of Light within a living vessel.

Constantly engaged with the Field, communication happens instantly via Energy transmissions. One way we communicate with the Field is through the language of emotion; the heart's language. Each emotion has its own unique Energy Signature and each emotion and every beat of your heart influences your Signature in kind. When my mind had been influenced by nonsensical chatter, I know now it served to dampen my Energy Signature. The darker or more negative the thoughts, the more my energy was dampened. I also realize that this was the cause behind much of my chaos. I could not change the potential energy deficits if I remained unaware of the powerful energies in and around me. Each life form has power and potential - individually and jointly. To leave all of these dynamics to chance doesn't seem to fit the Devine Design. Can you imagine the kind of changes our collective Energies would create if we could consciously coordinate it?

Unity Drummers

After Mom's death, I began dipping my toe into the First Nation community whenever I could. I was drawn to these people for reasons I couldn't understand at the time. I saw a Native drumming group at a booth at a local festival. They were looking for members. Hey! I had a drum and I would love to learn about this part of my heritage. I respectfully asked if I could join. They didn't ask if I was Native before they said yes.

I visited one of their practice sessions at a local high school. I felt out of place, of course, and sat in the gallery for the entire session to watch and listen. I had no idea that this kind of respect inside of me came from the culture inside of them. I returned to the next practice and they invited me into their circle. I had attended only a couple of practices when I was invited to play with them at one of their gigs. I humbly declined saying I could hardly be ready for a stage performance. They nodded their heads and insisted as if they knew something I didn't.

Much to my surprise, the performance was at the convention center. And just before entering the hall, I again tried to decline. They clearly weren't going to accept my hesitance as a reason to not perform with them, so away we went together. We sat on the sideline for a time, and then were welcomed to the stage. There were a mere 2,000 people in the audience and my feet wanted to run in the opposite direction really bad!

Our leader stood at the front, and I raised my drum. We started playing, and as though I had known the various songs all my life, I played right along with them. I even knew when to stop and when to change the beat. No one was more shocked than I was. I was so grateful to be part of this experience and not because of the audience but because the music came from my Spirit as if I'd been drumming all my life.

Sound is vibration. If you are familiar with the Flower of Life you are looking at a pattern that is created by the highest frequency of sound vibration. It can be visually shown how sound frequencies create shapes. Using a metal sheet and sand, attaching a speaker to the sheet and playing a series of individual frequencies, you can view how each hertz level creates a different pattern in the sand. These shapes can be seen all around us. Energy vibrations create the shapes of all things and Light animates them. Light and sound are powerful energies each with their own properties and purpose that were about to come together.

"Sound frequency and vibration organize matter
into sacred geometrical shape." **Parkah**

The Field is made up of endless vibrations and frequencies which then form shapes that house Light and which create unique Energy Signatures. This Energy Signature is a combination of all other energies that make up the collective energy much like an orchestra. In an orchestra, each instrument and note is a unique vibration while the whole orchestra is a blend of all instruments forming an Energy Signature unique to the Whole. Discord by one, affects all others.

Estranged

To be estranged from my family brought years of sadness. The loss of my father and my sister from my life in particular was heartbreaking. Dad and I had been buddies and it was no secret that I was his favorite. I was the one who worked in the garage with him. I had helped him build the bar and renovate the basement. He had taught me how to do many things – because I always made it a point to be with him when he was home. Heather and Dad however rarely saw eye to eye, and it was clear that they were like oil and water.

Dad married a woman who had been circling even while my mother was dying. She would become the wall between Dad and me. After being estranged for nearly ten years, to say I was astounded when I learned that he would move in with Heather and her husband in his later years would be an understatement. Not even being informed saddened me more than anything else. Yet all I knew about anything had been assumed. Whatever they were thinking, saying and doing would be without my inclusion or knowledge. After I quit trying to reach out, I blamed Dad because after all, the phone lines went both ways. For ten years I struggled with how I could reconnect with him as he was nearing his eightieth birthday. I knew his time was limited, and I wanted him in my life and me in his. More importantly, I needed my Dad back and I agonized over how I could make it happen for too many years.

I worked hard at visualizing our reunion. I wondered if I should write, so I composed lengthy letters and poured my injured heart all over the paper. I sent an emotional poem in a frame as a Christmas gift: a tribute to my Dad.

Nothing changed. He never responded. I wracked my brain trying to figure out what I might have done that he wouldn't just call and reconnect. I never heard from anyone about selling our family home of fifty years or their move to live with my sister after Dad's retirement. It seemed I had no family left. In desperation, once I had connected with the Light, I posed the question for how I could end the pain.

Sound and Light are electromagnetic energy. Just as there are sound waves the human ear cannot hear, so too are there light waves that the human eye cannot see. Light is always there - whether we see it or not. According to the Heisenberg Uncertainty Principle, in this energy, it is said that there is always a tiny, tiny bit of electromagnetic jiggling which adds up to a dynamic force within the Matrix. This is consistent movement and sound vibration. If you could view an atom with the naked eye, you could see this jiggling. And if you could quantify and hear those ceaseless movements, you would experience the background Sea of Light of the Universe and an energy total that is enormous. This is part of the entire Matrix of the Universe again. When focusing a giant Energy Collector toward outer space, for instance, this Sea of Light is the white noise.

Not only does the Matrix exist, it is in constant flux while it fills the Universe with this noise. It is said to be continuously computing much like the macrocosm of the internet. Was this the stuff of Consciousness? Was this Energy Field supporting the fundamental Conscious Intelligence of the Universe? Spirit had written it, so it was true. By the time I finished typing Spirit's book and understanding my own tests and experiences of the Light, I was certain this was exactly what was going on.

Influenced - Influential

With the Energy Field influencing and being influenced, continuously computing, exchanging, balancing and rebalancing from the minute to the whole, and the Light being vibration and frequency, it was all starting to gel. This Coherent Light energy was the Intelligent Consciousness of the Universe. This must be the unique dynamic of this amazing and vast field of energy. The messages would ramp up and validate that it was so. Let's remember the Mind and that it is not housed within the cranium. Remember it is the antenna that connects each Light to everything in the Field from the tiniest of particles in our biology to the vast orbits in the Cosmos. Why would we not have such a connector to the Energy Field of which we are part?

Finding Peace

The day I found a way to make the first move to reconnect with Dad a warm milky peace slipped softly into my chest. That's it! Yet today I can barely remember how the new strategy changed my confidence. I do remember that it felt right and from Spirit, I was big enough to do it.

I called Dad to invite him to lunch; plain and simple. He accepted and suggested we meet half way. During our lunch I explained how I had felt over the past ten years and how hard it had been to be without him. He nodded and listened and said little as I spilled my grief. In the end, his only comment was, "I understand how you might have felt that way." And the rest would be history. We would spend lots quality time together after our luncheon. And if the stepmother, sister, niece or brother-in-law were there when I went to see Dad in the future, I was respectful and cautious and always mindful of why I was there.

After my father's death two years later, I also had plans to reconnect with my sister and then her family. Today we have moved on and are now taking this spiritual journey together as if we never missed a beat. As for the past and the reasons or the details; well, those days are behind us.

We all think we know about atoms. We have an understanding of their basic shape and how they come together to form more complex structures called molecules. But did you know that atoms don't look like the pictures we used to see in text books? Atoms are small clouds of energy, not a nucleus with concentric orbiting bits of energy. Also, if you took a marble and placed it in the palm of your hand to represent the nucleus of an atom, in relative terms, the closest electron would be two miles away. The stuff in between, what we have been taught was empty space, apparently is anything but. There is energy in that space; considerable energy.

The volume of an atom is made up of
99.99% empty space that is filled with energy.

I am clearly not a physicist, and I can only speculate on the laws but for the time being Energy seemed to be adding up. Light Energy is everywhere, all the time. It was the animator of the primordial pond that kick-started the first single-celled life form. Light was the spark of life, and it remains the energy that maintains it. We would not be here if it weren't for the light of the sun. The internal laws of light and energy create its intelligence: the electromagnetics, kinetics, physics, physical, weak and strong forces and entanglement, the Higgs Boson, quantum and quantum mechanical law, gravitational laws and everything in between.

"Life is not evolution or creation. It is both. The Light must evolve and it was destined to fuse a gene so that one would become another." **Parkah**

Scientists claim the difference in human DNA was formed when 2 genes fused into one. There are many who claim however that this fusion has never been seen in any other DNA from any other species. Yet it is this fusion which accounts for our intelligence and our ability to create and learn and logic. This fusion separates us from all other species. They also claim it proves Creation. Spirit says it proves Light is proactive and ever evolving.

Einstein's most famous equation, $E = MC^2$ means the evidence of energy equals mass times the speed of Light squared which is a basic fundamental of the Universe. It shows the common thread of all energy and that it is connected. Further, the stability of the Universe is due solely to this real currency; a constant exchange of Energy always working within a set range toward a specific balance. Nothing is created or destroyed - merely changed. Einstein's theory of Cause and Effect stands up too. With every Cause, there is an Effect. We are intricately connected through the same. What is done to one is done to all. As nothing is ever created or destroyed, the Light became a very important catalyst to what we are and why we're here.

We can now extend our understanding to combine a few concepts:

- All Energy is varying degrees of frequency and vibration.
- Light is Energy; made of frequency, wavelength and vibration.
- Visible Light is a specific frequency, wavelength and vibration.
- All Light = Energy, and therefore All Energy = Light.

- God is the greatest Energy, and Light = God = Light.
  - Light/God is everywhere, all the time
  - This energy is unmatched in the Universe
  - It denies all other laws
  - This energy contains all knowledge and wisdom
  - Light lives within each life form
  - The quality of the Light cannot be altered
  - Light is the Conscious Intelligence of the Universe
- Sound energy creates shapes.
- Light inhabits and then animates these shapes.
- There is an Energy Field in and around all things in the Universe.
- Light is everywhere. Each star emits light, and as there are stars above, below and all around us, Light is everywhere ...for as long as there are stars that shine. When the light goes out, so does life.
- Mass, what we have considered the material weight of reality, is actually infinitesimally small in relation to the space between the nucleus and the electron in each and every atom.
  - 99.99% looks like empty space but it is really Energy while a mere 0.01% is mass.
- There is no emptiness in space as space is filled with Light Energy.
- A square meter of space has enough energy to boil all the oceans on Earth.

With Light everywhere; within each body and inside each cell, Light is evolving; coming from nothing just before the Big Bang on a long journey toward Ascension or Perfect Light in physical reality. This progression or evolution unites both Science and Spirit in a Universal dance. It would be further along on this journey that Spirit would inform me that nothing comes from me, only through me. The Theory that seemed to be percolating within me wasn't a theory – merely the Light and how it is our next leap in understanding. It was when I would be reminded that Spirit didn't need to do theory. Right! Interesting!

Energy = Spirit = Light = Consciousness = God = Energy

This was fodder for Light and Energy being the same, and so the terms are interchangeable for our purposes. It was about this time when the next part of my Theory started to gel. Once this happened, I was able to receive more and more evidence of the Theory than I could have imagined. One day I heard a new voice, almost singing;

> "As Light lives within, you are the **Evolution of Light.** The Coherent Beam of Light that resides in you is the Conscious Intelligence of the Universe and it is revealed through your biological expression." **Orella**

Even John Audette confirms in Ervin Laszlo's recent book, The Intelligence of the Cosmos, all the answers are waiting patiently to be discovered within each of us. Laszlo argues too that physical reality is pure Consciousness facilitated by the Field and that this Consciousness is the substance and intelligence of all living things.

Life wasn't always as intelligent as it is today. If Consciousness equates at all to Intelligence, there must have been a connection from the single-celled amoeba of the primordial pond to that intelligence. Consciousness had been expressed through all life forms. It had taken up residence inside the first cells. Movement led to a reason for a brain that later through Consciousness would coordinate a more complex organism. Consciousness was the Light which was connected to the super conductor of the Mind which expressed the Light in all forms and creativity. This was creative evolution at its best and it proved a profound connection between the Light and biology. A symbiotic evolution was at work in real time. It appeared to be fundamental to everything, especially who we are and why we're here.

In her book, Frequency, Penney Peirce confirms the varying degrees of frequency, how one influences another and how we, not unlike tuning forks, pick up on, or resonate with these frequencies. She writes that if your Energy Frequency is high, life tends to unfold easily and beautifully as it was designed to, while a lower or distorted frequency results in conflict and disappointment. Peirce even goes so far as to validate the inner feeling I have had all my life that - there must be something better.

> "You are hard wired to seek the Light within you." **Wahwaskenah**

Penny alludes to the varying degrees and levels of vibration within the human body from the physical down to the quantum. The smaller quantum entities, like molecules, atoms and neutrinos are higher frequencies compared to the breath and heart of things on a larger scale. One still influences the other through the grandest scheme of everything. This was a key too. If energy can be affected and influenced, why aren't we more actively working on the best energy possible? Why are we so stuck with violence, greed and hatred when these energies are extremely low and destructive to the one who harbors them? I didn't have to be a scientist or brain surgeon to conclude that we seem to be missing something very fundamental in our understanding of our world and reality.

We are all aware of the varying frequencies of the brain waves ranging from Delta, or sleep, to Beta or alert and awake. Peirce discusses how these frequencies change and likewise how they change what we are aware of. The more worried and fearful our brain becomes, the greater we are distracted and the less we are aware. In conclusion, the slower the Brain wave is the greater the ability of the Mind to connect to subtle kinds of energy, such as Spirit Energy. This follows closely with the benefits of meditation when we turn off or pause the brain so the Mind can connect to subtle Spiritual Energy. Few people know of these vital energy properties of the Mind. As such most of us have a limited understanding and have had even fewer experiences of the Mind.

As seen in this picture of intersecting waves, each circle of Energy flows outward and influences the next as the waves connect and cross each other. The same is true of all Energy throughout the Universe, including ours. As nothing is ever created or destroyed but merely changed, the energy of the Universe is a dynamic interwoven field, a total field, forever being influenced and influencing. In fact, it is the usable and accumulating currency of the Universe. That we should be resonating within a certain frequency range suddenly became common sense instead of fantasy. We had a purpose, a very certain and calculated purpose in the grand scheme of it all. And we are meant to harness it.

Entanglement or Non-Locality

Einstein called Non-Locality 'spooky action at a distance,' while quantum physicists call it Entanglement. And in short what it means is that once quantum particles make a connection with each other, they remain dynamically connected forever - influenced by each other - regardless of how much distance separated them. This discovery has been verified several times since 1982. It means the heart that is donated to another will forever be linked on a quantum level with the donor. This could account for why organ recipients will often experience unfamiliar traits or behaviors that were known to belong intimately to a donor.

It is interesting that First Nation people have long acknowledged the world exists as a vast web of interdependent and indivisible relationships. This single principle has far-reaching implications too. From a baby in the womb to an astronaut on a spacewalk to strangers thousands of miles apart to a loved one who has just died, once connected, we remain connected forever, perhaps not in blood and bones but certainly in our Spiritual Energy. As well we must consider the atoms of oxygen and water that circulate around and through everything. Once a water molecule is connected to something, it too will remain imprinted. Here is substantial validation of our interconnectedness. Many who have experienced those special spiritual connections with someone can now understand why they are so real and what the dynamics of the connection really is.

Sentience

We have more evidence of the sentience, the heart and the soul of animals too. Recently a man who had rescued a herd of elephants a number of years prior had died at his home in Africa. Somehow those elephants knew of his death. Those he had saved trekked several days and nights to his home guided by something unknown. Arriving, they stood vigil for several days then quietly walked away. This was evidence of the Energy bond and its depth of power within all of us. Animals go with the energy. They don't fight it and aren't distracted from it by life quite like we are. They are open and they allow the energy to flow through them and they are not distracted by the physical illusion. They are reminders of what is possible for us too.

We may now fully appreciate the quality of the connection we have to ones who are loved and who feel so much a part of us and why we can sense them after they have passed. I have often wondered what is meant by the 'other side.' Certainly it feels as if there is a curtain or at least a veil created at death. Though we can no longer see or touch those who have passed, there will always be a time when we can truly sense them. When the biology is no longer functioning, the Light from within the body is freed and retreats back through the coherent beam to reconnect with the Matrix. The quieter the chatter of the brain and the more focus we can muster on the Mind, the better we are able to tap into their energy conversations. Sometimes we can even converse. Entanglement plays a supportive and important role via Water, Spirit, Light, Energy and the Field.

In Masaru Emoto's book on water crystals called The Secret Life of Water, he explains that blood stored for two years developed the same properties as the blood from the original body. Water in blood and the quantum particles, once connected remain influenced and influential beyond time and space. This concept alone is intriguing as it links all and everything in a very simple yet physical way to validate it is not possible to be separate or apart from anything. Consider the air that filled the lungs of Jesus long ago may well be the exact same molecules you breathed today. Our full and complete understanding of this is hindered by our paradigms of old or those beliefs based on outdated information. Many people have been led to believe that acquisition of material things will satiate their deepest, inner need or that things of this world will fill the void they sense within themselves. So false and temporary is the satisfaction derived from the material world that those who mistakenly pursue the external do not realize the experience they seek is found solely through the internal.

All of the matter that has ever been here - is still here! Understanding Entanglement means we really are more equal and connected than we ever could have imagined. Our dynamic potential, the true Akashic record of all knowledge could well be found in a single drop of water. The issue then becomes how aware we are of such phenomenon so we won't miss our ultimate potential, our precise balance, our true equality or our Perfect Vibration. Over the time of life on Earth, we have accumulated part of the wisdom, grace and healing of these Laws. As we accumulate incarnations, and as our physical life repeats over and over again, surely the water, the air molecules and the Light are doing their part in our evolution. What is it then that stands between us and our potential? One guess is simply not being aware of the truth within.

"There is potential to consciously influence and be influenced. Connecting allows you to become Master of that influence." **Buck**

In that water does not discriminate and records good and not-so-good messages, blessing what you put into and near your body will make sure you are delivering just good messages. The Energy within you and surrounding you, including but not limited to food and drink, can all be blessed.

Thoughts & Words

When everything is known to be energy, we can go back to the Bible once again. It was written in Genesis that God thought about a Universe, and then created it. He spoke of the Light and the Light happened. He spoke of the first humans, and so on. I find it very interesting how many times concepts about the Light are referenced. The unique fusion of Chromosome 2 was such a fact of the Light and its purpose to evolve.

As well, each thought and word contains a unique energy. At the beginning of this book is a 'Note' that the words, concepts and thoughts in Spirit's book will create good energy within you, and as such will shift and increase your Energy Signature. If you read the whole book over a week or two, the resulting energy shift may happen in a shorter timeframe but might not have the fullest effect of the highest energy possible. If you read it slowly over a few months and digest and contemplate the concepts, your Energy Signature will benefit from the extended immersion. From the time you begin the book, listen closely to what you hear in your mind. Take note of, and write down, the concepts in your Mind and the new thoughts and ideas which return to your ears as your Spirit begins to speak to you.

"Be mindful of each shift you experience." **Sarah**

The Last Letter

Robert's last letter from the South Pacific would arrive just before I left for Mom's final days in 1989. He wrote that he would be home by mid-June behind his apologies and loving wishes. This is an excerpt from his final letter.

"A warm hug is a good way to wake up in the morning. I can't wait to wake up next to you. Take care and think of me. My love as always, Robert."

Thoughts and words are highly influential energies because many of us have them bantering about in our heads all the time. Constant negative thoughts bring your energy down as surely as laughter lifts you up. Being aware of the thoughts and words we use helps us to choose the best ones for ourselves in order to keep our energy high. One of our challenges is to live in the moment and be aware enough that we can retrain our habitual brain and our tongue to put forth only high vibrations.

Water

There was another energy that was emerging too and it would prove to be almost as important as the Light. Masaru Emoto studied interesting aspects of frozen water. His book shows how water is influenced by the Energy of its environment. At the time I was more interested in thought and biological Energy, but I was also very pleased to learn that water seemed to be a fundamental compound of considerable value too. Not only is it the most unusual compound on Earth, I'm sure we underestimate its entire role. Some dots were about to link up that would startle.

Emoto froze water droplets onto slides. Each drop had been drawn from a different location or environment. The slides showed that the location of the droplets influenced the frozen crystals in remarkable ways. Negative energy from an industrial area, for instance, created crystals that were broken or incomplete. High energy locations like the head water of a pristine river created startlingly beautiful and intricate crystals. The affects that the surrounding Energy created in the water crystals provided evidence that water is a highly sensitive **tape recorder**. This linked Light with Water - two interconnected essential energies of all life.

Lynn McTaggart confirmed in her book The Field that water molecules will polarize around charged molecules. The water can capture and retain the Energy Signature of these molecules, again being a recorder of information. She writes that molecules speak to each other in vibrating frequencies, both non-locally and instantaneously. Light and water were suddenly intimately interconnected.

A French Doctor, Jacques Benveniste, while studying allergies in his lab, stumbled upon another aspect of water which led to more evidence. One of his researchers had made an error while mixing a drug in sterile water to produce and test a homeopathic dilution. In error, the solution had been diluted to well beyond the targeted 1:1000 parts. This meant the liquid could no longer have held any molecules of the drug. Even when they realized that there could be no original drug left in the diluted solution, they found the effects of the compound as strong, if not stronger, than the intended dilution or the pure drug itself. This became the first real evidence of the dynamics of homeopathy: the less drug remaining in the aqueous solution following a dilution process, the greater the effect. This was also more evidence of the tape recorder quality of the water. Even with no discernable molecules of the drug left in the water, it retained the energy signature of the drug and likewise its intended effect.

Benveniste, and other scientists performing parallel experiments were also beginning to prove that the digital frequency of a compound was as effective as the compound itself. This could mean that instead of ingesting a dangerous drug, we could transmit the digital signal of a drug to a patient with the same or better effect than the drug itself. Again, it all came back to the Energy. If we know the Energy Signature of a substance, like a pathogen or cancer, we could perform tests for their presence in the body based solely on finding its Energy Signature in a serum, likely blood as it circulates throughout the entire body. The water in the blood would naturally imprint the Energy Signature of a pathogen or disease. A stunning statistic is that the total number of **deaths** caused by conventional medicine is an astounding 783,936 per year in the USA. Matching the disease with the frequency of a treatment without the contraindications could decrease death due to medical treatment considerably.

In another study at the University of Stuttgart, several students each took an eye dropper of water from the same beaker, placed droplets onto glass slides and allowed them to dry. Once dry, the droplets were viewed under a microscope. It quickly became apparent that the structure of the droplets left on each slide was unique to each student. In other words, each individual student could be identified by their water droplets. The University study included placing other items, such as a flower, into the water which resulted in a different pattern in the respective droplets too.

The only suitable conclusion was that the Energy Signature of a student, or whatever item was somehow engaged with the water, had been captured by it. Water became the star of the show recording the energy of other influences in its vicinity.

Pile everything else so far upon the new understanding of energy, and we could rewrite more than just physics, biology, medicine and theology. Experiments with water droplets validate that one frequency influences another. As well, the frequencies of other elements such as flowers, colors and even written words in proximity to water have the same effect. This could speak to intention as well. This brings us to consider that water in conjunction with Light Energy behaves much like the Internet of all living cells.

Light & Water

Now, link the water to the Light. Every living cell contains both.

The implications for Light and water suddenly became huge. Consider that in our first nine months we are surrounded by water in the uterus. Consider the implications and influence of the mother during this time. Consider the energy that a fetus is subjected to in the amniotic fluid, or energized water, of their mother. Think about breathing in the Light and water as you walk a forest path. Every living thing in Nature is imparting Light and water to your being. No wonder we feel energized when we are in a forest or on a beach. Solutions like homeopathic dilutions suddenly became important. Water will continue to transmit the energy signature of an original substance even after 1,000 or more dilutions. This is Entanglement at its best. Water is a life-giving fluid we cannot live without for far more reasons than we thought. Could these discoveries become a path for such things as healing, health and even reaching our dreams?

Water must be communicating all kinds of things back and forth to and from the fetus, like fear, love, dreams and even intelligence. As a fetus is akin to a blank slate, Mother Nature designed the environment of the womb to begin a vital role of imprinting to baby what it needs while simultaneously bonding it with its mother. This means that thoughts and words, emotions and the mother's internal and external biological environments are just some of the influential information that will be accessed by baby. A fetus begins to learn language and recognize its mother's voice in utero. This is all the more reason to not only eat and sleep well, but to live, love and think well too.

In The Biology of Belief, Dr. Bruce Lipton, a cellular biologist, writes about how the cell has an amazing intelligence, how it responds and adjusts to its environment. He describes quite eloquently that the brain of the cell is the membrane. The membrane conducts and regulates everything coming and going - in and out of the cell. It is this structure that responds and adjusts directly to its environment to support the survival of each cell. Lipton explains how none of this could take place without the medium of water. He writes about proteins and how these little compounds are the stuff that facilitates movement. As water is the ultimate tape recorder, this is another world of information being transmitted without our knowledge.

The human brain and the all-important spinal column are bathed in cerebral spinal fluid, a clear, watery liquid. Inside of each cell and in between each cell is the interstitial fluid, the water that bathes everything, transports substances, decreases friction in movement, cleans and washes, and now we know supports instant communication and ultimate health. Once this water has been in contact with various substances and energies, it will carry this information into the minute corners of not only the body, but everywhere it travels too. To have a clear understanding of this important substance should be imperative for understanding how health is even possible, let alone life.

> Light is the Great Commander
> Water is the Super Conductor

Internal Light

Rupert Sheldrake, a British Biologist, has been touting Energy Fields as the answer to how biology takes specific shape and form in the way that it does, a question biologists have not yet been able to answer. What exactly causes cells to form a hand versus a foot at the end of an arm? Sheldrake hypothesized that there is an energy scaffold which has a memory that the body then uses for shape, form and communication.

"The internal Light sustains each vessel for its purpose." **Little Reign**

Popp also showed that light was a communication tool which orchestrates the body. Gurwitsch, a Russian scientist, theorized that a morphic field, not a chemical or biological reaction in the body was responsible for the structural shape of the body, which would also be verified as true.

There is other evidence as well of the presence and power of the Light, but for Spirit's purpose, let's say there is Light everywhere. And the Light is not only vital and powerful but precious. It contains the shape of its vessel and provides the water with internal rivers in which to flow while it bathes everything in information and records even more.

Evidence like this had a tendency to overflow to other areas. More questions arose: how many other roles did water have, and what sort of other crucial role did water play in the body? The human body, after all, is 60–70% water. Water fascinates us. It calms us, rejuvenates us, cleans, moisturizes and softens us. And Light energizes, warms, vitalizes, awakens, excites and inspires us. Together it is no wonder these two energies are pivotal to understanding the entire Energy Field in which all life swims. I would be hard-pressed to ignore these two from here on.

G. F. Thornton

Chapter 12

Points of Light

EACH COLLECTION OF ENERGY is coherent and never fully dissipates. Instead it stays as a bundled entity even after the death of the body. My beam remains as the Energy Signature of this incarnation. It is also the same beam which will return in the next. Each beam is meant to eventually evolve to Perfect Light upon Ascension in the distant future. Meanwhile, each beam of Energy retains its cohesion and remains as a unique Soul after death of its vessel. This Energy may stay here near the Earth, retreat far away from the Earth or travel to other astral planes and some will return to a new biological form almost instantly. The ultimate goal of ascension is only possible when one's Light achieves its zenith. This is when the earthly Consciousness can break free from the tethers and distractions of the physical. It is only then that each beam rejoins the divine wisdom and blends wholly into The Source in clear open space, here on earth and on all astral planes at the same time.

Home 1989

Shortly after my mother died, I fell headlong into a giant Biology text of over 500 grueling pages over six weeks, memorizing, reading and re-reading until the words would spill out of me upon command. It would distract my brain at least. A few weeks later, I knew Robert was back from his tropical island. I knew, not because he called, but because I sensed him. I phoned his best friend a couple of hundred miles away, and sure enough, Robert was there. My heart started beating so fast as I heard his voice for the first time in nearly a year. "Why didn't you call?" I asked as a smile spilled over my face. There was a long, empty pause before he answered. All he said was, "I'm going to marry her." It was the hardest, shortest conversation we had ever had.

That would be the last time we would speak for quite some time. I would cry for seven years. I would never stop missing him or loving him. And Robert would never fully leave my life. Every now and then he would call, invite me to coffee or dinner on his way through town. On occasion he would even show up mysteriously when I really needed something as if he was still tapped into me. He never lent money to anyone. It was one of his rules. Yet there was a time that I was in desperate need. He suddenly appeared, handed me a fistful of money and said, "Take what you need."

1989 stacks up as the worst year of my life. I lost my mother in May and my love in July. There wasn't much else life could take.

When someone says that in middle-age, they still feel as they did in their prime is evidence that our Consciousness is contained in the body but it is not a part of our body. We retain our Energy Signature throughout many incarnations. The Light doesn't age as the body does. The Light isn't born as a vessel, nor does it die as one. Its presence is a catalyst to our need and ability to connect with it. We get to tap into the Light and it seems to adjust, add, subtract or balance its knowledge through our expression. Simply, life is the cause of the veils between our consciousness and our Light. Only when we reconnect with the Light, recognize it and know it for what it really is, embrace it and breathe it in, can we become aware of its consciousness and benefit from its wisdom. Paying attention to its presence and allowing the Light to shine from within us allows our Conscious Intelligence to come out to play.

The body is a vessel and a way of Light accessing physical spaces to evolve and progress in, through and eventually out of this dimension. The true dimension of Consciousness is not the body. It is the Universe. When we say we are first Spirit, nothing could be truer as Spirit is Light and Light is Energy that is then born into a vessel. This Energy is focused, or coherent within a given vessel, validates that each life containing Light is a Point of Light that will one day lead to Perfect Energy. There is no other purpose for our physical expression than to progress Light forward, ever higher and brighter, gaining more and more knowledge and wisdom recorded within it and rising beyond the base physical space. The purpose is to express the Source, Perfect Love, on all levels of existence; intellectually, emotionally, physically and Spiritually.

Ancient texts tell of the many layers of existence: the Seven Great Planes and the forty nine sub-planes which they claim constitute the Cosmic Physical Body. All Energy layers and even the layers of time and space will affect this life and the next in the form of energy conversations that are written in each coherent Light beam. Such conversations constitute a vast record of various Energies such as emotions, experiences, lessons, events and challenges for instance, stacked one upon the other in the order they happened. We call them memories.

Light that can travel at 186,000 miles per second animates all life and feeds life its vital energy. Water heals and records information and transmits messages instantly and both serve the Conscious Intelligence of the Universe. Profoundly, could this be God experiencing physical reality?

The Math

Many of the greatest minds in Science spend their lifetimes describing everything in the Universe with a math equation. From combustion to the temperature water freezes, from the numbers of electrons of an atom and how they relate to other atoms all the way to the paired combinations within our DNA and the ones and zeroes used in computer technology. The world is expressed in specific relationship to numbers. With Einstein's Theory of Relativity where $E=MC^2$, nothing is ever created or destroyed but merely changed. This bodes well for the theory that Light and the Source will always be here in various forms or states. It is fascinating that everything can be explained with numbers, values and equations, and that the Theory of Relativity also seems to support that each life is a unique Point of Light. In Numerology, we can see how all energies in the Universe affect every other. Values given to a specific time or space will show up in time and space. We are part of both and we are affected by the ever changing values of both.

The Matrix

Once you cross the fine line from unknowing to knowing, the whole world will appear very different. As you take the time to contemplate each dynamic in your life from the perspective of Spirit, you will begin to notice a new understanding that seems almost elementary the moment you recognize it. As if you can suddenly tap into some of the vast Universal wisdom, Spirit opens up an expanse of understanding that is clearly fundamental and profound at the same time. The further I travelled along the road with Spirit, the more life made sense and the more questions found suitable and sensible answers. Voila!

The Matrix is a term used for the Energy in which we swim. This Matrix is the vast web of interconnected Energy that has been called the scaffolding. And it is found everywhere, including within this book. This grid of energy supports the structure, shape, continuity and communication of all things. The Mind when focused can tap into this Matrix and into all information from the past, present and future. As such, there is nothing that is invented or created that does not already exist, even if in another form. Einstein commented that he was not so much a genius but that he would spend a lot of time thinking or concentrating on something. As Einstein's Mind had the ability to focus intently and his Energy Signature became just the right frequency, he was able to tap into Universal wisdom on an exceptional level. In essence he willed the brilliance.

The Matrix also helps to explain Karma, reincarnation, past life memories, genius, miracles, Savants, intuition, psychics, premonitions, and all other supernatural phenomenon. Think of the possibilities with such a Matrix of Energy, an actual Field that connects and expresses everything. With the

Matrix, Light, Entanglement and Quantum Physics, why would there not be Intelligent Conscious conversation that operates across vast dimensions?

Brain or Mind

The brain is an organ. Its main function is to run the vessel and to ensure movement: to keep everything functioning perfectly and in balance, to provide information about the environment and a way for the brain to calculate, reason and logic in order to survive and procreate in a physical realm. This very complex and highly effective collection of systems is like a futuristic vehicle; one that functions completely on auto-pilot. The brain is the command center of this vessel and it is responsible for the entire function and balance. The body is a vessel which can respond, move and function to facilitate the coherent and laser-focused Light housed within it. But don't confuse the body or the brain with the Light.

Your brain is focused exclusively on the functions of the body in its physical space for survival, nourishment, dwelling, moving and safety, working, driving and talking and so on. As such, it is busy enough. The Mind (or the antenna) will fall into the background and become more like white noise if we're not focusing on it. We never lose our connection to the Light Source but we can certainly distance ourselves as life's distractions place barriers (or veils) between our physical reality and the Light. Inner Spirit is the only aspect that is tapped into your unique mind; into what has meaning to you and what your capacity and purposes are for this physical incarnation.

The Mind is the link, the vital link, between this vessel, the inner Conscious Light and the outer Conscious Intelligence of the Universe. The body is merely a vehicle to facilitate this consciousness. The brain is found within the cranium [skull] whereas the Mind exists both in and outside of the body and links the brain and the body to the outer Matrix. The Mind connects the brain, emotions and the entire body to all else. It is an antenna that functions within and outside of the each vessel. The Mind is therefore connected to every part of the body and the entire Matrix simultaneously. Does anyone care to guess the potential this embodies?

We are only now learning of this complex energy field. For centuries we have witnessed psychic ability, a plethora of unexplainable phenomenon: coincidence, the supernatural and paranormal. As humanity has been focused totally on the physical brain's understanding, few are practiced at connecting with the much larger and more powerful energy of the Mind and the Matrix.

Life also easily distracts us from our Mind. Meditation is one way to turn off the focus on just the brain. When we connect with the Mind is when we rise above this chaotic physical realm to soar with Spirit with very little effort.

Life on a Continuum

We met in 1998 and became instant friends. Rose showed me a single piece of paper one day as we talked about my turbulent past. It had three columns on it. She called it "Life on a Continuum". I glanced over the page. The three columns were headed "Inspiration, Coping, Surviving." Within less than ten seconds I was reading the column titled Surviving which I quickly determined as a list that described my life perfectly; unable to focus, exhaustion, no resilience, aches and pains, all or nothing thinking, greatest problem or greatest solution, ever-growing self-doubt, and so on. I glanced up at her, and with shock in my voice, I asked her, "How did you do this!? How do you know what my life feels like that you can put it down on paper in a single column?" Her answer came from what she had learned from her clients. She had counseled thousands and she kept hearing the same comments over and over again around a maze of different details. She removed the details, separated the emotional dynamics based on severity into three simple columns and made a comprehensive list.

Following the attack in 1999, I asked her how I could get from Surviving back to Inspiration. I will never forget her response. "Start with what is doable." It was an amazing relief to understand what was going on from a totally different perspective. This paper saved my life and my sanity.

Only when we override and quiet the brain's chatter can we connect with more valuable information accessed through the Mind. This can be achieved many ways, only one of which is meditation. Many people glaze over when the word meditation is even mentioned because it seems impossible to accomplish. In truth, it was really not as complex or tortuous as I had been led to believe. That my brain had considerable limitations on the physical level would become an understatement once I learned how to separate its chatter from what my Mind was really doing. Suddenly both had their own unique frequency and I merely had to focus on the right one. The chaos of my limited left brain, with the veils and distractions, had stood in the way of accessing the higher function of my Mind. I was eager to learn. I needed to understand that if the direction of my focus was to the physical world via the brain, I would continue to be stuck in the mud. And I had wallowed enough over many decades without much purpose. I had to decide to accept the Mind and be willing to totally receive something else if I was to be done with the mud.

Understanding the Mind and its benefits on the physical plane is crucial for happiness. Happiness is an internal event that has little to do with the external world. Instead of taking on all the challenges of the world, I could have awakened sooner to focus on the higher purpose of the Light. This could have altered everything! It started to become really clear that this could only be accomplished using the Mind's connection. While many may blame the ego for blockages and self-sabotage, it is actually the lack of focus and the accumulating veils that create our separation from the self-wisdom in our own unique Light. The mud is real for all of us.

Touch Down

The Universe is such a vast space, it is near impossible for us to comprehend. We used to believe that it was empty, that there was nothing between Earth and other galaxies. Today we know that the Universe is a vast expanse of Energy. Each celestial body; planet, star, comet, or moon is a physical place where the Light has touched down. Imagine what else the Universe holds that can be attributed to the Light.

"Light became. It was vast and interconnected. It progressed to Coherent, then Conscious to Sentient and then Intelligent." **Little Reign**

Humans associate with their bodies. So physical is our experience inside of this vessel that it is easy to miss what is really happening. The autonomic Flight, Fight or Freeze response to danger is experienced electrically, emotionally as fear, physically as in running or escaping, and intellectually as choices to avoid the danger. Out sentience, or being aware of this physical realm, aids life to survive this dynamic physical realm. To be sentient fulfills our basic needs and maintains life's ability to survive. Consciousness is far more. It is the core Energy, the Source Light that has hitched a ride in an imperfect biological vessel. Consciousness and sentience compute all physical and intellectual energies to emotional and spiritual information: the fuel which furthers the evolution of Light. Can you begin to see how focusing only on the physical intellectual is like living with only half a body?

The material currency of this physical world became less and less valuable when I was connected to and focused upon my Conscious Light. I always had good intentions and lived an ethical life even without the Light. Consciousness would not be there because I acknowledged it. It was there because it was part of me, just as it is part of all life. The Light gets to shine when we are not inhibiting it in some way. We are so much more than the body we dress, wash, exercise, feed and come to know as us. Our true value is the inner Light; the full expression of Love which lives inside our past and present and connects us to our future. This currency can be incredibly valuable when used to heal and serve.

His Wife

Robert would spend only six months of each year with his wife and the rest of the year at his house boat in a small town about four hours north of me where he was a fishing guide. He built this business far off in the wilderness after he returned from the South Pacific. Even though I never made much sense of it, I never asked him about why he had built his wife a house nearly two days travel from where he would work. Yet I knew this man, and knew he needed space. At one point he had told me that she was sick. Still it wouldn't change anything. And after crying for seven years, and taking on a new partner more out of loneliness than love, a silence began to settle into my heart. Each time I saw Robert, I noticed the distance growing thicker and thicker between us. At one point I could barely even recognize the man I had once loved more than life itself.

His last visit happened in the spring of 2006 when he dropped by one day out of the blue. He seemed quiet and even more distant as we hugged. He was going to sell his fishing business and retire. His bones, he said, could no longer deal with the dampness. He invited me to visit him there, all expenses paid, so I could see his ocean hideaway before he sold it. It was an endearing invitation, but I had to decline. My life just wouldn't allow him in again. I also had to remind myself that he was married, and no amount of hope could change that. Being alone again with him in a secluded place was tempting to play with fire.

The Source

The Source: Life Force; Spirit; Universal Wisdom;
God; Soul; Light; Fire; Higher Self

And this brings us full circle and back to God. Current religious doctrine teaches there is an Entity that is responsible for the Universe and everything in it. As in my past religious experiences the clergy had claimed this Entity was separate from me, far superior to me in every way and functioned well beyond my limited human understanding. This Entity was endowed with the ultimate in perfection, wisdom, power and knowledge, and always knew what was happening; what I'm doing, saying, planning and thinking. This was the entity that was the recipient of my prayers and devotion.

Various religions believe they have an exclusive audience to their God and that He is different or better than any other. In many ways I could easily exchange the word Light for the word God, bypass the male part, the fear, the untold interpretations and questionable perspectives - and go straight to the Light. And I could go there - without taking any baggage. The result was unexpected: I am the way, the truth and the Light and I pray to the Light that lives within which is connected to all knowledge and wisdom – when I can rise above the physical and unleash and benefit from my Mind.

Regardless of what we call this Entity, there can only be one; one Source, one Light, one God. The only difference between the Light and God is the human element; the perspective from which each one of us views the world. The differences and the suspected details brought forward about God have been contrived in our attempts to understand that which cannot be understood. For some, God has become a commodity: a ways and means for building kingdoms of devoted followers and increasing the power and wealth of those in control. Corporations have adopted many of these techniques and are using the same strategies to build and solidify vast material empires. Clinging to limited or out-of-date paradigms or doctrine, many believe they can separate their God from the others. And so far, that hasn't worked out too well either. Take away this human perspective, human interpretation and cultural slants from the subject and what you have left is the Light.

In First Nation philosophy, The Great Spirit is everywhere and in everything. First Nation understanding is inclusive and circular. It is about supporting the entire circle, of the Earth and the Tribe rather than pursuing everything in a straight line as in Mainstream's better, bigger and faster. Called the Great Spirit or Creator, this essence is singular, one and the same everywhere. While I hadn't been directly taught First Nation belief, I had always believed my relationship with God would be intimate and personal and that I was solely responsible for it and to it. I always felt that who and what I am in this physical life is what builds that relationship with the Divine. I am the decision-maker and I am tasked with a great responsibility to be honest with myself foremost. I can see now that these beliefs could only have come from the First Nation in me rather than whatever else I had learned. Not one of the churches I had joined had brought a lasting sense of peace like the Light. It was a key reason I stuck to my conviction that I was responsible and would need to do this on my own.

> "The Creator is the Light within you and that which is
> your true heart and intention." **Little Reign**

The concept of God is a human invention, an invention which has changed many times. Each artistic attempt has been an expression of something that was intuitively felt yet could only be half-known. When connected to the Life Force, the Eternal Energy and the Light, we can experience the Energy, which is much greater and more mysterious than ourselves. When I contemplate the Universe, I feel stretched far beyond this little reality to where I can entertain that everything is possible. We have always intuitively known and believed in something greater. I now know there is something greater. I can call it whatever I want - for the name changes nothing.

A rose by any other name would smell as sweet. Shakespeare

The Light is multidimensional with many levels of expression which our limited physical brains have only been able to partially comprehend. Today, humanity is preparing for the next leap forward in understanding. All of the Laws of the Universe allow everything to exist just as it is. Someone who claims they know the full truth of The Source is likely only fooling themselves or trying to fool others. Just as with comprehending the Universe, the depth and breadth of The Source is the greatest and most profound mystery.

For those who have escaped this plane during a Near Death or Out of Body Experience, their revelations of The Source will always change their human expression in profound ways. And likely this is the closest we'll get to understanding until we reunite in time. I fully expect that upon my death, when my Spirit Energy fully returns to the Source, I will once again have access to the wisdom of the Universe without any of the limitation or distractions of the physical. I expect the revelations will be equal to the experience.

Being a Point of Light separates each Consciousness, each incarnation, each memory and each experience from our biology and our Earthly senses. If we have dominion over anything, it is how we connect with and utilize this powerful source of information in our little, insignificant physical lives.

The greater realm is that of the Light, the ultimate energy and Conscious Intelligence of the Universe. How small we are inside this body but what a magnificent challenge to rise to grand and heavenly Light and exemplify this love, grace and wisdom on Earth.

I am Consciousness within an imperfect biological vessel, a human, and this vessel is mortal. This life has a beginning and middle and will come to an end one day. I will remain exactly how, who and what I am and can only progress by choice to whatever level of insight I am capable of achieving.

Like the tide that quietly washes higher and higher onto the shore, there are many unseen forces, not unlike the force of the Light. They are always present. Each tide pulses and changes the beach in unison with the heartbeat of the Universe. How perfectly special are the rocks, warmed all day long by the sun, as they offer up their heat to the water. The Universe is filled with just such tides; invisible forces that are profound, meaningful and purposeful …whether we are watching or not.

Chapter 13

Evidence

FOR CENTURIES we had placed them on their own exclusive roads but today Science, Philosophy and Theology are merging. They can no longer be separated as each one is now validating the truth of the other, of who and what we are and how things operate.

The Circle of Many

We are not separate, individual or alone on this journey. We are all part of The Circle, and we are the Many; one complete Tribe of Life, cycling in and through this biosphere, ensconced upon a planet we have called Earth. We are interdependent, not just in our family, our community or our country but in the entire environment of which we are a wee tiny part.

The 21st Century will be a time of realizing how destructive and impossible it will be to continue to maintain borders, divisions and conflicts as we have in the past. We exist because of systems that ebb and flow and sustain each other in a viable metabolism called Mother Earth. This planet is a living bio-eco-system. It breathes, cleanses, builds, replenishes and renews just like each life form upon it. This Earth is a self-regulating biological web of life that serves each part and the whole all at once. All life is essential to sustain all life; plants, animals, insects, fish, birds, bacteria, virus, fungi. The Earth is one being, a macrocosm of many microcosms, each as vulnerable and valuable as a single human on Earth or one planet within a galaxy. The Earth is the macrocosm of trillions and trillions of microcosms; a multitude of layers in the fractal geometry of systems from the quantum to the cellular, from the being to the Earth and beyond. Humanity is a single layer in the multitudinal strata of an entire Universe.

Light and water are essential elements which animate and sustain this layer. These two critical pieces are housed within each life form in all cells and DNA. Light is coherent, or laser-like, and assisted by water, provides instant communication in and throughout each life form. Both are critical to the health, maintenance and balance of each vessel. Each being develops a unique and fluctuating Energy Signature which is constantly influenced by its own inner and outer environment. It is also influential to its environment through those same energies. And all human beings live within the Earth's environment, and are influenced and influential to its energies too.

"On the Universal scale, biology is fleeting and inconsequential while the Light exists with a purpose to ensure Ascension." **Parkah**

Confirmation

In a very recent book called The Intelligence of the Cosmos, Ervin Laszlo, a highly regarded philosopher and systems scientist, twice nominated for the Nobel Peace Prize, confirms the Perfect Light on this physical planet. He confirms that incarnations happen; our Light does continue from one life to the next, ever evolving and advancing in wisdom toward ascension. You are Light, The Light and the Light of life and you are the Conscious Intelligence of the Universe. He confirms our need to understand and move past old paradigms and to reach for the truths we desperately need. The sacred mystery is moving toward its solution, one bit at a time. And Laszlo's latest answers to why we are here, from a science perspective, are likely to astound you too. For anyone who might still be skeptical that you are the evolution of Light, read Laszlo's book and then reconsider.

Peak Experience: The Path of One

Moving forward now to August 2006 and the sudden death of childhood friend. I had grown up with Brian and his family that lived across the street. I babysat him and his brother for years. The adults had spent many hours partying and neighboring over the years too. On this day, my sister called to say Brian had been in a car accident and was hooked up to life support which would be turned off on August 27th. He was 46 and a father of two teenagers. It was the day I started crying.

I had no idea why Brian's death was affecting me so deeply. He was a great person and a long-lost friend but I hadn't seen him in over twenty years. This tragic accident was still very sad. My tears kept falling and my heart felt broken and pained and I was grieving like I never had before. I wondered if Brian's death was connecting me to Mom's death. That must be it, I thought. I made my way to his funeral with Heather, and I cried the whole way, and not just sobbing, but full-on crying from my boots.

"I just don't know what's going on. I can't stop," I told Heather. At the funeral, my heart snapped open and the pain was like nothing else. My grief continued to grow and lasted many more days. Then, slowly, after a few weeks, I was able to return to my life and put Brian's death behind me.

The following February, in 2007, I received a manila envelope in the mail. It was addressed to me personally in an unfamiliar hand. Inside I found an 8 ½ x11" photo of Robert on his boat. I wondered what on Earth he was doing sending me such a picture. Had he lost his mind?

I turned the photo over to look for clues. In the same unfamiliar hand was written:

G. F. Thornton

"I thought you might like this recent photo.

Robert was scheduled for open heart surgery in November of last year but he died of a sudden heart attack at his summer home on August 27th."

Chapter 14

How to Reconnect

THIS SECTION offers practical and conscious strategies to help you reconnect with your personal Light. While there are likely many ways to accomplish this, these are intentional strategies you can employ to get things started. Taking a conscious, pro-active approach in the beginning will help you recognize the various energies of the Light and how to access them. This section will also help you to identify the sources of lesser vibration that have hindered and blocked your journey in the past. This section however is not about problem solving. You have likely had plenty of experience with that already. Every journey is about remembering the Light; how it works and its true purpose. It is about being right here, right now and knowing it is possible to bring your Light forward into your life when you are ready to embrace it.

This entire book speaks to Spiritual Healing. Spiritual Healing means you are open to knowing about all the energies, good and not-so-good that have made you who you are today. Using Energy Healing in such modalities as Reiki and crystals and the like will rebalance and enhance your Energy Signature, but how long will the balance last if after treatment you return to the same imbalanced life? Your mind has the greatest influence over your Energy Signature even when you aren't aware. The reason is simple. Your brain chatters away constantly and is often unknowingly stuck in lesser, habitual vibration. Spiritual Healing via the mind, when applied to the complex dynamics of your life, will rebalance your Energy Signature and teach you how to maintain your personal balance for the long term.

It is imperative to understand that healing is an internal affair. All of your healing happens within you. Your decisions, considerations, emotions, energies and purpose happen within you because they are based on the wisdom in your Light first and foremost. As said before, no one can take you to the Light any more than they can remove you once you're there. The healing is yours and the journey to it is yours. You are the decision, the dream, the peace and the love that will happen, or not. And these all exist within you first.

So where do you start? It is fundamental to view the world and this spiritual journey with an honorable and honest **intention.** A strong commitment will keep you on track as you set your intention to finding your self-wisdom hidden within you. As you travel this path, you will find much that will validate that this wisdom has always been there and that it is meant to be discovered. This section will help you to see how you have already experienced this Energy many times and in many ways. The suggestions encourage you to jump start your reconnection in the here and now - today. But first, try to look at everything as though you know nothing of it and view your past as the candle in a Chemistry Lab seen for the very first time.

Here is a quick example. Assess yourself by selecting one of these three words in answer to this question: How are you right now?

Inspired - Coping - Surviving

There is absolutely no doubt that you came up with the right answer. How long did it take you and where did you go to find the answer? This kind of experience provides simple evidence to help you trust there are many, many answers within yourself and your being.

Intention

There are many other clues. We have a 'gut instinct.' Think about intuition, coincidences, Déjà vu, predicting a phone call or knowing when a loved one is injured. What are you really accessing? In your past experiences, you can find numerous clues to your Light too. Think of events that seemed like miracles. Take a walk through the past as if you're viewing a movie. You needn't get caught up in the trauma of the past to search for these clues. Stay centered with the intention of finding information that will validate your own Light. Take a look at how you hurt to find out how to heal.

Life is complex. It can be challenging, difficult, happy, joyous, confusing and sad – and all at once. I made a promise to find a better way through this life. For many decades however, I found no indication or surety of another way. I had to look and keep looking. If a better way did exist, I was determined to find it. This drive eventually brought me to the Light and I had no idea how much it would change absolutely everything.

Your intention is critical to your search. Behind every decision we make and everything we do is our intention and it is always connected to what something means to us. More than anything else, your intention will determine the quality of the energy created with each event. I found evidence of this fact from my ex-husband, Tom. He believed in and practiced Positive Mental Attitude (PMA) and meditation daily. I watched as he consistently made an effort every day to harness the power of his mind. Yet after six years, his affirmations and visualizations had not enhanced his reality as he had expected. He had not brought about the wealth or the fame he craved.

After walking with Spirit for several years, I would come to see what had been missing for Tom. There had been no honorable intention in his actions. There was no honor or good intention in how he achieved anything. He was clearly disconnection from the Light. His low vibration and questionable intention blocked his success at every corner. Again, Spirit has its own passcode! And the proof happened the night of the attack. Tom had beaten me up out of his mounting fear and insecurity as he could see me easily gaining what he had longed for all his life; people who sought him out for help. On that night in 1999 his true intention showed his fear as he used his anger and his hands around my throat to force me to stand behind him again, to return to being lesser and submissive to his power. It was the only way he could find his own value because he could see that people were starting to seek me out, instead of him.

Malala

Malala Yousafzai speaking for education for all girls around the world inspires us with her courage and conviction. Malala is clearly connected to the strength and wisdom of her Spirit. She said that her fear and anger died the day she was shot in the head by the Taliban in 2012. Upon awakening from her coma, she had been reborn with even greater courage and purpose for her life. She was only 15. Winning the Nobel Peace Prize, she was rewarded for her mission for every child; education. She knows that education brings goodness, fairness, happiness and abundance, no matter the race, gender, status or state. This is an inclusive embrace seen through Spirit.

Here is a list of ten strategies I applied from the start that would one day prove critical to connecting with the Light.

10 Point List

- I was determined to find a better way to do this life.
- I made a commitment to myself to go the distance.
- I worked at living in the moment. I became aware and conscious of everything, and wrote everything down because I was certain the insight and wisdom I needed was in my own story.
- I worked at having an honorable intention. Doing something with the wrong intention, whether or not it was successful could not add value to my life. Good intentions through service, kindness, compassion, caring or love bring rewards – every time.
- I consciously monitored every interaction I had with others and became aware of when I would do or say something that did not come from good energy.

- I gave myself permission to take the trip regardless of potential pitfalls. I would still win and lose, make errors, bruise my ego and scrape my knees. It just wouldn't be as frequent or as devastating as before.
- I was patient with myself. I was still a human being on a physical plane attempting to reconnect with what had been covered over for a very long time by the many veils of living life on autopilot.
- I always believed that the connection to The Source would be personal, private and intimate, and I still do. Now I have much more evidence that this is true.
- I stayed realistic. I was realistic about taking time, making an effort and remaining with good intention, awareness and commitment. I wasn't critical of the time, just aware that I remained in a forward direction as much as possible and that all good and worthy tasks take time.
- I stayed the Course until I reached the Light. I continued to put one foot in front of the other as I made my way along this path and I refused to be knocked off track for long.
- Today, I am committed to the Light and will continue to be for the rest of my many lives.

Decision & Commitment

If you were standing on one side of a large room full of strangers and saw your best friend come through the door on the other side of that room, you would want to make your way over to her. If she was just an acquaintance, you might start out but stop somewhere along the way, perhaps distracted or interrupted by someone or something. If the person was your very best friend you hadn't seen in years, you would make a far more concerted effort and wouldn't be deterred halfway for anything. The meaning, or the degree of importance to complete your journey, would determine your level of success. The exact same dynamics happen with everything. If doing something is important enough and holds sufficient meaning, you will not let anything stand in your way. And the journey toward the Light is just such a process.

Every journey begins with an intention. Reconnecting with the Light is no different. It has to begin with the intention to stay the course, to be honest and to not give up when the going gets tough. We can arrive at a time when we find ourselves at the end of our rope, lost and alone in the abyss or when something happens that readies us for a change. In our darkest moments is often when we reach beyond ourselves and life's challenges to entertain another way. We are hardwired to survive, so we take survival very seriously. If or when we can let go of our dire focus on the outer world, on all the material trappings is when Spirit has room to slip in. One day we will all forsake the material world and allow the Universe to move in.

When there seems no possible way for life to begin, it does. Grass will grow through the tarmac as if nothing could possibly stop it. A tree will root on the side of a cliff hanging on by mere grains of sand. Creatures find ways to harness life in the darkest depths of the ocean, in deserts and arctic tundra. Algae flourish in the acid waters of a geyser. A baby will be conceived against all odds. Life is prolific and plentiful, teeming throughout the Earth and with very few limitations. The Light is the powerful force that pushes for a way, any possible way to express itself. It creates momentum, vision, meaning and purpose …in addition to being the fuel of the eternal fire. How can we be complacent, angry, sad, alone or abusive when this energy inhabits every cell?

Your path however must include the necessary commitment because the journey forward will still come with obstacles. Your success will depend upon your desire, intention and commitment. As if you were setting off on a journey across an entire country, you will find many hills and valleys, mountains and boulders along the way. There will be many challenges to overcome. Yet you will arrive if you stay the course and do not waver in the quest.

Once you can recognize a single event of the Light it will validate your journey and secure your commitment. The best news is that we have all experienced these events in our past many times over. We only need to find it, open it up and gather the energy from within it. Once you recognize the miracles and the many messages you've already experienced, you will become reassured and curious about what else is possible. Validation always brings an inspired and motivated energy that will move you forward with determination. Discovering those miracles and significant messages in your own past will fuel your search for greater understanding, just as they did for me.

"Look through your expanded Spiritual lens to identify
the messages and miracles of the past.
Think on them and consider the wisdom within each." **SoSo**

Someone who 'falls' into something that is great is experiencing the Light Energy. The arts and music are activities that will connect you with inspiration energy which is the Spiritual Energy of the Light. These contain high vibrations that you can actively harness simply by remembering and appreciating where these activities take you. Life without the Light is barren, fearful and unsafe. Life in the Light is freedom, happiness, wisdom, faith, trust and grace. Learning to notice the differences and beginning to seek will help you change your focus and your experiences.

"Choose to live - with or without the Light." **Simi**

Most of us are still waiting for others to say we can, that we should, or gee, that we're doing something great! We think that just because we have a dream, doesn't mean we can put ourselves in the right frame of mind to accomplish it. And therein lays the missing piece from Positive Mental Attitude. How do I believe, especially without any evidence, that it's possible at all, let alone for me? Faith or belief rarely come first because we spend our first twenty or so years waiting for others to give us permission or to validate that we are on the right track. And this is a paradigm that won't go away easily.

It is also important to give yourself permission to step into your own truth and that the Light is not there to cause harm but to free you from the mud. Understand the road on this new journey can be a bit bumpy as it will be unfamiliar to start. Sometimes digging through the past can bring up old emotions attached to past events. It is important to know you can protect yourself by preparing to simply **observe** the past as you look for the jewels.

"Bear not the theft of your inner self
by those who seek to exploit." **Little Reign**

Preparation: Removing the Veils

Preparation takes the form of handling ahead of time anything that might block your progress. In other words, it is best if you clean your closet first, so to speak. This journey begins with clearing a space in your life so you can focus on you. It will be all about you and no one else. You are the vessel, the brain and mind, the emotion and heart of it all. You are the "I Am." You will know when you are ready because you will begin taking the first steps and you will find a determination to continue. If you are not ready, you will experience the resistance in some way or it will be too easy to stop or turn around and return to your life as it was.

Reflect on whatever resonated for you in this book. Consider my 10-Point List from your own inner wisdom and from the perspective of your Spirit first. These are accessible, immediate and empowering. We will prepare for this spiritual journey too - just like any other trip. Cleaning your closet means to inventory and assess the things in your life that could create road blocks. Take notes as you categorize and assess everything that might get in your way as well as those things that propel you forward with ease. Being clear about what motivates or scares you is imperative. These two opposites are powerful clues.

> "Pack for this trip as if your life depends
> on arriving at your destination." **Lucy**

Investing

Today, I see how every element of my life has brought me to this day and to this task. Had my lot in life been different would I be who I am? Would I be as convinced or committed to this mission or this project? Would I still be bringing these words to you if I hadn't had the same incentives for them? Would this book have been written had I invested in other things along the way? My lot in life would be determined more by my capacity to respond than any of the details or my experiences. I admit however, I may never know the exact answers to these questions until the other side.

The details, the events that happen in life are common to us all. We have all lost loved ones, been tempted, hurt, betrayed or conflicted. We have all changed jobs, moved, opted in or out, joined, quit and cried a river, felt unloved, lost and alone. All of humanity feels the pain, grief, joy and happiness of life. The details may be different but the dynamics are the same. We will all have to endure being wrong, reaching out, hiding away and being tempted. That which will determine our journey is not so much the color of the car or the road we take but rather by our capacity to drive at all – and stay between the lines no matter the mood. The details would not have changed my destiny, only my choice to seek or not.

As you seek to find the Light, you will discover the veils that have been blocking it. The first step in a Spiritual journey is to look at, assess and remove as many of the veils as possible. Your success will be determined solely by your commitment and honesty to yourself. Become a witness to how you show up in your life. Be curious instead of scared and witness that you come from the right intention when you reach inside to the Light.

"Shake your head, your eyes are stuck!" **Bill**

This little sentence from **Bill**, a dear departed friend, was meant for the referee at a softball game but it reminds me daily that when I look at each moment of my life, I might not be seeing what I need to see.

Life can steal our ability to see beyond the veil of the physical or what we need to see. Sometimes we need to shake our head and get rid of the cobwebs of complacency so we can see again. To remove the veils, we must be willing to do whatever it takes. We need to be willing to meet ourselves in the truth, and perhaps for the first time! This part of the journey doesn't have to be scary if you think that looking back at your past will be filled with pain. Start in Observer Mode, and take a look as if you're simply watching a movie. Do not engage or connect to the emotion of the past. Just look for the clues. Begin to listen carefully and with curiosity, not criticism, to your complaints and questions. Our self-talk can offer powerful insight into what we need to change and what we need to know about how to change.

You have had a lifetime of experiences and there will be those which have left indelible marks. To clear the veils will require you to travel all the way back to your family of origin to take a true look at what made you who you are today. You do not have to traumatize yourself as you revisit this past. An acknowledgment of an event and a clear decision about what to do with it today can be enough for it to recede and be gone for good. Identify what the veil was about. Ask yourself if this veil is still needed. Address an old issue with good intentions and self-respect without being critical. Here is a sampling of the kinds of question to use as you explore your truth.

- How was your relationship with your mother and father?

- How did you feel about yourself growing up?
- Were you in a balanced and healthy place, or what was imbalanced about it?
- What made the greatest impact on how you are today?
- In what way is the past still with you today?
- What are the things you wish you could change? Why?
  - Questions like this one will provide valuable clues.
- What always crops up that bothers you or gets in your way?
- What strategies have you built out of need and out of fear? They served a purpose at the time ...do they still?
- How fearful are you, and of what? Why? Where did this fear come from – yourself or someone else? Is it your fear or theirs?
- Do you know what you value most? Can you make a list? What does it tell you about how you have responded to events in your life?
- Can you name what holds the most meaning to you and why?

There is a lot of magic in the right question and great insight in a truthful answer. These are the kind of dynamics that are helpful to clear the path. I needed to identify my behavior, what kind of energy each characteristic presented, how each dynamic arrived and how each affected the big picture. I had to decide when I no longer wanted the veils that were hiding my Light. Once each one was identified, contemplated and dismissed, I didn't even notice when they dissipated. It wasn't until the old emotions like anger, resentment, fear and judgment suddenly stopped surfacing that I realized something important had occurred.

It can help to have a gentle guide to ease you through the mud. Someone's validation can keep you on track, usher you through the thicker mud and help you to identify what you need in order to heal. Sometimes others can hear what you can't - until you can. Someone else can also remind you to walk past or remove what no longer serves you.

> "You need not experience the pain of the past
> ...to be done with it." **Parkah**

It's important to be able to keep your eye on the prize and on the truth through Spirit so you can ease yourself beyond an event. From a step away, without the emotion, you can witness the old energy and the emotional echoes that pop up from an event long after it is over. This sometimes takes a guide who can help you recognize and understand the energy of trauma and how to navigate it Spiritually. It can be helpful to know that someone cares and can validate that you are on track. Their support should feel valuable. If someone makes you feel ashamed, guilty, wrong or blamed - move on for they are not coming from Spirit's energy. I am proof that we can still do this on our own with just a little encouragement. Your determination can be the fuel to keep you going.

This Spiritual Quest requires that your mind is clear, open and ready to receive insight. As Spirit wrote in a previous chapter, it is important to clear yourself of as much lesser energy as you can in order to balance and raise your frequency. It is important to not get bogged down by details. Be on the hunt and look for the underlying value or the emotional meaning of each event. Remember that emotions are the bridge to your Light. Emotions will alert or remind you of what has meaning and what needs to be addressed and how. Understand we have a well-developed and powerful relationship with our emotions as a way to guide us and keep us safe. You have employed and experienced your emotions on many occasions with just this purpose, aware or not. Take the time to validate this is true. Slowly, intentionally and with self-wisdom and care, look at your emotions from the past and let them become the clues to guide you forward.

Knowing how you hurt brings the insight
to what you need - in order to heal.

Let the Process Begin

Begin by discovering yourself. What motivates and inspires you? What can you learn about the dynamics of who you really are? What do various aspects of your life mean to you?

Live in the Moment

These suggestions offer many ways to connect with your inner Light. Some activities require engaging within to your core in solitude to still the energy and expand your Spiritual experiences. Other activities are about coming from, or connecting to your core to engage with the outer world pro-actively with intention and safety. The daily challenge we all have is to engage in the world and remain balanced, centered, connected to the Light and conscious enough to stay safe and at peace.

It is valuable to chart your progress. To capture the meaning will take living in the moment and being conscious of where you are, what you're doing, what you're thinking and how things are happening. Start by practicing living in the moment for periods of time each day, increasing the length of time and/or frequency as you progress. Begin to journal and take note of emotions, internal questions, intentions, and meaning versus the details of events. Observe your world and take notes on your responses and reactions to the outer world. Whenever you are working on the following processes, being in the moment is crucial to clarity and truth.

Here is a list to begin working on. The time it takes to work through these is up to you, but be serious, concise and honest. Remember, the passcode!

Assess Yourself to Start

1. **Values:** moral points of reference such as kindness, compassion, patience, fairness, loyalty, gratitude, honor, respect, etc. Choose at least three values that are of the utmost importance to you. These will then become your reference point to use as a filter in all things.
   a. Take the time to identify and then test each possible value.
   b. Consider why each is meaningful. Your answers are what you are made of and what is meaningful to your core self.
   c. Search your past for those values that always seem to show up (Example: I was adamant with my son for years that he always tell me the truth no matter what. After testing how important truth was to me in other areas of my life, I was able to identify truth as one of my three highest values.)

2. **Meaning:** identify what has the most meaning in your life.
   a. On what do you give the most energy, time and attention?
   b. Build a page of empty circles on a piece of paper and place each issue, good and bad, in its own circle.
   c. Assessing mindset – What mindset to you experience when dealing with each issue? Assign a color to each circle: like

blue for inspiration, yellow for coping and red for surviving.

d. Assess your Energy Signature knowing High frequency is Inspiration energy and Surviving frequency is the lowest.

e. Assess the meaning of each to identify which issues bring the most value and purpose. Focusing on these are catalysts to take you to the Light.

f. Assess which issues raise your Energy Signature to a higher vibration?

g. Assess if you are ready to shift your energy consciously.

h. Assess physical, intellectual, emotional and spiritual energy. Mark each circle based on these to show which dynamic is underneath each one.

i. How do you spend more time focused on high vibration?

Take a step back. Place the chart several feet away on the floor. Look at the chart from Observer Mode to gain an impartial emotional distance to decide what needs more or less of your attention. What are the red flags or the achievements? How big does each issue feel in a day versus how big are they in reality?

You can use this chart to assess a full range of qualities for life events to create clarity for when you are overwhelmed with detail, circumstance, emotion and complexity.

3. **Identity:** identify your external, internal and core self.

    a. **External:** Do you identify yourself by your career? a certain status? as a family? through your children? spouse? Are you really just an employee, boss or servant?

        i. Is this really all there is to your identity?

        ii. Do you identify yourself by behavior; worrier, fearful, skeptical, optimistic, intelligent, anxious, creative, boring, angry, etc.?

        iii. Be careful what you take to heart as you will be found in how you talk and feel about yourself.

    b. **Internal:** how do you experience yourself?

        i. What do you hear yourself always saying?

        ii. Did someone validate that you were a worry wart, fearful, skeptical, second-best, unworthy, etc.?

       iii. Are you introverted, taking life to heart, reflecting on life at a deep level and requiring solitude to regenerate the energy you spend at life?

       iv. Are you extroverted, processing life out loud, talking things through and gaining energy from exchanges with others?

       v. Did you buy into what your parents said about you? Do you still? Is this still right, or fair?

       vi. Is there something you always confirm to yourself? Is this really true, or is it something someone else imposed upon you years ago? Are you really a worry wart or are there things in life that cause you to worry? [Did you notice a difference in the words?]

       vii. Being a worry wart is there but why, and is it really true? Things can cause you to worry, but it doesn't mean you're a worry wart.

       viii. Can you see how we can fall down the hole into self-doubt and habitual thinking that doesn't serve us?

  c. **Core:** Spirit, Light, Enlightened Self fosters;

       i. Moral intention which is reflected in your values.

       ii. Honorable intention to value life.

       iii. Faith in the process and trust in life.

       iv. Making meaningful choices to add to the quality of your life and the lives of others.

All three identities contribute to your overall identity. Coming from your Core Identity, your Light, you will experience what resonates for you. This is your Truth.

4. **Purpose:** Can you identify something in your life that has always been with you? Example: for me it was writing this book. Once I started looking at me, I began to see the parts of myself that made up the whole. I could see how everything in my past had led me to this place, this time and this task. It took many years to discover it as something so important. So don't give up. Give yourself the time

you need to fill in the blanks and come up with what your life says about you. Remember you are the dream already.

Today, I fully believe everything happens for a reason. There is so much value at looking at the process and not near as much in the end product – which is opposite to what we're taught. We're taught to focus only on the destination, and in so doing many of us aren't able to enjoy the trip or find value in how it happened that they arrived at all.

Signs

There are signs when we are off track. As strange as some of these might seem at first, they are hallmarks to be aware of that will let you know when you are strictly in the physical and have fallen off the path. Identified, you can take the steps to correct the course.

a. **Exhaustion** - the desire to fold up physically, to protect your heart or your inner self, to need to sleep more than normal, and to still feel tired when you wake up. These are sure signs that you're smack dab in the physical world, and you have landed hard. Have you 'exhausted' all the reactive ways to cope and are you ready to look at something different?

    Note: when we are constantly trying to orchestrate life, when we are always smiling or pretending, there will be days when we collapse because the energy it takes to keep the pretense going is *exhausting*.

b. **More aches and pains** than usual as the body responds to an imbalance in energy. When you are feeling the stress, pressure, fear or resentment of the physical (to name only a few) the body responds with aches and pains, colds, cramps, nausea, tiredness, etc. which are the result of an energy imbalance from what you are not tending to.

    a. When the **brain's chatter** is scattered, habitually negative, or when it's racing, fretting, worried or fearful...

    b. **Emotions** can bring a definite energy with them. Being aware of those emotions that don't add to you or increase your Energy Signature are reminders of what needs to be addressed to balance lesser energy.

i. I had focused in on spotting stupid people …and I lived in resentment, frustration and anger as a result. My focus didn't affect the stupid people but it kept me in a state of emotional turmoil!

Strategies

a. Observe while not investing or believing; listen from a distance; what do you want to change [complaints], what do you need to know [questions]? There is insight in both.

b. When you hear habitual chatter shift to Observer Mode to distance emotionally from it. This allows you to listen objectively to see if there is insight in the chatter.

c. You can listen to the chatter but you don't have to be influenced by it or believe it. The psyche offers chatter as an opportunity to observe, consider and respond by accepting or utilizing a thought or challenging and releasing it if it's not helpful or no longer is needed. Success will increase your energy and change your chemistry for the better.

d. Words and thoughts have energy. Fill your mind with words and thoughts which will maintain a more balanced and higher vibration. As you become more conscious and successful, intentionally begin to eliminate the negative or habitual words and thoughts and instill inspirational ones to continue to increase your frequency.

e. Healthy Intolerance shows itself in resistance, defeat, imbalance, resentment and break down. These are not pleasant experiences but experiencing a healthy intolerance for toxic things is the good news. It shows that you're ready to address what has been revealed that is clearly not working for you.

Influence Your Energy

Energy is fluid. It can be influential and influenced. The dynamic of energy can be your greatest ally. If you accept that you can influence your own energy, that you can increase it at will, would you not want to?

How are you already influencing your energy …intuitively and naturally? You already change your energy by doing things like; taking a deep breath to calm yourself; energizing yourself to become playful; listening to uplifting music. Your previous successes go a long way in creating confidence that you can influence and change your energy when you want to or need to.

How can you pro-actively influence your energy?

- Thoughts and Words create a consistent impact upon our energy as they live within us and through us all the time. Every thought and word comes with a distinct energy. Can you feel the shift in your energy when you switch from thinking of a word like joy to a word like anger? Words and thoughts will resonate and influence your Energy. Being conscious of being surrounded by good ones can make a big difference.
- Consciously spend time thinking about high energy words: love, happiness, hope, sunshine, peace, gratitude and so on.
- Meditate or take a walk in the sunshine – calm and eventually quieten the inner voice. It doesn't need to keep talking!
- Practicing gratitude prayers every day or night will change the chemistry of your brain and mind and consequently your Energy Signature.
- Color has energy. Witness and embrace the energy of each color to add quality to your experiences.
  - o Surround yourself with the color/s that you crave or love or the ones you are attracted to at the time for they will hold the energy you need.
- Some of the things you can change to bring those colors into your life are:
  - o Clothing, wall colors, blankets, pictures, home décor and accessories.
- Some colors are universal and available everywhere all the time.
  - o Nature, sky, flowers, sunshine
  - o The color black will immediately dampen and draw out your energy. Look around and see how many people wear dark colors. What does a dark color express and what do you sense from it? What is your experience of blue? of yellow or red? Note that black reflects all Light back while white is the combination of all colors in the Light.

- Sound has energy:
    - Fill your space with beautiful sounds.
    - Nature, music, birds, water, whatever soothes your energy.
    - Eliminate sound and colors that don't add to you or resonate with your core in good and high vibration.
    - Some television and media, most newscasts, violent entertainment, adrenaline games and heavy-metal music will always lessen your Energy Signature.
    - Classical music and natural, beautiful sounds will always increase your Energy Signature whether or not you feel a connection with them.
- People have energy:
    - Surround yourself with kind, caring, supportive and loving people.
    - If you must go somewhere questionable, prepare yourself to be in toxic energy in order to protect your higher vibration. Always consciously protect your vital energy.
    - Don't allow people to dump on you – protect your right to be here just as you are and extend the same right to all others.
    - Own your journey …it is yours to make.
- Live in the moment and make sure each moment adds to your Energy.
- Places have energy:
    - A country road has far different energy from a bustling city street – select your environment with this in mind; what will add to you? Practise first on the quiet road so you can survive the energy of the busy road when you need to.
    - Your office space, bedroom, home, yard and outside areas can add considerable energy as nature is always the right color and energy. Create the sounds conducive to peace and good energy, and look for what literally feels good to your soul.
    - Nature's Energy is the best: the ocean has energy that moves you, wind will fluff up and energize you, sunlight will warm and expand you, and green foliage cleans and brightens your energy, and so on.

- o Go out for a quiet stroll whenever you can… and take notice of how you engage and what best fills you up.
- Shut off the television, computers and cell phones. Enjoy talking with your friends again.
- Crowds have unknown energies. Protect your energy with a bubble of peace before you venture into a crowd.
- Animals have beautiful energy:
  - o If you have a pet, you're on your way: playing with, sleeping with, cuddling, spending time with your pet while being conscious and aware. Animals can lift your spirit instantly because they are pure Light.
  - o Humans are good at doing, animals are good at being.
  - o If you don't have a pet, you can visit one: walk SPCA dogs, sit with their kitties, adopt a pet or foster one: animals are pure spirit. Be conscious and aware of their energy and drink it in as much as possible. [Having a pet is a great responsibility so being prepared to properly care for any animal you bring into your home comes first.]
- Crystals and have energy:
  - o Become familiar with nature's crystals and how their energy can enhance, heal and energize your own.
- Scents have energy:
  - o Become familiar with essential oils and learn when their energy resonates with yours. What else can they offer you?

Allowance

Finding the code that unlocks the abundance promise has been the dream of millions, if not billions. I had experienced the Positive Mental Attitude protocol and something hadn't seemed quite right. Something was clearly missing in the mantras "you bring about what you think about" or "what you can conceive and believe you will achieve." If this was all it took everyone would be living in Nirvana by now. In my research it became clear that it is not just what we conceive and believe that produces abundance or success, it also requires that **we allow the Universe to fill us up**.

"Your mission will fill your heart with reward, joy and peace." **Parkah**

How can abundance enter our lives if we keep the door closed? When we are shut down, angry or afraid, our Energy Signature decreases and abundance energy just can't get in. It's as if we have built a wall between us and potential. Anita Moorjani's book was clear that we can and do influence our energy quotient with thought, emotion and word energy as well as with energy from our external and internal environments. We can therefore actively be in sync with the higher frequencies in order to benefit. Let's take a closer look at what this means.

Embrace and Lean In

In order to allow abundance into your life, one must embrace it. This means we need to unburden ourselves from fear, anger, greed, want, desire, pain and other reactive and lesser vibrations from this physical life. Through the Light means you have found faith and trust in the process of life and can embrace it again. To lean in means you are not afraid to move into your life and to know you will be alright. Leaning in to your life may take courage at first as it's not what we are accustomed to. Leaning in however and living with gusto will become the greatest gift and reward. As you journey along this path toward the Light, you will begin to accumulate instances where you experience more trust and faith, bit by bit as the Light shows the way.

"Abundance does not come to you, but rather flows through you." **Willo**

In order to be a recipient of the abundance of the Universe, we need to lessen toxic fear, greed and anger energy. We need to be more aware of our own Energy and keep it in balance. Focusing outside of ourselves is the opposite direction for our attention to be placed. Our focus on the artificial material world is the very reason we are moving further away from the vitality of our inner world. When we are fearful, angry or focused on the physical we are operating in a Spiritual Desert. We literally tighten up physically. We tense and draw ourselves inward in an attempt to protect our vitality. To know and accept abundance, we must allow it and tightening up physically will block the abundance. Faith, trust in life, abundance, joy and happiness cannot be found outside of us. These arrive only when we open up and allow their good Energy in.

Embracing is floating on the thermals like an eagle, so assured that the invisible wind will hold you up and not let you plummet to the ground. The

Light softens all other things including the harshness and imbalance of fear, anger, pain and sorrow.

> "It is your faith and trust in the wind that supports you
> more than the wind ever can." **Wahwaskenah**

Healthy Fear

In this physical life, we have been conditioned to focus on our own little world. We are very physically connected to our experiences. When we are afraid, even our posture expresses our fear. We draw ourselves inward, sometimes to the fetal position, hang our head, isolate from others and even hold on tightly to our pain as we shrink away from what we fear; real or imagined. This is our healthy fear triggering Fight, Flight or Freeze reaction for instant survival. Healthy fear is meant to alert us to take quick action and release the adrenaline once we are safe again. Our consciousness and our biology know it is unhealthy to remain trapped in this lower vibration for very long. Energy like this cuts us off from the benefits of the greater energy that heals and comforts. We often find ourselves in unhealthy and fearful places or are around unhealthy people. And we are being convinced we should just put up with it. We feel powerless and pressured to keep pace, to avoid taking a stand and to keep our opinions to ourselves. Thus, we live in an atmosphere of fear and lesser energies.

When we become captive in a reactive state, our aches and pains, postures, thoughts, words and emotional expressions become toxic, work against us and make us feel powerless. These shut us down from balanced healing Energy. Sometimes when we think we are open minded, accepting and positive, we can be anything but. Abundance shouldn't feel impossible. Abundance is meant to flow through us and it is vital to our health that we open up to let it flow.

> "The more fear that builds up in your head,
> the more veils there are to obscure the Light." **Parkah**

Distraction

We know that life distractions obscure the Light. One of the other critical distractions of the modern world is when technology focuses us into cell phones and computers. As valuable as this technology might be in certain places at certain times, it is removing opportunities for young people to turn inward to their Spiritual Energy as their minds are critically and steadfastly focused on the portals of chaos from the outer world.

In fact, technology is the new addiction for the 21st Century, and it may well take decades to understand and address the worst addictive 'drug of choice' to come along yet with over 305 million users in US and Canada, a whopping 85% of the population. Focusing on the outside physical world sets us on a downward spiral into the darkness and it can trap us there. Training young minds to be totally captured by technology like they are today, is robbing them of all their skill sets; social graces, morals, ethics, interrelations, and even love and democracy. Many victims are validating the toll that this focus has taken already. Suicide is the 2nd leading cause of death of young people and anxiety and depression are at record highs with 350 million people suffering around the world. And these numbers are increasing exponentially. Two key reasons are their prolific outward focus and creating an inner Spiritual desert. More than anything else, this robs us of our collective strength and power and our ability to unite. This is a very dangerous game and one of the highest offences to the whole of humanity.

United we stand. Divided we fall.

Anita Moorjani, while on the other side in her Near Death Experience, learned that we are meant to allow life to unfold without fear. We therefore have to usurp our fascination with artificial fear and violence in order for everyone to find abundance. While we cannot live without fear entirely and it serves a very important role in survival, we must be selective. We should make every effort to live void of unhealthy and toxic fear. The level of artificial fear imposed by the outer world is already taking a huge toll in how safe we feel. We are not designed to handle artificial fear in great quantities because the hormonal cascade that happens as a result is powerful and is not meant to be continuous. Our automated responses can't tell the difference between real or artificial threat and we will always react. The adrenaline rush that comes as a result can be as addicting as a dangerous drug if we're not aware or watching.

Many people don't know how they can open up and let go in the face of adversity and threat. We've been taught to nurse our wounds, pull away from the world that hurt us and sleep off the exhaustion. Exhaustion is a sign that we're trying to orchestrate, control or push our world against the grain. To maintain an unnatural state all the time, to pretend all is well on the outside while fearful on the inside takes considerable energy. This is not 'allowing' anything but rather becoming a battle 'against' everything. Exhaustion is a healthy sign we have become unhealthy. It is also a clear sign of the B - Mindset.

We have two fundamental states of mind:
A - Inspired/Healthy Mindset tapped into Expanded Resources,
or
B - Fearful/Unhealthy Mindset with access to Limited Resources

What we are intuitively meant to do is adopt the A - Inspired/Healthy Mindset and open up, even throw our hands in the air, and let abundance fill us up with love and Light and peace. We are more comfortable in 'A' where we are Inspired and Healthy and have unlimited access to many other key resources. So how can we ensure the A Mindset when we're often unknowingly pushed into 'B' Mindset by life's challenges?

"The Light fosters peace and happiness, safety and awe, and it
fuels your faith that it is safe for life to unfold." **Simi**

Once you reconnect with the Light and realize you are the energy within, you will naturally trust life and have faith in the physical experiences. Safety, faith and happiness are then possible. Moorjani was convinced too much unhealthy fear single-handedly allowed a cancerous disease to ravage her body. Toxic fear should be limited. If you can save money for a rainy day, you should. If you can save your adrenalin for a real threat, shouldn't you?

Dream Meeting

One winter night several years after Robert's death, I slipped silently into one of our special dreams. I was travelling a long and winding road that was reminiscent of the many back roads we had travelled together. I would come to a small fishing village where everyone knew his name. I entered a restaurant, and found him moving across the crowded room toward me. The sound of his voice was becoming clearer and clearer as the warmth of his energy was reaching out to touch me. We hugged, my heart feeling his. He started to speak and said what I had no idea I would ever hear.

"We made a pact that we wouldn't be together this time. We would travel this life separately. You wanted to find the Light," he said. "We would be apart so we could both do it differently this time."

I felt acceptance fill my chest even though a slight doubt creeped in too. Could this be true? Or was it my imagination trying to find another excuse for why he hadn't loved me back? Then I realized it had been 23 years ago... and I didn't really need an answer from the other side to heal any longer. Yet, there it was.

One day after another special dream with a similar depth as this one, an Elder would explain something it would take me some time to understand.

*"You have the ability to cross the divide that separates you from other realms. Robert pulls you into his realm at times when he needs to help you understand." **SoSo***

One day I would make the link that these dreams are most certainly Out-of-Body Experiences. I had travelled to another realm, another dimension of energy, every time I connected with Robert in this way. Transcending this physical world was why they felt so real.

Imagine how powerful being a soulmate is when we can come back to this place, in new bodies and new lives, totally separate and apart, and still manage to find each other. Why had he chosen her and not me? We weren't to be together in this incarnation and both of us had made other plans. Nothing else mattered. How could I have accomplished my destiny of learning about my own inner Light if he and I had devoured each other in the powerful ocean of an all-consuming love yet again? It even made sense. The further I looked into my past, the clearer it became that this was true. I wouldn't have been so adamant about finding a better way to do this life – if I had found it with my soulmate again as I apparently had so many times before. The plan was to be here on our own – both of us. And we had followed this plan as closely as we could. Astoundingly enough however, we would still find each other.

Forgive

Old paradigms taught that in order to move on from a trauma, it was necessary to trudge back through the event to relive it all over again and to forgive. This usually feels nothing short of unfair and again painful as the victim is often enmeshed inside their own suffering. Let's clarify a few things from the perspective of the Light.

Let's take a look at healing. First of all, we are in this life to learn and grow and understand the physical experience from a Spiritual place, not just from a physical place.

> "You will learn the Light changes your perspective.
> The Light offers the physical world from
> the safety and shelter of the Spiritual." **Parkah**

There will come a time when we will all disconnect from the illusion of the physical and we will place the Spiritual as first and most important. Being comfortable in the armchair of our lives means we are connected to our trust, faith and purpose within the safe harbor of the truth in the Light.

Forgiving is not the same as condoning, setting aside or lessening the act that was perpetrated. Wrong is wrong. Forgiving facilitates the victim's healing and letting go of the energy the victim associates with the act *and* the perpetrator. There are two stages of forgiveness: the intention to forgive and being ready to forgive. They are important parts of our healing process and they alone will determine how and when to proceed. Forgiving is most possible from the understanding and safety of the Light.

Over recent years I went to my Light many times with the intention to forgive, heal and move forward. Each time, I explored how I hurt so I could tell what I needed in order to heal. Layers of complexity, confusion and trauma were brought to light in each experience. With clarity and guidance from the Light, I found a different meaning in all those past experiences and I could recognize what no longer served me. Forgiving was possible, even exciting and had little to do with the perpetrators. I could finally understand the love within me and how to move on to resolve the pain of the past. If you are a victim of trauma, to intentionally connect with your Light can buffer you from the pain. In the Light you will become more resourceful and able to avoid lesser emotional vibrations for long. Our psyche will protect us from the full onslaught of the pain until a time in the future when we are ready to process it. Healing will take place in the safest and best way in the presence of your Light.

A traumatic event may freeze a victim's maturity at the age and emotional capacity of the event itself. This happens as the victim often remains captive by the pain and suffering of an event and is not able to progress or move past it. Although traumatic events can be complex and difficult to heal, the effect of freezing in time offers time and space to gather the insight and strengthen our resolve and safety first. When you are aware of these dynamics, you can regain your inner power and take back your life when you are ready. To become aware is half the battle. Healing will come when you are consciously ready to release the trauma through the power of understanding and the safety of your Spiritual energy. To open up and allow the healing is a blessing you can accept. The psyche knows when you are capable of processing a trauma and will introduce reminders, or echoes of a past event, when you are in a safe place and ready to process it.

For Mom

Prejudice is a subject that is huge in the media. We far too easily become judgemental of others based on details like the color of their skin, their faith or address. I am reminded of the scars and pain my mother bore and how she had worn her pain like a coat of heavy armor. Prejudice is the ultimate state of insensitivity, arrogance and ignorance.

There is currently a hot topic in Canada about juries needing to be fully representative of the community. Our neighborhoods today are not mostly white, but rather a blend of many cultures like Hindu, Muslim, First Nation, African Canadian and others. A radio host recently was saying how all cultures are invited to sit on a jury, but many just don't show up for the selection process. In this particular instance, the court case was over a white farmer who shot and killed a young First Nation boy in the head for trying to steal a vehicle. While the crime was wrong, death was a huge and inappropriate punishment to pay for trying to steal anything. The radio host was coming from his own perspective and was shaming the First Nation community for not showing up for jury selection. The farmer's jury was 100% white and he would be acquitted of all charges.

This is prejudice. It is unfounded ignorance of monumental proportion. Did the radio host understand, or even think about the fact that in First Nation culture it is not proper or right to sit in judgment, tell on or speak ill of another? Did he realize that First Nation people have no process to incarcerate offenders but rather prefer to counsel and heal them back into the community? In good conscience, jail is not something they would contemplate, let alone do. From Mainstream perspectives it looked as though they didn't care about this deceased young man, yet nothing could be further from the truth. We are rarely well informed enough before we make judgmental calls or give opinions on others. In fact, the entire genocide and assimilation of the First Nation people is fuelled more by the fact that the two cultures could not have been more opposite on many subjects. Neither understands the other, but only one has the power.

Rupert Ross, a Circuit Court Lawyer wrote my favorite book called **Dancing with a Ghost.** It was from his work in Northern Ontario on the Circuit Court that he learned amazing aspects of the First Nation culture. With great respect he earned from the people he met over many years, he speaks of these differences and how they have been the cause for incredible injustice and prejudicial perspectives toward First Nation people - from the beginning. I cried over and over again as I read. I was shocked, surprised and incensed at how the misunderstanding and ignorance of one culture by another is often the catalyst of hate, disrespect and prejudice. Where was our faith and where was our moral or ethical heart?

Mainstream culture is about hot pursuit, a straight line toward bigger, better, faster, higher and new and improved. First Nation culture is about the circle of life; taking care of each other, being mindful and respecting Nature and all creatures. It is about compassion and kindness, fairness and inclusivity, and it is round and full and filled with Light. Since reading Ross' book, I have been amazed that regardless of how many thousands of miles that lie between tribes, how many oceans or the size of the continents that fall between them, they all have the same philosophy. Now that – is something to think about.

Heal from what hurts you by moving forward and leaving the trauma to the past. Let the trauma subside for it will only steal your energy and prevent you from moving beyond it. That person, those people and the trauma do not deserve to hold power over you. So, take it back. As you begin to soar above Earthly cares through the Light, your true beauty will begin to emerge through the fog of the past and the rainbow colors of life will return. It is a promise given to you by God.

Emotions are not the Enemy

As we slowly become adults we get to experience more that life has to offer. Not all experiences however will be happy ones. We will all be let down, betrayed, ignored, left behind, cheated on and bullied. We will all lose a loved one and we will all experience a plethora of emotions unique to each event, good and bad. As life doles out more hurtful events over time, the accumulating pain can make us shy away from the sort of events that caused us pain. Sometimes, we can even push others away just to avoid the possible pain that comes with relationships. Shutting down our emotions in any way however, also shuts down our greatest resource for happiness.

If you stub your toe, you will feel the physical pain. It is a serious warning to pay attention to what caused the pain. You put ice on your foot and put your shoes back on, turn on the lights and walk more carefully. Emotional pain is the exact same warning device because emotions are the bridge to Spirit. Spirit communicates with us through our emotional responses to life events. And each and every emotion is a very telling and important message. Negative emotions like sadness, fear and anger are valuable clues of exactly what we need to pay attention to. If we avoid these emotions - because they don't feel good, we will shut down the guidance from Spirit toward the lessons we need to learn on this journey.

Emotions therefore are valuable clues and signposts, questions and answers, crossroads and reminders that laden every path from the abyss to the Light.

Chapter 15

The Best Kept Secret

MANY PEOPLE have offered the greatest secret to the world - many times over. All words have already been used many times over and redefined as many times. The word 'secret' is one such word. While our knowledge of what makes the world spin may have increased, there are still secrets we need to discover. Spirit, right here and now, is revealing the next 'best-kept secret' in what will very likely be a long line of additional ones in the future. The next evolution for life on Earth is here – yet it is still a secret if no one knows what is happening.

Never Satisfied

My mother had often commented to me, "You're never satisfied." I took her words to mean there was something different about me, but today I see this statement in another light. She was right: I was never satisfied ...with the mediocre, being a victim or crying the rivers that filled my pillow night after night. She was right and so was I: there was a better way to do this life, and while it would take me six decades to figure it out, ah, better late than never!

The fact that I never felt satisfied, especially in one place or doing one thing was likely why I was able to stay the course until I found an answer that worked. The unquestionable resolve I seemed to possess to keep moving forward and not get stuck in the mediocre was one of the Golden Threads that ran through my entire life. I had never been stuck in one place for very long. In fact, it seemed easy to find reason enough to move on to 'something else' and remain ever hopefully for something better. I can see only now that this resolve had always been the desire to connect to my own Inner Light. I just wouldn't know it until I found it.

Actually the next best kept secret is that the power, purpose and meaning for your life are safely written in your own Light. This incredible information is kept safe from all outside influences. The information is protected and cannot ever be manipulated or changed. My truth had always been safe within until I could capture it for myself. In order to discover your best resource, your own Life Manual, if you will, and the best guide for happiness, turn toward your own dream, open up the window and let it out.

"Nothing leads to peace better than an honest dose of Light." **Buck**

Understanding this fact motivated me too. Knowing that my essence was within me and that it had remained untouched by any outside influence gave me hope. Feeling and experiencing the Light, growing in clarity and self-wisdom and having this different perspective of the Universe was freedom. When I could clear the chatter, remove the veils and move through each event with my own strength and wisdom guiding me, more doors could open. I knew it but only after I had reconnected. What actually made me had been written in the stars and I was about to experience the benefits of reading them. I would be able to power-wash the tears and pain away to get ready for some good news …for a change!

Being

Moorjani also saw from the other side that God is not a being, but rather a state of being. Light is made of Love; Perfect Love. Being in good energy should feel good. And being in a state of Spiritual Light should feel even better.

"Little will motivate you more than validating your brilliance." **Willo**

This state of being happens more as one lives in each moment. The benefits and being aware of them are ways to help identify and capture the Light even more. Getting excited about the changes as you progress adds to your inspiration energy which also means your Light is shining even brighter. I felt like I was twenty – okay, maybe forty then, filled with faith and hope and strength. And I could trust again.

Perfect Light

Removing Consciousness from our spiritual teachings changed the course of human history. It changed our identity from the correct internal identity to the outer, material and physical world. We had always felt teased by our gut instincts and our innate sense of knowing but we never fully understood or developed this resource into all it was meant to be. This loss of the truth about our Consciousness changed us from being Spiritual beings first to not being able to identify our inner Light as anything significant. We sense when we're being fair and compassionate and when we're living right, but we're often not aware of why or how. Grounding within the Light means something strong, powerful, loving, soft and precious is moving inside of you and it will become very real and strong the longer it's there.

What is it that gives us our moral center, our inner code of ethical goodness? Why do some of us have it, and others couldn't be further from it? The inner Consciousness that we have been meant to acknowledge, harness and utilize needs to be rediscovered. We can all find our internal compass. We feel the emptiness in our center all the time and we actually have an innate knowledge of what should live there. We actually know we should turn away from the fascination of the outer world and reconnect to our internal Light to find what has the greatest meaning. Those who continue to miss the mark however may have too many veils between them and their Light. The veils can be so thick and heavy they may have to work extra hard if they are to cut through them all. Still, the promise is the Light is accessible to all who seek it.

When we welcome a new baby into the world we can actually see and feel our connection to Spirit energy again. We think babies are just really cute. We are instantly overjoyed with this tiny new creature that lights up a room with giggles and bright eyes. We cuddle and coo and watch so  closely, yet we're not aware that they are fascinating because we are seeing the Light in them that we forgot so many years ago. Tiny new creatures, all babies, are direct from the Perfect Light and they are the closest to the truth. We see this Light in dogs that are simply joyous and we are drawn to this energy for a reason. We think we love our dogs because they love us, but we will always recognize Spirit first.

The most egregious error I made on this physical plane was to not know the Light. It seemed like a major crime that few were teaching this, and I hadn't run into any teachers in all of my sixty years. Yet we are first Light and first Spirit. To not know this or acknowledge it or to not have that internal connection is akin to believing you're in hell when you're actually in heaven. If, or when, you are in a bind next time, stop and ask yourself what the event looks like from Spirit. Then realize how differently the entire experience can be from your Spiritual presence. Why is that? Try it out as it is a short trip back to the center of the Light - where you began.

Faith

They say faith is the assurance of things hoped for and the conviction of things not seen. More truthfully, faith comes naturally and easily in Spirit. When we know the Light we regain pure faith in many things. Suddenly life is how it should be. It is the Light within me through which all my experiences should be viewed. Life is safe and I can be comfortable. When one is able to accept that this physical incarnation is one of many and that the Light that shines in this one will return over and over again, we can let go of the fear of living and dying. We can spend more time polishing our brilliance and less time worrying about it. Anytime we can let go of the fear that stops us from dancing – it is a good day. Faith will happen naturally too as more and more of the fear fades into the material funk of the past. As it fades our Energy Signature increases, opens up and allows the greater Universe in. And partnered with the Universe, all things are possible.

Parkah spoke to me one day about why my tears flowed when I was in the same room as the Elders. "You have the same energy. This," he said, "is an important clue to who you are and to the understanding that has been imparted to you through many generations. Drift down the river as they do, be loyal, kind and steadfast, and bear that gift with honor."

As you begin travelling the Spiritual road, look for the changes inside of you. Life will feel lighter and you will sense a new freedom. Life will even smell better and be more colorful. When you are in the moment, you will notice these subtle changes pretty much as they happen. The day you find yourself smiling for no reason while walking through the grocery store will be a day you will likely mark on the calendar, just as I did. As we begin to feel more comfortable in the armchair of our life, we gain more faith in the process. We will realize that regardless of what befalls us, we are on this ride for a reason. We can make the very best of it and we can lean into it even more. The pain will begin to slip away. Life itself will become less serious and less stressful. The air will feel cleaner, colors more vibrant and the burden you have been carrying for years will lighten bit by bit until there is no longer anything pressing down on your shoulders. Your faith in life will compound and grow as your path is validated. You will sleep like a baby again.

In the context of a modality, it is not necessary to force faith upon anyone. You don't have to feel you are going against the grain or denying Spirituality if you don't have faith… in the beginning. Allow Faith to grow naturally as you experience more and more of the benefits of the Light in real life. In the beginning you only need to have faith that faith will come.

Trust

As life throws things our way, it is easy to lose trust. As resilient as life is, we worry about a lot of things, particularly in today's world of instant everything. Global horrors are reaching us as the media sends sensationalized drama to our door every moment of every day. I have often wondered about our fascination with all the bad news while miracles are happening every day too. Each dire circumstance that reaches us reinforces our fear. The world can be a violent and dangerous place. It is however even more so when we're trapped and forced to see nothing but the drama. Our experience of the world is largely artificial, made up of incoming messages spurred an agenda to divide and conquer us all. To be aware is helpful as you begin to reassess what you really want in your life. You do have a choice and it is okay to give yourself permission.

Power Dream

This morning I woke up from a dream with a feeling of divine power inside of me as if I had crossed over to the other side in my sleep. As I was waking, I recall feeling as though many pieces had fallen into place, questions would have answers and even though I was in the forest all alone, I sensed love and appreciation. The peace at that moment - was captivating.

> "It is one thing to learn of or speak of truth
> and quite another to experience or live it." **Little Reign**

We have been conditioned to negate the violence factors in our day to day lives in the name of entertainment and news. Video games, horror movies and cop shows are way too abundant. And contrary to what Hollywood claims, these sensory inputs do damage our energy. In fact the military is now using tools based on this fact to desensitize soldiers to the horrors of war before they even leave for battle. Each onslaught of violence collapses our ability to trust, not only energetically but Spiritually. The more fear and worry, anger, anxiety and apprehension we are fed, the more our Energy Signature decreases. We become more likely to hide from life, get into a worsening and habitual dialogue with ourselves about how worried and afraid we are and to cower and pull in instead of opening up and trusting or allowing life to happen. After all, we are hard-wired to brace at the hint of risk or threat. It is time to overcome these counterproductive and dangerously intrusive agendas to spread our wings.

The Light showed me that I am safe. The Light softened the edges of this brittle world so I wasn't inclined to worry or fret about tomorrow. It protects me, fills me up and brings happiness and trust over worry and fear and anger. I divorced myself more from the challenges of the material world for I was no longer tethered to its chaos. When I took control, when I returned to caring for what lives within me, from the words and thoughts to the emotions and energies, I became stronger, happier and safer. When I found myself smiling for no reason, I knew I had changed. Everything was softer the further I moved away from the darkness.

There are times when I just sit quietly for a while. Just like nature takes a break once a year in the winter to rejuvenate, we are meant to take breaks too. Everything is cyclical, and every life form should sit back and rest now and then. When we let new wisdom and good energy seep into us, taking a break allows it to sink in and take up residence. We need time to ponder what we learn to let new Spiritual knowledge and understanding grow roots and build a strong foundation. Life is not a race and true learning cannot to be rushed. Take the time you need to contemplate the steps along the way, to form a solid foundation so the next time you are challenged, you can rest easily upon it knowing you will be supported. Spirit is profound; it always knows what you need when you need it

Others have expressed similar experiences once reconnected to their Light. A feeling of peace and lightness moved into their body and their minds quietened from the chatter. They would begin to understand and experience things differently and from another perspective. The questions would fade because suddenly the answers were no longer necessary or they were becoming softly apparent. They marveled at how quickly fear could subside and how natural it felt to heal. After they crossed the fine line from the darkness to the Light, they wondered why they hadn't known sooner. Fear slipped away into a distant memory. Best of all, they began to trust again too.

All of this and more happens as a result of embracing life as an expression of Light, and not just a physical presence. Life held greater meaning for me as I began to appreciate it from the level of the physical to the higher levels of the Spiritual. Once I accepted that my Light was eternal and will continue to exist, the fear and mystery of life and death subsided too. Each physical life soon becomes more of a singular experience rather than the end-all or be-all. While life is a privilege and an amazing experience, it is a platform for learning how to center in the abundance of Spiritual Energy - regardless of the physical. This also spurs a natural distancing from the material aspects of the physical world. True wealth will one day be internal wisdom and silence. Being materially wealthy holds few benefits for Spiritual people. Service, compassion and kindness become the greatest wealth and the most endearing reward.

As you progress through the process of reconnecting, become aware of the trust that is engendered by the Light. Again, rather than a modality, trusting in the life you are living, having faith that you will be alright and allowing abundance and the Conscious Intelligence of the Universe to assist will materialize many benefits.

Abundance

Abundance is the natural and automatic benefit that will flow through us when we focus on opening up our energy to allow the Light to fill us up. We become guardians of our energy when we understand and live consciously. A higher frequency is required in order for the Universal Energy to resonate within us and teach us its mysteries. Such a resonance increases our feelings of safety and of all good things of this life. Once resonance validates the music is when the dance of abundance can begin.

And once connected, abundance will take on new meaning too. We will no longer feel needy, alone or empty. Your idea of filling your life with the superficial things of the material world will subside as your needs change. Things of this world does not abundance make. Abundance is about basking in the sunbeams and being surrounded by the benefits of this physical life like the rewards of being able to serve and love and to know gratitude, grace, wisdom and humility, to name a few. We are meant to tiptoe and not march. We are meant to be delighted and to touch the world softly, not to bulldoze a way through it. This does not mean that you are not to enjoy the material things of the physical world. It means that you no longer depend or focus on them for happiness or fulfillment. Abundance therefore is more a state of consciously being than a state of acquisition, financial success or material gain. We will all leave the material world and everything in it behind upon the death of these bodies but our Light will remain for all eternity. Upon which should you invest?

An Exercise

Practice taking a deep breath and feel the energy enter your body to calm your inner self with peace. Ground yourself as you place your feet flat. Become aware of your physical presence. This will bring you back into your body and into this moment. Focusing on being within will remind you there is safety and peace inside even if the world is spinning. Focus on your breath. If this is difficult, focus on something or someone who calms and centers you first, like your pet or best friend. Invite the energies of peace and comfort to move into you. Stay in this state for as long as you can. Return often enough that being in the calm becomes easier and easier.

Practice living in the moment and being in your body; open up, feel, smell and sense each moment. Breathe in your empowerment, strength and balance. Feeling stable, balanced and peaceful is an important sensory memory to build up for the times when the storm reappears.

Love

The ultimate Light is Love. When someone returns from a Near Death Experience the one thing they noticed on the other side is the Profound Love. This love is indescribable in Earthly terms. The Light one will return to at death or when their energy leaves their body exists at one end of the Light spectrum where purity, perfection and truth reside. This means all things in this end of the spectrum are ultimate states; love, wisdom, grace, humility and union, to name a few. There is transcendence of all Astral Planes when we reach the Ultimate and Highest Levels of what is possible. This is what is experienced when we reach the other side and are suddenly enveloped by the Source. The Love there is so profound we are unable to find words to adequately describe it.

Love experienced between two people on the physical plane is physical love. It is the biological force of survival that attracts one to another. Its base purpose is procreation, to ensure survival of the species. This is a biological need first. Physical love is hormonal, psychological and based in the biology of a body on the physical plane. Humans are attracted to certain body types, personalities, eyes, voices, scents and even gender, and so on. This attraction is to ensure life continues. Soulmates are attracted by deep Spiritual connection across many incarnations.

"Spirit to Spirit love on the physical plane is the ultimate gift." **Parkah**

 There is a kind of connection on the physical plane that when experienced is magic. This is a Spirit to Spirit connection. We live through intellectual, physical, emotional and spiritual aspects on this plane. Often times when couples meet, they connect on opposite levels such as a physical level to an emotional level or an emotional to intellectual level. These kinds of connections can be quite attractive in the beginning as one person fills the void in the other. The dynamics of this kind of connection however will eventually start to show up as discord when one begins to live more often on a different page from the other. Eventually the physical person tires of the emotional drama or the emotional person's needs are not fulfilled by the intellectual focus of the other.

By divine design, we start with a balance of all four: physical, emotional, intellectual and spiritual. In actuality, few of us remain in such a balance if we don't know we need to work at it. This kind of balance isn't taught as such. Rather, men are taught to buck up and to avoid the emotional and being Spiritual is seen as weakness or submission. Women aren't supposed to be intellectual or physical as they are deemed the weaker and those meant to be submissive. Yet we all have these four dynamics in each of us. Who is tending to this balance?

A spirit to spirit connection is when the fireworks happen. We experience the deepest possible love when we connect one spirit to another. When two connect intellectually for example, there will be a strong bond because they are on the same page and will likely remain so. Yet relating to another Spirit from yours there is a depth of love long sought after but rarely found.

Within this bond there is no jealousy, competition, anger, control or fear. A spirit to spirit connection is a powerful fundamental connection that we naturally crave yet few can explain or identify inside the chaos of complex relationships. Those who seem to be missing something in their relationship are seldom able to identify exactly what is missing. They merely have a deep yearning inside that eventually shows up as conflict. Yet more often than not it will be the depth and power of a Spirit to Spirit connection that is missing.

Spiritual Love is the greatest love. This kind of Light connection includes all knowledge, wisdom, purpose and fulfillment. From the physical plane, love is the unbridled evolution of the Light to the highest vibration possible. Two working together is always stronger than one alone. This is an Ultimate Love; the greatest expression of the full spectrum of the Light. Breathtaking and overwhelming are some of the superlative words used to describe this kind and depth of Love.

> "Spiritual Love rivals the stars, unites the cosmos and
> gathers the Universe into one eternal hug." **Parkah**

With a Spirit to Spirit love on Earth there is no jealousy, no limitation; no pain, conflict, anger, fear, jealousy or need to control. This Love is the epitome of all the answers to all the questions, of all the solutions to all the problems and the grandest purpose for life itself. Finding this Love on the physical plane doesn't happen often enough because it's an unknown quality of which we are only now becoming aware. Looking back I can see why I was frustrated in all relationships if I look at them from the perspective of Spirit to Spirit. I had only once connected Spirit to Spirit and we weren't meant to even meet in this incarnation. I chose the intellect or the physical man instead of one that would match my Spirit. I hadn't realized what the difference could mean, of course, and so I missed the mark many times. I had barely known of my own Spirit let alone to look for one in a partner.

Still, love on this physical plane has its own purpose and meaning. Surrounding yourself with those who love you will enhance your Energy. Being Spiritual and in service to others out of compassion brings an expression of love both on the physical and Spiritual planes. The higher vibration of love is likened to a clear golden tone while lesser vibrations like frustration and anger are so low and chaotic they become annoying dark noise much like radio interference. Love Energy is a soft warm tone that is a rich, full, soothing energy and it is very purple, pink and warm. In fact, the highest vibration one can experience on this plane is the Spiritual vibration with its deep violet Light. The second is love. The higher the frequency and vibration, the greater is the love. Finding Spiritual Love with someone on the physical plane is the ultimate experience, akin to soulmates. Remember what true love does. When you fall in love colors are brighter, the sun is warmer and the flowers are more beautiful than ever before. When we fall in love we open up and connect instantaneously to the Light. Enjoy the benefits!

How can you increase your love experiences on this plane? Surrounding yourself with those you love, with those who love you, doing things that express your love and that you love all help to raise your vibration. Your love energy will culminate in the love being attracted to, and returned to you. Such is the best brush stroke upon your canvas and the most golden thread within your tapestry.

Respect each other. Offer kindness and compassion, patience and empathy always and to everyone. And in doing this you will experience the greatest self-love in return. Never let your Light fade beneath veils of doubt or fear, anger or greed, frustration, jealousy or resentment. How you are in the world will benefit or detract from your own energy. Be aware and cautious of lesser energies that do not value the Light or add value to you. Protect your Energy and prevent the loss of the higher frequency. Just shine.

Touching the Other Side

Robert continued, "And when you reach the other side, we find all the answers to all the questions we could ever ask. We finally learn all about the pain and we will come to know the secrets of each journey. I now know of the love you held for me and how much pain you endured because of it. It is why I had to remind you that it was our pact. I will be here when you are done, and you will see how I have honored your pain. Your life is good and you have found the Light. Take the time to breathe it in."

I returned from the other side remembering what he had said ...and can tell you now about his words from this vibrant memory. The next morning there was a quiet peace in my heart, as if we had come full circle. His message had let my heart settle with a renewed confidence and peace for the rest of my journey. To understand set me free. His energy returns regularly to this realm now, even in my waking moments and when it does, a warm glow takes me home and away from whatever I'm doing. I can feel when he leaves too as his energy fades slowly and silently back into a corner of my heart.

I know we'll be together again, and for now that's all I need.

Gratitude

At night as you lie in your bed, thank the Universe. I express my gratitude of whatever comes to mind at the moment: white bunnies, purple flowers, Dad, eagles, summer breezes, kittens, chocolate, and so on. It matters not what you are grateful for as the very act of being grateful will fuel your internal fire. Be sincere as the right intention fuels it even more.

This simple exercise will begin to open up your Energy and will actually change the chemistry of your brain in a matter of days. This change can eventually turn habitual and repetitive negative chatter in your head to that of more positive, useful and beneficial energy too. Gratitude can even shut down the chatter altogether. It usually takes a few weeks to begin noticing a difference in how you feel. Consistency and commitment are the keys. Then be aware of the subtle differences that result - like smiling for no reason, feeling more energy and sleeping soundly. Recognizing the slight differences within you as you practice is a sure and powerful way to connect even deeper and to move up the pace of knowing and learning.

Remember

Remember you are not working your way to a distant shore far off in a land of super psychology and understanding when you seek the Light. You are returning to where you began. The Light remains within all of us from the start. Connecting with it takes an about face and a return to within ourselves, which is actually a very short trip when you think about it. The hardest part is letting go and forgetting the mind control and conditioning given to us over the decades, accusations that you are bad, unable, sinful, useless, powerless, damaged, stupid, awkward, clumsy, fat, short, and so on. These cannot nor do they define you. These are names, titles offered by others who are lost in the wilderness of expectation and status quo and they are clearly not connected to the Light either. Remember, there are far more of them than there are of you.

Remember you are Spirit first, Light first. While you learn about this complex world, the Light is there, still communicating, no matter what. Learning about this resource and the powerful guidance it offers means you can decide to focus intently on finding your own and learning how to listen for yourself. Spirit is your core, your heart, your guide, your resource and your fulfillment. Returning home to Spirit is like apple pie, a warm fire, fleecy blankets and a room full of laughter and love.

Come on in.

Chapter 16

Take Charge

SARAH BREATHED A SIGH, "Your journey is yours to take, and Spirit will let you know all you need to know. Do not be afraid to reach out and know that teachers cannot lead you to where you want to go. Only you can decide to go there.

Being centered and quiet and connecting with your core will help you hear the messages and confirmations intended for you regardless of how they arrive. The wisdom is there within you and your trust will build over time as you witness it. Be mindful of how something feels and cherish the words and messages that resonate …and then leave the rest for now. Do not automatically assume that everyone who talks of Sacredness will have what you need. Your journey is yours and each is unique. Be protective of what you take in and let Spirit guide you always. If someone is preaching but not saying much – walk on by."

G. F. Thornton

A Personal Message

I had searched the world. From Japan to Whitehorse, Montreal to New York, Seattle to Miami and Hawaii to the Caribbean and Europe, I looked as far and wide and as intently serious as I could for a better way to do this life. I moved over thirty times, held well over sixty different jobs and rarely did anything like parasailing, horseback riding or skiing more than a few times. I found only two true friendships in all those years, one that ended after ten years and the other is twenty years young – so far. I married twice and lived common law with three others, the longest relationship being a mere six years. And I ended each one because of abuse. I was becoming an expert at nothing but the pain of the search. Still - I never gave up. This would become the catalyst for the book I knew I would write one day.

Learning about my past, starting at the Bubble of Peace in 1999, I became laser-focused because I was finding exactly what I had always believed; that a relationship with the Source is personal. The past pain and betrayal would become powerful clues to what went wrong. I began to see that I had to look at how I hurt in order to find what I needed to heal. And I would find much wisdom in my own story. I would eventually wake up to embrace the messages that were coming from another dimension. Perhaps they were from the other side or maybe even further away but certainly their energy was very different. I will be ever grateful to the Elders for their support and gentle guidance as they helped me to see that the space around us all is filled with pure and precious Light.

My journey was to write this book, first and foremost. And I have lived each page. The message that I am the dream and all I had to do was open the window and let it out, was a very recent one. It would be the day I would understand this book and each word within it held unique and personal lessons. And each word, each thought, each page will resonate differently for every person who will read it, just as the Elder's wisdom had reached out to touch my own heart so intimately. You will learn in stages as did I, and you too will add one revelation to the next then to the next. You too will come to understand that no one holds your truth except you and that there is nothing as important in this lifetime than the dream you came here to express. Within the dream is the magic, the inspiration and reward. Take your time to discover it for yourself.

Brain or Mind

Influence which neural net you focus upon. You are likely very aware of the constant chatter in your brain; the running commentary about all things useless, worrisome, tiring, scary, old and critical. The voice that chatters away in your head is a habitual dialogue that we often allow and rarely think to question. It's just there. Here in the Western hemisphere we have not even started to appreciate the value of a quiet mind.

The Mind (not the brain) is the antenna that transmits information to and from the Source. Quieting the brain and letting go of the need to always be active and functioning can help clear away the chatter so the real messages can find their way to you. Identifying the messages from The Source is beneficial in many ways: not only are they wisdom but guidance, resources and much-needed love too.

Frequency / Vibration

Energy waves, the frequency and vibration of everything like sounds, colors, emotions, thoughts, people, and words all influence your Energy Signature. Knowing this, it becomes all that more important to surround yourself with high frequencies and eliminate as much of the lower ones as you can. Taking in a horror movie for instance will only serve to cut you off from the higher frequencies in direct proportion to its lowest vibration. Such energy causes exhaustion too which can remain for some time. Once you can recognize the amount of work involved in returning from the low Energy, you may think twice about the next horror movie. The adrenaline rush from certain sources, like a horror movie or an extreme sport, can be a short-lived substitute for the elevation experienced in the Light.

To instantly bring you closer to Light energy, do something, a task or activity that 'inspires' you, that will 'take you away from the world' and that will stop the clock. Connecting with Inspiration Energy such as being creative is the quickest and easiest way to reconnect. If you are creative and do things like painting, gardening, dancing, babysitting, or playing an instrument, you will already now the energy of the Light. You are connected with your Light and are in the Zone when you are connected to your passion or your creativity.

Be aware of what is happening in your Energy each time you practice these modalities until you can easily recognize the most successful ways for you to connect with your Light and exactly what it feels like to be there. Repeat the ones that work best until you can call up the energy instantly.

Love Again

Love at first sight became the test, and the power of being soulmates became the answer. Somewhere...out there, to this day, is my soulmate. His name in this lifetime was Robert. I so appreciate the fact that when we are connected to our Spirit, we get to realize that even though we can't see those who have passed, we feel them beside us. We feel the warmth as their energy seeps into our heart. Even though I can't hug him or go fishing on the West Wind anymore, he is there today and in the future as I wait on this shore for the day. I feel his heart beating with mine and his arm is around me and when he visits, I am filled with the warmth of that hug.

Robert was in my life to be a catalyst and a guide. He brought me to connect with the depth of myself, to open my heart to the Love in the Light. I am anchored in this love now like never before as I begin to learn the many dimensions it will foster from here.

Energy is influential and can be influenced. Light Energy is love energy. You can enhance the Energy around you which will help you to open up to the Light. Again, be mindful of what resonates. You will have a favorite color, for instance, and your Spirit will be drawn to it because you need its influence or it resonates within. Contemplate from Spirit, be grateful for everything you receive and live in the moment so you don't miss any of the magic. Become conscious of what is around you, who or what is influencing you, what environment you're in and how it is affecting you. Don't mistake criticism as care. Don't let others rain on your parade. You are not the only one who needs to be responsible. Take notes. Write everything down that is significant until you learn what you need to know. Surround yourself with your favorite colors, with beautiful sounds, words and thoughts and music that fills you up. Be present and fall in Love with your life - again. Then lean in for more.

It is easy to say 'go for a walk', but the impulse can be difficult when you are carrying the weight of the world. Once you can understand how a walk in nature will help your Energy, you will be more encouraged to take that walk intentionally. The next time life is looming, take a walk in the forest and find a hollow log. Pick up a stick and beat a rhythm upon it for a time. Focus on the rhythm, and begin to feel it in your chest. Let it resonate through you like a heartbeat. Begin to chant. Make no notice of what or how; just give yourself permission to be. Turn off the self-judgment and relax into your Mind as the rhythm takes you to a simple place deep within. Notice how the cares of the world fall away and become less intrusive. When you are filled with life energy, remember how it feels, what you discover and what is happening in your Mind so you can take it with you. Make notes on all revelations. Be in the moment. And remember, practice will make it more meaningful and easier to identify each time.

You can find magic in these moments. Notice the subtle effects and changes and write them down as a reminder. Being in Nature is energizing because all those living things share the Light with you and bring it closer to you. Surrounded by the forest you are connecting with a field of high frequencies of air and water and Light.

Clean Out the Closet

We all have things in our life that annoy us and keep us awake at night, that make us feel guilty, worried, frustrated or angry. And so one thing we can do to be rid of the decreased Energy is to figuratively clean out the closet.

I had to work on the anger that would flare up inside of me without warning or invitation. I used to get into this energy by noticing stupid people or whatever was unfair. We all know how much of the world is unfair and how stupid we can all be so I was pretty busy with the resulting anger and frustration. I would come to see how being in an angry state was only ever damaging to me as I huffed and puffed around in my life. The subjects of my focus had convinced me that I was a target for everything that was stupid and unfair. I found it easy to spot stupidity and unfairness in the outer world and having no power over any of it would turn out as an exercise that kept the anger festering – *inside of me*. If I wanted to be done with the anger, I had to stop being focused on what triggered it.

Taking a step back to undo the complex web of mistakes, emotions and events in the past was liberating. As I spent considerable time focused on each, it was like removing a pair of skinny jeans that just didn't fit anymore. It really felt good to peel them off and not care about tossing them out. I recognized the reasons for my anger and decided I didn't want to live in anger anymore. Stupid suddenly disappeared and unfair started to take on a different meaning as it slipped to the back of my attention to be replaced by what is fair and humorous. Life *can be* about what is good.

Trust Life

Celebrating our 60th and 65th birthdays in Mexico, Heather and I were in the pool waxing profoundly about life and all the things we had shared over the years. She looked up. High above us were seven birds gliding on the thermals. She said, "See - that's what this is all about. We need to have an unwavering faith that Spirit wind will hold us up too, just like those birds know that the wind will hold them up." We watched them for a time as we lingered deep in thought about their unquestionable faith in what they could not see and knew absolutely nothing about.

In that moment, we understood we could trust in life too ...even at the worst of times as we had always found a way through whatever had happened and now we knew why. Events had not been road blocks, not even the bad events. Rather they had been doors that needed to close or clues about what needed to change before the Universe could open us up to new and better insights. We would learn to spread our wings and to trust that an unseen Spiritual wind would support us. Those birds and that moment in time and space became a powerful message to let go so we could soar too.

If there are things in your life that remain unfinished, that are angry, conflicting or burdensome or have created a block between you and happiness, these are to be dealt with first. If low energy remains, it will hold you back and interfere with moving forward. Take time to deal with each one. Name a problem; give it over to the Light, ask for a solution and wait for an answer. You will need to live in each moment in order to catch the answer when it arrives. And when the milky warmth moves into your chest, know that you have found the answer. Living in the present is always more valuable anyway. If you have events from the past that were traumatic and you're still struggling with them or are not able to process them and feel you need help, seek the assistance of someone who understands the

Light or who is a Spiritual guide in good standing. Remember that the greatest Spirit in the room will be the quietest.

What has been received for this book is being received by many. It may no longer be a psychic connection as much as the evolution of our energy. Every day I find more and more validation of Spirit's wisdom in so many places. I am grateful and humbled as I recognize the messages far and wide. This alone will offer great hope for the future. The Inuit people confirm that the sun is rising and setting at different places on the horizon. It is true that the electromagnetic poles of the Earth have shifted and this is causing the Earth to literally shift in energy. This is one cause of the new energy we are experiencing and it is helping to change everything.

This is a time of great Spiritual awakening. We are seeing evidence as millions take to the streets. One day, maybe in the near future, more of us will awaken to the power of Spirit for it is our destiny and our purpose. We are, as given before, the Evolution of Light. Rather than feeling responsible for the outer world we have learned we cannot change, perhaps we can become responsible for the change we wish for the world by starting with ourselves. There is no other direction, purpose or mode for life but to move forward with the Universe. It will happen whether we are willing or not. The question then becomes "How long will it take to pack?"

A Prediction

On September 13th, 2016, I received an email from Heather to call her after work. While our ancestral history had been locked behind a wall no one had been able to penetrate, Heather had met a member of the Squamish Nation, the tribe from which our ancestors had come. They had found themselves simply standing beside each other at a conference. They started a conversation and came to realize they were related. He knew of our great-great grandmother's maiden name - and he could even spell it! This was something we had never been able to confirm. In fact, our records have as many as twelve different spellings for Sarah's name. Yet there, standing beside Heather that day, was a man who knew the name and even how it was pronounced. He also told her that his brother had been given the task of maintaining seven generations of information about our ancestors. He told her that Sarah, our great-great grandmother, had been a Hereditary Chief.

Heather recounted a story told in our family for years that Sarah had been a Princess. He replied that the word princess was a mainstream term. Indeed, he said, the correct term was Hereditary Chief. He went on to explain the lineage of Hereditary Chief is passed down through the first born females. As first born, Mom had been a Hereditary Chief ... and so too am I.

Another First Nation friend added some important fuel to the fire. After she recounted this event to him, he told her about how important it is to own who we are, to say that we are First Nation and to be open to talking about our heritage. By owning our past and modelling it for others, it is hoped that those who have been lost would find their way back home so they could help. The lost, he said, are badly needed at home to help their Tribe. By this time the tears were running down my face, my throat had swollen shut, my heart was sobbing and its beat was suddenly audible in my ears. My mind filled up with all the clues from the past. "Of course" was all I could think to say. Then between the sobs came, "Everything is what it is!" I had always known there had been a greater connection to these people than I could even imagine.

Circle of Many

There were several Golden Threads that ran throughout this life. Being nearer the end of the journey as I am, it seems most of the vital pieces have been found. I can see now that Spirit had always talked to me and had always touched me. It had been my singular focus on the outer world that had stolen my awareness and thus my happiness and truth. Robert came along to let me taste love and wonder and ancient energy enough to wake me up to something else, something more, and to draw me to seek my inner self. The final day in the abyss of darkness in 1999 with absolutely nothing left to lose was the day there was a crack in my armor just big enough to let the Light in. I was so ready. The Bubble of

Peace opened my eyes and heart and caused me to commit to finding my way home.

Regardless of what life had presented, I had been internally driven to find something better. I can only attribute this drive to being guided by the Light. When I see others who are stuck in the darkness, I am reminded; 'there but for Grace, go I.' I do not take credit for the internal spark that moved me forward each day in search of what I could not name and of which I had searched over many decades. It was as if the greatest lesson for this incarnation was to remember – to remember the Light from which I had come so I could be freed from the grip of this lowly physical illusion. And one day, I would find my own freedom and love for myself in the very same place. I am grateful that on the next incarnation I will be closer to remembering all of it again.

Lean into each moment. Show up in your life as if you want to be here, even when you don't. Be aware of the brain and how the chatter can keep you from hearing the voice of Spirit. Know that the details or the chaos of life are the greatest distractions that can keep you from being connected with the Light that will inspire you to your greatest things. Remember that there are many, many clues in your own story that can shed Light on your future. Stay clear of anything that brings a negative, lesser or lower vibration with it, including words and thoughts. Take back control of the Energy in which you swim. Fill your space with windows through which your Light can shine. Turn off the television, the cell phone and the computer. Spend time thinking of the beauty of this place and how grateful you are for this miracle... then be amazed as everything changes – right before your eyes.

My understanding of the Light continues to change and grow. Even this book - that Spirit wrote – would come in waves, each lesson building upon the one before it. It has evolved over the five years it took to write just as my life has over the past eighteen since I started on this path. I am creating a tapestry that will continue to be made from the many diverse and colorful threads I will discover along the way that will make it unique unto itself. I am excited to see what the weave becomes from here. Regardless, I will be forever grateful for the history written in its weave. I am beginning to understand the depth of this great ocean of Energy.

The Circle of Many is composed of all Lights, of all Spirits, you, me, the neighbors, family members, Fido, friends and co-workers …and every life in between. The Circle of Many represents all life and every Light. Humans have come here to remember the Light, to move forward, to learn and teach, to support and love and give of themselves. The Circle of Many includes those who are on this journey, those who may have lost their way and those who lag behind or others who are still in the dark. Those who are not able to serve their Light for whatever reason are the lost souls amongst us. They are our charges – our brothers and sisters we are meant to help along this path. Regardless of where we are or how we are in our lives, we will always be part of the Circle of Many. Lost, whole, sad, angry or joyous, rich or poor, or of various colors or addresses, we are one.

The Path of One, from the title of Spirit's book, might be seen as my path, yet it is not. It is your path too. It is a single path and every path - all at once. While the stories and details in this book may be from my life, the color, the wind and the depth of each story rises up from within yours as you connect with our commonality - our basic needs, desires and fears. We all feel the same pain, the same loss and grief alongside the happiness and joy. We all know the emotions of this physical life, no matter our age, gender or address. Our stories will be unique to each one of us but they are only the details as we each weave our tapestry in the exact same way. The empty feeling within is Universal and it alone ensures we will seek until we 'find something better.' Know that The Circle of Many surrounds and influences each one of us every day. Seek and ask and you will find the promise too. Let the Elders guide you from the darkness to the Light. Sit in silent repose and listen to the wind to find their song.

Even when you are sad, lost or angry, you can affect a change by being mindful of the energy in and around you. You can begin to fill yourself up with high energy by doing things that inspire you, being around high frequency people who make you smile, by being out in nature and actually connecting to the energy of Mother Earth. Book a date with a horse! Go camping - alone. Play your music and sing your song. Think good thoughts. Meditate. Believe that you are wise beyond measure. Stand on the top of a mountain and breathe in the Light. Learn how to stop the chatter. Listen to the wind as it plays music in the trees. Pray to the sunset. Remove all the masks of the status quo and forget the expectations of others. Decide to live within the quiet center of the vast material tornado. Be mindful of the colors that embrace you. Stare at the moon. Stand in your faith. Throw a rock into a pond and watch the waves spread out perfectly and remember that its energy changes the water just as Spirit Energy will change you, just as the energy of the words in this book will change you too. Be proactive, take charge and take your life back. You have everything inside that you will ever need for the journey. And most of all, remember …you are the dream.

"Balance is a key. When you are connected to the Light of Spirit, the Source, the Life Force from which you have come, you will fill up with a love and happiness that will stay with you. These are the hallmarks of true Spiritual growth. Let these be your yardstick... if you insist on something to measure." **Wahwaskenah**

You can connect to the Light within you; everyone can. The Light is in every life form. Written in your Light are the gifts you came here to play with and the love in which you want to be immersed. The journey is yours, and right now could well be the moment in time you decide to take this fork on the proverbial road ahead. Jump on board and sail your ship into the future of Love, Wisdom, Joy, Peace and Abundance.

Robert

I could never discount the love I had for Robert. The depth to which he touched my soul was and still is undeniable. Learning that we made a pact to not be partners in this incarnation would spur me toward an even greater truth. So, what about Robert rocked my world to the core?

In 1993 I sat down to take a stab at writing the book. As if on a mission I set out to compose our story so it would have another ending, a happy one. Remembering this story today, I realized it had some amazing parallels to all that had transpired since. Having written that 350 page book in a mere six weeks, I see now that it had been channeled too. It foretold of how everything had been connected and interconnected and applicable. The First Nation connection and that ancient blood connected us from the stars ending deep within the many circles of our lives together and apart.

The pact had been a vow ...and it had a significant purpose; to make me focus on the void within that had been left when he was gone. This had been the basis of my undying love and affinity for Robert in that story and in the real one. We were much more than just lovers who had met on this physical plane. He was my catalyst, my drummer, my guide on the search for the Light. Our Spiritual connection had been an undeniable affinity that we still have to this day. And yes, we meet in Out-of-Body dreams to reignite that energy.

Our greatest connection was through the First Nation blood which had always moved us as if it flowed through one heart. Nothing could have prepared me for the truth of our relationship... at the time. My soul knew where he'd be and when, and it felt the loss at the moment of his death far, far away. This alone speaks to the depth of our energy. The Elders would tell of why we came together in this life and that we had shared many incarnations before this one. They would also foretell of those incarnations we will share in the future. That I would learn of being a Hereditary Chief solidified the ancient understanding that flowed through my bones that I could no longer deny. The greatest tragedies in my life which had opened such deep and painful wounds would become my full breath, a purpose and a truth and my personal inspiration in the Light.

His presence follows me to this day. I find Robert in the ocean when I sit upon the shore. I find him in the forest as the mist envelopes the flora. He is in the scent of the cedars and in the yellow sun as it streaks between them. I find him lingering inside a movie and within a simple line of poetry that reaches out and touches my heart. I see him in the eyes of my kitty and in the face of a flower. I find him in my own Light... and I would come to find him again - in this book.

The Path of One

Our instant connection was more than just love on this Earthly plane or being soulmates over many centuries. It was the Light, the Water, the Entanglement and the truth that made our connection so deep and strong. It was about the sacredness and ancient wisdom from beyond many generations. It was about a common understanding and a philosophy we shared from the depth of the Universe that we will bathe in again – in time.

Regardless of our pact, the power of our connection had drawn us together - against all odds. It mattered not that there were seven billion people in the world or there were millions of possible miles between us. I had been drawn to search relentlessly for what I could not describe or name. And I would come to find my truth a mere two miles away from the back door I kept returning to in Dashwood. We were destined to find each other in this lifetime - regardless of the mountains, oceans or winds that lay between us.

His constant presence in this lifetime kept my heart alive and open and it kept me searching. Even as his memory would slip to the back corner from time to time, he would always show up again as if he knew exactly what was next. He was the angel tasked with keeping me awake.

I did not answer the call to the Light for another ten years beyond losing Robert until I was alone and broken yet again in 1999 and had absolutely nothing left to lose. I had missed the call for decades until my story really ached for another truth, until all the pieces were in place and I truly wanted to reach out and touch something else. The Elders would send thousands of messages and most I could never have imagined. The wisdom they would share would evolve and grow in depth and meaning with each word and each passing day. And they would spend many weeks and months and years waiting patiently for me to catch up. Then, in their gentle and precious way, they would save the best and most important message for the final page of their book.

"In your realm - I was Robert." **Parkah**

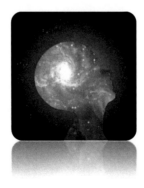

G. F. Thornton

Epilogue

Every day is an adventure now as the Elders continue to speak and send information. This very dynamic made it difficult to stop writing, close the computer and send the manuscript off. They said there would be more …much more. And just yesterday I was filled with a picture of my life in relationship to Heather's. We will have much to talk to about soon. And just today, I was given details about evolution, time, space and the Light that I simply couldn't leave out of this book.

The Elders exist in another realm, one of Progenic Energy and they maintain time and space on the 11th Plane. They are able to communicate by lowering their vibration substantially in order to cross a cathartic plane to resonate with the energy of us on Earth, which they say is a considerable feat. To bring information to us is quite timely as they have become aware of the perils that perhaps lie ahead. Their greatest concerns are around the lesser vibrations, the violence and the Earth's shaky environment as they sense humanity's direction toward the Light has stalled. They know the shift in the Earth's Energy is helping us escape from the masculine to the feminine, from patriarchy to matriarchy. An Earthly plane such as ours, they say, is a special place for Spiritual growth and it is imperative places such as these are kept viable for this purpose.

"Humanity has been at this place many times yet continues to turn a blind eye to their truth. It is time." **Parkah**

The most recent message was about evolution and ascension. Ascension is the realization of Pure and Divine Spiritual Light while existing on a physical plane; in other words, being fully Spiritual Energy while inhabiting a physical place. And Evolution does not happen exactly as we understand at present. A far more accurate term would be 'progress.' Regardless, Evolution, the Elders say, would not be sufficient to bring humanity to Ascension as we are "still tethered far too tightly and blindly to the illusions of the physical." We will need a greater energy to lift our sights enough to see beyond the fog of this reality. They also say that Evolution is not something that moves us forward; as in time we will evolve. Rather, Evolution moves toward us. Progress falls upon us like a light mist which melts through the tough outer shell of the physical and all

the veils to reveal the Pure Light beneath. This is so because there is Pure Light within all life. It merely needs to be revealed beneath the dust and illusions of the physical world.

The Elders offer, "This is the time to focus upon your inner self, to direct your attention and time to something of value other than the cold metal and plastic houses that no longer hold your warmth.

You may have lost your faith; in life and God and each other and even in the miracles and the magic. And thus, there has been a shift of Energy to rebalance vital vibrations on Earth. This adjustment will cause a refocus and reconsideration on that which is of higher vibration; value, love, compassion, cooperation, unity and truth, all which are necessary for peace and grace. Unite and stand firm knowing that there is only one Source, one Truth and one Way to progress, and it is behind you - from whence you came in the beginning; journey there to find the Perfect Light."

Go Forth
…past the door, beyond this place...

Self-worth is open, the heart inspires
and purpose true to fuel the fires
... of wisdom.

There is a Light that burns so bright;
it gives meaning to your flight
... fly high.

The day is near, the time has come;
It's true where the Light is from
... stay free.

Bless this journey, past this door;
It's just begun - awake for more
... have faith.

Go forth all thee to bless them too;
the path is set, there's much to do
... and trust.

Follow along each day that falls;
this path is straight and Spirit calls
... be brave.

Do not look back, don't ever fear;
the future's bright and oh so near
... know love.

Hark the Light, take to the sky;
the die is cast, and it's time to fly
... go forth.

[Channeled from my Mom in 2016]

Services

Dr. Glenda Faye Thornton, Sho'wasa-mae, has a private practice for Spirit Healing and Counsel in Victoria, B.C. and she travels to teach and speak. She has earned a PhD in Philosophy and Parapsychology from the University of Sedona, Arizona. She is a member of the International College of Energy Healing and is a Minister through the International Metaphysical Ministry. She is Founder of the

Awe Inspired Publishing House

which publishes spiritual and related books.

Dr. Thornton and the *Awe Inspired Team* of practitioners are available for Key Notes, Seminars, Workshops and speaking engagements.

Please email for information at: info@aweinspirednetwork.com to connect.

Sign up to receive our Free eMagazine, *Awe Inspired Minds;* a vibrant platform for the purpose of showcasing good work, inspirational stories and powerful messages and works from around the world. Visit us at www.aweinspirednetwork.com for the Magazine, *Awe Inspired Retreats* and a host of other services.

Hummingbird by I. Dimdi, Italy

Bibliography

Adam. Dreamhealer 2. Toronto, Canada: Penguin Group (Canada), 2003. Print.

Audette, John/Laszlo, Ervin. Intelligence of the Cosmos. Chapter 9. Inner Traditions, Rochester Vermont. 2017. Print.

Bartlett, Dr. Richard. Matrix Energetics, The Science and Art of Transformation. New York: Atria Paperback, A Division of Simon & Schuster, Inc. 2007. Print.

The Physics of Miracles. Atria, A Division of Simon & Schuster, Inc. 2009. Print.

Braden, Gregg. Deep Truth. New York: Hay House Inc., 2011. Print. The Spontaneous Healing of Belief. New York: Hay House Inc., 2008. Print. The Divine Matrix. New York: Hay House, 2006. Print.

Emoto, Masaru. The Secret Life of Water. New York: Atria Paperback, A Division of Simon & Schuster, Inc. Reprint Edition 2011. Print.

Gordon, Richard and Duffield, Chris. The New Human. North Atlantic Books, 2013. Print.

Goswami, Dr. Amit. Physics of the Soul. Hampton Roads Publishing Co., Inc. 2001. Print.

Haisch, Dr. Bernard. The God Theory. York Beach, M.E: Red Wheel/ Weiser, 2003. Print.

Holy Bible. King James Version. Oxford, England: Oxford University Press, 1997. Print.

Laszlo, Ervin. The Intelligence of the Cosmos. Vermont, Inner Traditions. 2017. Print.

Lipton, Dr. Bruce H. The Biology of Belief. New York: Hay House Inc., 2005. Print. Lipton, Dr. Bruce and Bhaerman, Steve. Spontaneous Evolution. Hay House. 2009. Print.

McTaggart, Lynn. The Field: The Quest for the Secret Force of the Universe. New York: Harper Collins Publishers, 2002. Print.

Mercola, Doctor. http://articles.mercola.com. February 7, 2014. Web.

Moorjani, Anita. Dying To Be Me. New York: Hay House, Inc., 2012. Print.

Osbon, Diane. Reflections on the Art of Living, a Joseph Campbell Companion. Harper Perennial, 1995. Print.

Peirce, Penney. Frequency: The Power of Personal Vibration. New York: Atria Paperback, a Division of Simon & Schuster, Inc. 2009. Print.

Rankin, Dr. Lissa. Mind Over Medicine. New York: Hay House, Inc., 2013. Print.

Ross, Rupert. Dancing with a Ghost. Penguin Canada, 1992. Print.
Ross, Rupert. Returning to the Teachings. Penguin Canada, 2006. Print.

Roddenberry, Gene. Star Trek, The Next Generation. Season 5, Episode 20. Television

Tolle, Eckhart. The Power of Now. New World Library, 2004. Print. Torus definition: From: http://www.thrivemovement.com

Vallyon, Imre. Heaven and Hells of the Mind, Volume 1 & 2. Hamilton, New Zealand: Sounding Light Publishing Ltd., 2007. Print.

Wikipedia. https://en.wikipedia.org/. Worldwide Web

Zukav, Gary. The Seat of the Soul. Simon & Schuster, 1999. Print

World Wide Web references:

Atom: Volume: 99.99 % of an atom is empty space filled with energy: http://education.jlab.org/qa/how-much-of-an-atom-is-empty-space. html

Biological Statistics: http://www.makemegenius.com/cool-facts/ human-body--systems-biology-interesting-facts

Bolte-Taylor, Jean: https://www.youtube.com/ watch?v=UyyjU8fzEYU

Consciousness:https://www.quora.com/At-what-age-does-a-fetus-begin-to-experience-consciousness; https://www.scientificamerican.com/article/when-does-consciousness-arise/ in The Scientific American publication.

Death by Medical treatment; www.webdc.com/pdfs/**deathbymedicine**.pdf

Einstein Quotes: https://www.brainyquote.com/quotes/authors/a/ albert_einstein.html

Fetus begins learning language: http://www.washington.edu/ news/2013/01/02/while-in-womb-babies-begin-learning-language- from-their-mothers/

Genocide: https://www.theglobeandmail.com/globe-debate/what-canada-committed-against-first-nations-was-genocide-the-un-should-recognize-it/article14853747/

Human Genome: https://en.wikipedia.org/wiki/Chromosome_2

Heisenberg Uncertainty Principle: Background Sea of Light. http://enthea.org/library/ brilliant-disguise-light-matter-and-the-zero-point-field/

Lovelock, James: Gaia Theory: https://iai.tv/home/speakers/ James-Lovelock?gclid=CMrtltyNttQCFYZcfgodErEDmQ

Plastic Surgery for teens in UK: http://news.bbc.co.uk/2/hi/health/4147961.stm

Removing memory of rat brain: http://www.intropsych.com/ ch06_memory/lashleys_research.html

Shakespear: https://en.wikipedia.org/wiki/A_rose_by_any_other_name_would_smell_as_sweet

Sheldrake, Rupert: Morphic Fields: https://en.wikipedia.org/wiki/ Rupert_Sheldrake.

Sentience: https://www.reddit.com/r/askscience/comments/45kjkh/is_there_a_point_when_children_become_sentient/

Suzuki, Dr. David: Born Good?: https://www.utoronto.ca/news/ babies-born-be-good

Two-Spirited: http://bipartisanreport.com/2016/06/19/before-european-christians-forced-gender-roles-native-americans- acknowledged-5-genders/

Yousafzai, Malala: https://www.biography.com/people/ malala-yousafzai-21362253

Images are from 123rf.com and personal albums